# Welfare and Citizenship

# Politics and Culture

*Politics and Culture* analyses the complex relationships between political institutions, civil society and contemporary states. Individual books will draw on the major theoretical paradigms in sociology, politics and philosophy within which citizenship, rights and justice can be understood. The series will focus attention on the importance of culture and the implications of globalization and postmodernism for the study of politics and society. It will relate these advanced theoretical issues to conventional approaches to welfare, participation and democracy.

SERIES EDITOR: Bryan S. Turner, University of Essex and Deakin University

Published in association with *Theory, Culture & Society*

# Welfare and Citizenship

## Beyond the Crisis of the Welfare State?

Ian Culpitt

SAGE Publications
London • Newbury Park • New Delhi

SAGE Publications Ltd
6 Bonhill Street
London EC2A 4PU

SAGE Publications Inc
2455 Teller Road
Newbury Park, California 91320

SAGE Publications India Pvt Ltd
32, M-Block Market
Greater Kailash – I
New Delhi 110 048

Published in association with *Theory, Culture & Society*,
School of Health, Social and Policy Studies, University of
Teesside.

**British Library Cataloguing in Publication data**

Culpitt, Ian
    Welfare and Citizenship: Beyond the
    Crisis of the Welfare State? –
    (Politics and Culture Series)
    I. Title II. Series
    361.6

ISBN 0–8039–8617–3
ISBN 0–8039–8618–1 (pbk)

**Library of Congress catalog card number 92–056381**

Typeset by Photoprint, Torquay, Devon
Printed in Great Britain by Biddles Ltd, Guildford, Surrey

To Ginny, my wife, friend and intellectual companion

Also to my children, Emma, Jeremy, Martyn,
Nicholas and William

# Contents

# Preface

In New Zealand, where I live and work, fundamental changes to the political structure of the welfare state have been made with very little public debate. Both of the major political parties, Labour and National, have made significant changes to the pattern of legislation that supported the welfare state. These were not signalled or debated in election manifestos. We are now in a post-'crisis of the welfare state' era in which the political reference points, particularly those of left and right, are no longer useful. Social policies have had a certain air of moral timelessness about them in that they stood outside of the normal rhetoric of political debate. The function of the neo-conservative challenge to this almost magisterial function of social and welfare policies was to ask awkward questions about their utility. The 'scrambled' defence of the left, once it was clear that these 'immutable' patterns were being attacked, has been ineffectual. The left has attempted to use the same metaphors and intellectual tools that were so effective when welfare states were first mooted. However, these calls for solidarity and a commitment to the previous patterns of welfare services have fallen on deaf ears.

Western governments are no longer ethically driven by the social needs of their citizenry but by the economic imperatives of survival. The former protected markets which had guaranteed an effectively nil unemployment rate for New Zealand have gone. New Zealand's unemployment rate continues to grow beyond the 13 per cent level with no end in sight and many forecasts that it will go much higher. This book discusses the debate about 'welfare' and recognizes that new ways of thinking about these old dilemmas must be found. We need to draft social policies as experiments instead of trying to enshrine social legislation. The political structures of a mutually supportive community still have power to compel the imagination. However, social obligation will need to be rethought. We will need a new pattern of political discourse that gives place to obligations and not just to rights. Both the resurgent individualism of the neo-conservatives and the unbridled expectations of welfare rights groups need to be rethought and the primacy of their separate claims questioned.

This book arose from two pieces of research which were undertaken for the New Zealand Department of Social Welfare. The first was about the purchase of social service contracting and the second concerned the analysis and determination of needs assessments. Professor Leon Fulcher, Professor of Social Work at Victoria University of Wellington, was instrumental in negotiating the first of these research contracts and in stimulating my interest in privatization and contracting debates in the provision of welfare services. He was also very early aware of the undoubted benefits of the word processor and I am grateful for his support and encouragement.

Several other colleagues in my Department have been very helpful in the critical evolution of these ideas. I am particularly indebted to Professor Michael Hill, Ms Jenny Neale, Dr David Pearson, Dr Bob Tristram and Dr Kevin White. It is, however, to Jenny Neale and Kevin White that I owe an especial debt. Jenny was closely involved in the research that we used to prepare these two reports for the New Zealand Department of Social Welfare. She has been especially helpful in clarifying some of the technical issues involved in needs assessment research. Kevin joined me to read the whole manuscript and painstakingly helped me to edit each subsequent draft.

I would like also to pay a special tribute to my wife, Ginny Hickman, whose deft and insightful criticism has helped to shape my thinking about systems theories and particularly the epistemological understanding about 'belief' and belief systems. Emeritus Professor Robert Morris of Brandeis University has given me support and encouragement in this project for which I am also grateful.

Finally, I would also like to acknowledge my gratitude for the early support for this book from Professor Bryan Turner of Essex University. His succinct and clear criticism was vital in helping me to reshape the initial drafts for this book. Similarly, Stephen Barr and Rosemary Campbell of Sage Publications have always been helpful and supportive.

# 1

# The Rhetoric of 'Welfare Crisis'

## The eclipse of citizenship entitlements and social rights

> To say that none of the standard justifications of the welfare state will suffice is not to say that the welfare state is without justification. It is merely to say that its justification must be sought elsewhere, in less conventional arguments.
>
> (Goodin, 1988: x)

Political support for traditional welfare states is no longer an obvious feature of the public rhetoric of western liberal democracies. The theoretical rationales which were used to defend the welfare state and its traditional pattern of practical social policies have been challenged. The power of the old welfare coalition which promoted the public sector as the preferred – and indeed the only – way to deal with outstanding social problems has been shattered by their stubborn persistence and even growth, as well as by the equally persistent dilemmas of programme design (Pack, 1987: 527). As a result, the previous 'monolith' of state welfare has been attacked and dramatically restructured, particularly over the past decade (cf., Lipsky, 1984; Rein et al., 1987; Glazer, 1988; Goodin, 1988; Morris, 1986; 1988).

An essential aspect of this attack on the welfare state has been the complete rejection of those social ideals of citizenship rights and obligations which were encapsulated in the political and social structures of welfare states. The champions of the new corporate state, often loosely described as neo-conservatives, have criticized the welfare state predominantly because it is regarded as a 'coercive bargain between strangers which abridged the liberties of both rich and poor while infantilizing the poor' (Ignatieff, 1989: 63). This neo-conservative critical stance has spurned any emphasis on collective responsibility, or obligation, and has stressed the threat that its proponents believe the welfare state poses to individual liberty. It also denies the validity of any social policy analysis which tries to assert a claim for access to public services based upon traditional community ties of authority and obligation.

Not unexpectedly, most of the contributors to the social policy debate about the structure, functioning and utility of welfare states write from within entrenched and polarized ideological positions. The polemical nature of the debate has meant that little attempt has been made to develop an analysis that does not depend upon these rigid and polarized boundaries (cf., Goodin, 1985b; 1988). This reflects aspects of the current political struggle in western democracies between 'defenders' of the established pattern of welfare bureaucracies and those 'protagonists' who argue for the supremacy of market-led concepts of privatization and contracting. The former support the systems of social service provision developed since the formal establishment of welfare states and the latter seek to validate services through the competitive private sector.

The climate of debate is now dominated by the 'logic' of economic rationality rather than what mix of 'social obligations' ought properly to be supported by redistributive tax regimes. Part of the restless debate, intrinsic to the welfare state, is what pattern of social policies should be promoted that would provide an acceptable answer to the nagging question of how the state could continue to justify professional intervention in the lives of its citizens (cf., Watson, 1980; Obler, 1986). Governments are often placed in a paradoxical position in respect of welfare policy. They are appealed to for resources and policy direction while at the same time enduring criticism for not providing an equitable distribution of the nation's resources, or demonstrating effective 'leadership' to integrate the plethora of demands and needs into a coherent and universally respected welfare system (Beedle and Taylor-Gooby, 1983). Various attempts to experiment with the privatization of social welfare services, and the development of a 'user-pays' philosophy within an overall resurgent market and monetarist approach, reflect successive governments' disenchantment with the ceaseless complaint for more resources and services (Burkitt and Davey, 1980; 1984). The emergence of a general reproach of the public sector welfare bureaucracies, interestingly, is echoed in the welfare critiques of both the left and the right. So widespread is the intellectual attack on the political legitimacy of an interventionist state that queries are also raised about the legitimacy of any further policy research associated with state sector welfare bureaucracies (Loney and Bocock, 1987: 141).

One of the intriguing aspects about the implementation of privatization policies, which presupposes a fundamental review of the welfare state, is how they were introduced without significant public discussion about the value of the former policies. The rhetoric for change in welfare has been successful in pre-empting any debate about the role of the state, other than its reduction. The argument, almost as soon as it has begun, is shut down and it is declared that there is no contest! Given this current political mood, where the social value of former welfare polices is not seen as open to defence, it is important to understand how the 'knowledge' of the incontestability of the neo-conservatives' social policy was produced and to consider why such social legislation has been so successful. To gain some argumentative space it is vital that social policy be seen as an 'experiment' rather than the outcome of given ideological positions foreclosed by legislation (cf., Ferber and Hirsch, 1982). Only then will the debate around welfare policy be opened up to alternatives.

The absolute imperative of privatized and contracted social services, currently promoted as the 'answer' to effective social service delivery, makes no more sense than the former pattern of public sector responsibilities. Both have been argued for in an absolutist way which severely limits their usefulness. There has always been a conflict between definitions and perceptions of social need and priority. Merely to assert the priority of neo-conservative definitions over the old welfare 'liberalism' does not advance our understanding of the complexities of welfare policy and implementation. Contracting for social services will require governments to institute comprehensive systems of analysis in order to define social needs.

This book will discuss some of the issues surrounding the determination and assessment of social needs and the managerial questions that must be addressed in the restructuring of social welfare policies. However, before discussing these more practical issues the general context of the debate about the advent of a welfare crisis will be surveyed as well as the range of arguments about social obligation and the privatization of social service delivery.

**Paradigms and Beliefs: Old 'Obligations' and New 'Rights'**

The welfare debate has foundered on the diverse meanings given to social 'obligations and rights' and to differing concepts of citizenship. The current debate about the political viability of welfare states reflects aspects of an important shift in the social paradigms which are used to justify specific political choices. These paradigms create the current context for contemporary debate and research (Rein, 1983). Clear distinctions can be drawn between the initial paradigm which was used to establish the welfare state and those used currently to defend it. This book explores this paradigm shift and discusses how the politics of neo-conservatism and the expectations of social radicalism have 'joined' to defeat the old welfare consensus.

The development of welfare states represented the triumph of the traditional welfare paradigm in which the dominant assumption was that those with skills or opportunities were obligated to assist those who did not have such skills or opportunities (Ashford, 1986; Morris, 1986). Such beliefs provided the rationale for the growth of social work and allied social services as respective governments accepted direct responsibility for the welfare needs of their citizens. Aspects of this 'assumed responsibility' were reflected in the political arguments that respective governments used to promote welfare state legislation. Professional assumptions of 'assumed responsibility' are similarly reflected in the rationales used by social work to justify patterns of practice intervention in people's lives, particularly those used to validate intervention under the authority of statutory provisions.

A new welfare paradigm has emerged, based upon the notion of social rights, which has challenged the implicit beliefs in paternalistic and professional assumptions. This new paradigm seems to guarantee the rights of clients to be protected from overt intervention by professional and sometimes paternalistic groups. However, in the current climate of social services retrenchment and government withdrawal from the public provision of help, the users of services have been left in a politically vulnerable position. Importantly, they have been abandoned by those professional groups who previously advocated on their behalf. Community groups are weakened by a legislative process that apparently grants them autonomy but grants them little or no legitimacy in policy debates.

The paradigm shift in welfare provision, from paternalism to welfare rights, is reflected in the way that social policies have been identified and administered. The emergence of a welfare rights perspective has exposed the 'hidden hand' behind the benign paternalism of a professional practice that was an intrinsic part of the 'old welfare' paradigm. The decay of this old paradigm, and the emergence of a welfare rights paradigm, occurred partly because of the numerous social challenges that have been thrown at statutory and conferred authority. There can be no surprise that this 'attack' was aimed at the management of the social services, which have always operated within the double bind of professionalism. The assumption that 'we know what is best for you and you must accept it' simply will not hold (cf., Pearson, 1975a).

## Obligations, Rights and 'Moral' Experts

The old paradigm of professional obligation validated the power of the social expert to determine needs, and provided the intellectual, ethical and moral imperatives for several generations of social science analysis. This model authenticated the 'objective' stance of social 'experts' who determined what social needs were, how they should be met and what pattern of social service delivery should be implemented. This essentially 'paternalistic' model is thus sustained by beliefs about the social obligations by means of which those who have are required to give to those who have not. This involves entitlements to citizenship rights as well as rights to personal social services. Thus practical altruism was woven into normative concerns about the entitlement to citizenship.

The early political discussions about the formation of welfare states were dominated by questions about 'sobriety, thrift, self-help and temperance'. Such ethical and moral preoccupations led to beliefs that the social world could be 'divided between those who did good and those to whom good was done'. These beliefs created and reinforced the notion of a 'culture of poverty' which presumed that 'poverty had a moral purpose' (Ashford, 1986: 303). This orientation towards social obligation reinforced public assumptions that social service professionals, whether social workers, social planners or welfare administrators, were objective, expert and balanced. A new range of radical political opinion, particularly a feminist analysis of social policy and an ethnic consciousness, has emerged which seeks to undermine the former paternalistic, moral or 'racist' justifications for the old welfare paradigm. These contrary arguments have united both the left-wing criticisms, as well as those expressed by the right, in seeking to develop a critique of the assumptions underpinning the 'professional vision' which they attributed to the welfare state (cf., Richan and Mendelsohn, 1973; Anderson et al., 1981; Brewer and Lait, 1981). Such attacks have been intensified by the emergence of a general community bias against professionalism. This has challenged the social work professional's assumption of the power both to identify and to meet needs.

Awareness of 'welfare rights' and social justice has accompanied the emergence of a new welfare paradigm in which the organizing belief is no longer that those who have are obliged to give to those who have not, but rather that those who have not have rights to receive. Implicit in this belief is a rejection of the traditional justification for professional intervention. The rights of communities to determine their own needs are now forcefully asserted in a considerable literature (cf., Gough, 1979; Parry et al., 1979; Weale, 1978; 1985b; Plant et al., 1980; Watson, 1980; Soper, 1981; Withorn, 1984; Beresford and Croft, 1986). This paradigm shift leads to a 'democratisation of welfare' (Morris, 1986) where the emphasis on rights embodies an attack against the power of the 'detached and objective' professional and calls for an 'involved and self-responsible' community. A new consumer-based community 'voice' has thus emerged with expectations that community interests will determine their own needs as well as developing locally based methods of needs analysis. These paradigm shifts redefine the purpose and possibility of professional intervention as well as the value and purpose of social needs assessment and policy analysis.

## Rights and Obligations: The 'Lonely' Citizen

The political visions which accompanied the establishment of welfare states sought to transcend the essential individual significance that people make of their own lives. Citizenship theory was grounded in the primacy of the practical politics of universal social obligations and rights. However, at the heart of the neo-conservative challenge to this 'welfare orthodoxy' is the assumption that people are essentially individualistic. This criticism has been enhanced because the 'active' expectations of citizenship, intrinsic to the founding protocols of the welfare state, have combined with the 'passive' expectations of welfare rights. That is to say, the welfare states' initial contract between the state and the individual was not fulfilled. While the left was worried about professional paternalism and the right about the destruction of individual responsibility, the recipients of welfare policies came to assume them as a right. In this they saw no need for a reciprocity with the state. An emphasis on rights and entitlements rather than obligations has eroded one of the key initial assumptions of the welfare state, specifically that social rights and obligations represented the 'citizenship of shared entitlement' (Ignatieff, 1989). This gave rise to a situation in which the middle could not hold. It was seen both by those who had, and by those who wanted to give, as a non-responsive sector of society.

The eclipse of the welfare state cannot simply be credited to the more effective politics with which neo-conservatives challenge a ubiquitous 'welfarist mentality'. Their challenge exists and is a powerful one. However, as Ignatieff suggests, one major reason for the 'ruination of the socialist tradition' has been the steady trivialization of rights and obligations which were intrinsic to the ethical foundations of the welfare state. In this the intellectual left with its idealization of the working class, and the working class as passive recipients of welfare, are both to blame. If the political traditions of liberal and social democracy are ever to be able to develop robust alternative visions to market conservatism they must 'work themselves free of the seductive pleasures of moral superiority about the venality of the market and false nostalgia about the vanished compassion of the old civic contract' (Ignatieff, 1989: 72).

Criticism of the paternalistic and bureaucratic pattern of professionalized authority is incontrovertible. However, a renewed defence of mutual rights and obligations is required in order to maintain an ethically defensible society. Those who would attempt a defence of the welfare state must not only consider the nature of this new criticism but also look more seriously at the sets of internal contradictions that are exposed as the hopes for active citizenship became passive expectations. This book explores the inevitability of the ideological and rhetorical conflict which fashions the debate.

## The Politics of Silence and Exclusion

This new political climate has silenced those who have supported the traditional delivery of social services. Its pervasiveness can be demonstrated by pointing out that some governments refuse to participate in those sets of tripartite negotiations about wages, health and welfare matters that characterized the usual administrative policies of welfare states. Governments which support a non-interventionist stance can promote new welfare policies that aim to remove the state from direct responsibility for social service intervention. The successful introduction of market-driven policies into the welfare state policy debate reflects a political assumption that governments can only partially support the delivery of social services. The argument is that governments can never respond completely to complex social uncertainties and risks and that the 'true' social reality is the 'morality of the market'. In contrast there are posited the 'false' and ineffectual welfare systems of mutual obligation. Illustrating this style of argument is Lane's conclusion that 'the political method of collective satisfaction of wants creates more claims of injustice than does the market method of individual satisfaction of wants' (1987: 348). The role of the market in social service contracting and even the privatization of welfare services have therefore emerged as 'self-evident' social policies. The merits of these new policies are proffered on technical rather than political grounds. Those more limited welfare policies which have escaped the net of market logic are presented as the best that governments can do within the 'side effects of the enormous, almost "natural" forces that government could not be expected to control' (Lipsky, 1984: 21). These residual state activities leave some of the existing structures of welfare policy intact but the overall impact is to weaken the entire legitimacy of the state's role in the determination and delivery of welfare policy.

Advocates of private sector welfare systems weave their arguments against the inefficiencies of the public sector around two common themes. The first relates to the belief that welfare bureaucracies stifle individuality and the second is that private systems are better able to provide specific and targeted services.

### Malign Bureaucracies: The Loss of Personal Autonomy Under 'Welfare'?

Neo-conservative social theory constantly elaborates the theme that the public sector is dominated by an inept bureaucracy that is inefficient, resistant to decentralization and dominated by strong unions (Dorwart et al., 1986: 875; Wedel and Hardcastle, 1978; Savas, 1982; 1987). The general tenor of this argument is that public sector bureaucracies are too cumbersome and expensive; that they create an administrative structure which inhibits personal responsibility; and that they will condone inefficient provision of services. It is also argued that public welfare services may become so comprehensive that a 'homogenised undifferentiated "mass society" may result' which no longer discriminates social rewards on the basis of individual effort and initiative (Weddell, 1986: 14). Broadly similar and equally legitimate claims on the state, one of the essential aspects of citizenship rights, are denied. The usual patterns of welfare bureaucracy, it is claimed, will wreck personal freedom because responsibility is abandoned to the ubiquitous state which may then coerce its citizenry, engender economic inefficiencies within the private productive sectors, destroy individual integrity and social cohesion through the 'pork-barrel-line' of government favours and even contribute to the 'disappearance of the rule of law' (Friedman, 1981: 23)!

This critical opinion, reflected in public choice theory, also takes aim at the inefficiencies that result from inadequate incentives for the managers of public bureaucracies. These inadequacies are considered to be 'perverse' when contrasted with the private sector (Bennett and Johnson, 1980: 371). The core of this argument is that because there are no economic or external incentives for effective economic management public sector bureaucrats inevitably become inherent 'empire-builders' who seek only to enlarge the size and scope of their organization. Their managerial power is derived more from the administration of a large bureaucracy than from the efficient delivery of services. Part of this inefficiency, it is argued, arises out of the provision of different incentives for the managers of private and public organizations. Evaluation of the performance of the private sector manager hinges on the economic efficiency of the organization and the manager's ability to deliver services or products at minimal cost. Public managers, on the other hand, have a predisposition to enhance their power within the bureaucracy by increasing the number of subordinates who report to them.

## Bureaucratic Authority or Performance?

Perhaps the most influential summary of these arguments about an administrative 'crisis' has been presented by Drucker (1969). The title of his paper – 'The Sickness of Government' – is particularly significant, highlighting as it does the potency of 'sloganeering' rhetoric in the twists and turns of the enduring squabble about the relationship between public and private systems of welfare. Both left and right are culpable in that they avoid considered analysis in preference for sloganeering excess. Drucker sets out an argument for a principle of 'reprivatization' in which all institutions should be autonomous, and all social structures would have in common 'a principle of performance rather than a principle of authority' (1969: 19). This argument about the pre-eminence of performance over authority is echoed in the pattern of the welfare paradigm shift from that of structured and responsible authority to the legitimacy of sectorial interests and rights. The result is a curious dovetailing of a community rights perspective about appropriate and adequate service delivery with the neo-conservative rejection of bureaucratic authority. The denigration of all bureaucracy assumes the character of 'high rhetoric'. However, Drucker (1969), whose arguments are often used to justify such total antipathy to the validity of the public sector, does not himself assume such a stance. While commenting on the problems and constraints of bureaucratic rigidity he argues not for a 'withering away of the state' but rather for the re-emergence of strong government, for one that has political vision and not just administrative ability. Drucker's argument for 'reprivatization' does not imply the total destruction of the state sector, rather that it should be revamped into a more responsive organization, hence the arguments for contracted social services. One consequence of the controversy in support of these new welfare policies is that the classic assumption that the arenas of the private individual market and public communal world are intrinsically separate and antagonistic, is nullified. The choices for the economy, and the public sector welfare services, are neither total government indifference nor absolute government control but involve a 'new choice: an organic diversity in which institutions are used to do what they are best equipped to do' (Drucker, 1969: 22). Drucker does not expect a return to 'laissez-faire' because he argues that economics cannot and will not be considered separately from the public domain. This is one of the pivotal yet largely unrecognized aspects of this debate: it marks an acceptance that economics and social policy are indissoluble, creating valid reasons to seek new managerial and political solutions to welfare policy. Yet separation of public and private worlds lies at the heart of public choice theory.

### Private Welfare: Distinctiveness and Individuality?

The second major neo-conservative theme is the belief that private welfare agencies can provide a more effective means to recognize distinctive individual or group claims to services. It is suggested that they can contribute significant integrated functions when 'regional, ethnic or racial identities are highly salient (perhaps even on par with national identities) by providing a structure and purpose for such group organisations' (Gronbjerg, 1983: 774). The worldwide resurgence of the welfare claims of ethnic 'peoples', particularly those who are indigenous, represents the emergence of a unique set of political and moral claims for economic and social entitlement. It may well be true that citizenship responsibilities and duties:

> . . . with respect to primordial groups may be fully ensured only through the operation of the private welfare system, which can provide particular kinds of services and demand specific forms of contribution in return. The development of ethnic or religiously based welfare agencies then can be seen as an embodiment of such mutual, but specific, rights and obligations. (Gronbjerg, 1983: 785)

These perspectives challenge communitarian 'welfare orthodoxy' which has long assumed that the state is a much better 'guardian' of these responsibilities. Privately contracted welfare systems preserve and reinforce the voluntaristic nature of the welfare exchange and can therefore maintain group identity and purpose. Voluntary agencies can effectively deliver services to targeted 'hard-to-reach or controversial groups . . . whom government is obligated to serve but where fear or stigma inhibits utilization' (Kramer, 1983: 423). They can, more easily than the public system, support the growth of those intermediary and idiosyncratic cultural organizations necessary to negotiate the 'otherwise impersonal link between the individual and the state' (Gronbjerg, 1983: 784). In summary, because neo-conservative welfare policies are grounded in respect for difference and individuality it is no longer possible to subsume social differences and to continue to argue for general or universal social services that are based solely on the criteria of citizenship. There are more basic cultural patterns of allegiance, affiliation, identity and commonality that challenge traditional justifications for entitlement established solely on the grounds of citizenship.

## Paternalism, Political Power and 'Authority'

The commonplace rejection of the social work profession and the associated pattern of welfare administration, as we have seen, depended upon various political assumptions that derived their impetus from a more pervasive rejection of the 'legitimacy' of paternalism (cf., Saleeby, 1989). Both ethnic and feminist analysis of the respective problems and issues of the welfare state construct their critical arguments around this central dilemma of bureaucratic paternalistic authority (cf., Creed and Tomlinson, 1984; Mishra, 1986a; Pascall, 1986; Fraser, 1987; 1989; Dominelli and McLeod, 1989). The range of arguments about the institutionally racist and sexist nature of welfare professional practice supports Friedman's (1981) contention that the minutiae of welfare administration essentially represent 'policy without law'. The right to intervene was guaranteed by statutory authority and not through the ability of social service professions to gain public sanction. For the neo-conservatives the crisis of the welfare state was essentially fiscal – how would it be paid for? For the left the crisis was about accountability to clients and the 'transparency' required of welfare bureaucracies.

Criticism of the welfare state that focuses on the structural paternalism of services mediated by social service professionals is reflected in the separate critical social analyses of both the left and the right. Both imply that bureaucratic power reflects the arbitrariness of patriarchal moral justifications. The neo-conservative criticism more specifically focuses on the fear that the welfare state is 'totalitarian' and oppressively constrains individual freedom. Left-wing criticism focuses more on the whimsical and mercurial aspects of service provision, on the insufficient satisfaction of needs and a frustration with the social control function of the bureaucracy. It is assumed that professional social work intervention acts either to diffuse or to control the legitimacy of collective rights. Feminist theory, in its legitimate attack on the 'paternalism' of welfare bureaucracies, found an unusual ally in neo-conservatism which emphasized autonomy as well as fiscal probity. However, as Friedman contends, individualistic and collective orientations are 'analytically indistinguishable' within paternalistic welfare structures. She argues that the aversion to making 'explicit that society is a moral order rests on the vivid and threatening image of the administration of protection under a paternalistic moral order' (1981: 33). Sapiro (1986), however, points out that much of the debate about such patriarchal power is limited to how it supports the welfare bureaucracies. She broadens the base of the argument from an analysis about the paternalistic structure of inefficient institutions to how paternalism supports a masculinized view that 'welfare' is essentially the province of women (cf., Fraser, 1987; Baldock and Cass, 1988; Dominelli and McLeod, 1989). Friedman has suggested that the welfare bureaucracies combine 'paternalism with demands for obedience . . . . The protection the subject obtains is unceasingly contingent upon . . . service to the whim of the political authority' (1981: 28–29). That feminist theory is hostile to both paternalistic 'welfarism' and neo-conservative market ideology highlights the difficulty in developing arguments for socially cohesive policies that can sustain mutual obligation across interest groups. There are conceptual links between paternalism, political power and the emergence of welfare rights. Essentially the general attack on the structure of 'paternalistic' political power contributed to the destruction of the old welfare paradigm and ushered in the present paradigm of welfare rights. The welfare policy debate about privatization has destroyed the traditional collective pattern of universal support for mutual social obligations.

## The 'Inevitability' of the Market?

A quite separate defence of the neo-conservative argument for the privatization of welfare services avoids analysis of effectiveness and relies on the notion of historic inevitability. Reichert grounds an argument for neo-conservative social policy in an historical analysis of the welfare state. Those who would defend the structures of a welfare state political economy consider that the present crisis in support of the personal social services, indicates only 'a temporary aberration' in the maturation of a welfare political economy. Reichert argues to the contrary and links an analysis of the crisis of welfare to an historical context where we are 'experiencing the culmination of a long term development that is characterized by the ascendancy of market capitalism over the cushioning effect of a partly realized welfare state' (1982: 173). He concludes that analysis of this historical process shows the inexorable penetration of the health and welfare sectors by the 'rationality of the market' with its vastly different administrative institutions and styles of management. The operations of these health and welfare sectors were originally considered to lie outside the market system, but the privatization of service delivery has the capacity to 'undermine the values and distort the communal character of the social market' (Gilbert, 1984a; 1984b).

The belief that the developmental validity of the market is historically inevitable forms part of the substance of classic neo-conservatism. These arguments are not, I would suggest, completely sustainable. There is a recursive pattern in either individualistic or communal explanations of social policy that cannot be side-stepped by an appeal to the power of an historic linear ascendancy of ideas. Such an argument avoids questions about systemic process and how these explanatory models have oscillated historically. It is no longer possible to argue for the intrinsic 'truth' of one over the other; rather both are different, valid and, in certain ways, limited interpretations of the social world (cf., Glazer, 1988). The debate will not be resolved by a relatively simplistic appeal to the processes of historic inevitability.

It is an interesting speculation that the current ascendancy of market-led arguments in support of contracting and privatization represents what might be called 'the politics of nostalgia', a desire to re-establish the 'founding concepts' of private philanthropy. Ironically, these new proposals about the dominance of a rational market in delivering social welfare services reflect a yearning for a world that was supposedly less complicated, and one that was not over-burdened by a controlling bureaucracy. Supporting the privatization or contracting of social services, it can be argued, represents an attempt to create a political economy that respects idiosyncrasy, privacy, self-definition and difference. Ironically both 'left-wing' and 'neo-conservative' ideologies share common assumptions about the need to respect uniqueness and recognize difference. It is important to note how these common assumptions contributed towards the paradigm shift in welfare policy. The emergence of a 'welfare rights' paradigm is partly an expression of a coalition against aspects of bureaucratic indifference and self-serving. It is also influenced by the emergence of a radical opinion which finds an odd and paradoxical echo in Drucker that 'performance' is more vital than 'authority'. The demand for efficiency in service provision has made for odd 'bed-fellows'!

## Citizenship Ideals: Expectations, Hopes and Contradictions

The welfare state was founded on the criteria of the 'citizenship of shared entitlement' (Ignatieff, 1989). However, the translation of citizenship obligations into welfare rights requires that the former arguments for universal entitlement based on citizenship rights must be rethought. The concept of citizenship did embrace the corresponding concept of active political and social obligation. However, before we can argue validly for the moral logic of universal entitlement we will have to address Ignatieff's stricture that 'the more evident our common needs as a species become, the more brutal becomes the human insistence on the claims of difference' (1984: 130). If this assumption does mean, as he suggests, that this is 'the truth before which . . . politics has stalled' then perhaps the only possibility of resolution requires the valid acknowledgement of the welfare claims of these subsets and groups before proceeding again to argue for the moral universality of shared entitlement.

There is no single set of reasons that can be offered to explain the movement from the ideals of citizenship to the demands of claim rights. Questions about contracting and privatization reflect a more fundamental debate about the nature of the political economy. These questions cannot be reduced to issues concerning technical, administrative or programmatic efficiency. The arguments of both left and right in respect of the political economy are being redrawn because the justifications for clear distinctions between the public and private worlds are no longer viable. The welfare state is being substantially altered but so too are the historic imperatives of the market. The inexorable logic of the market-place is also being transformed by the emergence of those social and individual rights which, while originally guaranteed by the market, nevertheless transform it (Turner, 1986).

Imperatives for welfare reform are often interpreted and presented as if the central question ought properly, and only, to be about the efficient administration of these services. However, this managerial rhetoric obscures political biases because it advances, for the inferred 'benefit' of social welfare clients, a drastic reappraisal of social services that usually reinforces structural biases which are against their actual interests. One of the more significant pointers to the change in the traditional ground of welfare debate is that plans to introduce social service contracting have been accepted even by those who are the 'reluctant clients' of the welfare state. Attitudinal surveys of service users reveal that people, for 'fiscal and ideological reasons' (Kramer, 1985b: 380), want social services but prefer to have them provided by local community-based agencies rather than state agencies (Taylor-Gooby, 1985a; 1985b; 1985c; 1986a; 1987). There is fierce debate about the appropriate pattern of welfare services. Various reviews have shown that the restructuring, putatively on behalf of clients, has led to actual reductions in benefit levels or service access (cf., Lipsky, 1984: 22). Professional exercise of statutory authority is often met by a sullen and stubborn resentment from the clients of the public sector agencies. Yet these welfare encounters are not, as they are sometimes portrayed, 'a roiling sea of resentment and distrust' but rather reflect a bureaucratic tedium – a 'gray, ordinary, even boring reality' – where mundane transactions are routinely processed (Goodsell, 1980: 359). From a certain radical political perspective the professional activities of social service workers were seen to reflect aspects of the power of the state to use one class to control another (cf., Gough, 1979; Parry et al., 1979). However, client reaction and attitude to social services do not support the rigidity of such an analysis. Despite the inherent problems of statutory authority, and the imputation of a social control function, clients were not completely antipathetic to these statutory public services.

From a broader perspective we might consider why the various social security acts of the 1930s which passed such socially progressive legislation were 'implemented with almost no working-class input' (Quadagno, 1984: 645). The previous discussion about the normative 'conjunction' between church and state, and how that alliance contributed to the formation of what has been termed an old welfare paradigm, suggests a possible answer (cf., Morris, 1986). This traditional paradigm set out complex codes of social obligation which derived their social legitimacy from the normative linking of church and state, with both 'institutions' operating to define the nature of 'true' altruism and to propose 'appropriate' norms for social caring. Both church and state were still comfortable with the notion of informed obligation. The church established much of the normative criteria for the professional practice of social work, while the state introduced social legislation assuming that it had the political power to realize the altruistic aims of 'the social gospel'. The normative power of the state and the church jointly to determine the direction of social policy, which underpinned the original conception of the welfare state, has been superseded and is no longer so easily maintained.

An interesting historical digression is that both France and Germany provided respective research opportunities for major social theorists such as Weber and Durkheim because of 'the intensity of the debate over how states might fulfil their newly conceived social functions' (Ashford, 1986: 33). Ignatieff, com-menting on this theme of state intervention, reminds us that there are important theoretical differences between those social argu-ments where rights are conceived of as citizenship entitlements and those that treat entitlement as if it 'were a matter of moral generosity'. He suggests that:

> The language of citizenship is not properly about compassion at all, since compassion is a private virtue which cannot be legislated or enforced The practice of citizenship is about ensuring everyone has the entitle-ments necessary to the exercise of their liberty. As a political question, welfare is about rights, not caring, and the history of citizenship has been the struggle to make freedom real, not to tie us all in the leading strings of therapeutic good intentions . . . . The pell-mell retreat from the language of justice to the language of caring is perhaps the most worrying sign of the contemporary decadence of the language of citizenship. (1989: 72)

The 'decadence' of citizenship that Ignatieff refers to does not just depend upon the strength of the 'caring professions' to dominate the paradigm of welfare, with the result that citizenship becomes corrupted by, or recast as, 'moral generosity'. While the social service professions have acted normatively to reinforce dominant political ideologies, it is also true that those ideologies and their authority to fashion appropriate social debate about welfare have 'decayed' the notion of citizenship. The change from a paradigm of paternalistic obligation to a paradigm of rights is the consequence of a much wider political drama. The emergence of a welfare perspective focusing on rights cannot be laid solely at the door of social work as a 'caring' but 'controlling' profession. It also involves the political struggle between freedom and equality and the realization that recognition of common human needs has developed into rigid demands for the recognition of different and separate claim rights (Ignatieff, 1984). In sum, the problem is that the democratization of welfare has led to intense competition for resources and is unable to provide a unifying political perspective.

## The Rhetoric of Welfare Crisis

Much of the controversy in the social policy literature about the notion of a crisis in welfare states concentrates on the respective validity of either a left-wing or a neo-conservative analysis of the issues. Inevitably, much discussion about 'the welfare debate' is locked into a defence of a false dichotomy. The set of 'prevailing ideas' which are used to 'explain' social need and fashion the nature of social policy debates involve a lesser role for the state sector in the provision of social services (cf., Duke and Edgell, 1987). The influence of neo-conservatism in the general debate about the role of the state is particularly significant when it concentrates on the critical assumption that there is a 'crisis of legitimacy' in welfare states. The crisis is perhaps not so much about legitimacy as it is about economic viability, but the argument is more radical than issues of fiscal probity. As this debate continues to evolve it will be interesting to see if the rhetoric about 'crisis' does indeed collapse the distinctions between economic and social policy so central to the initial rhetoric of welfare states. The unintended effect of this may be to lay the ground for a political redefinition of community and social obligation that does not depend upon the 'tired' and hack-neyed rhetoric of either the left or the right. Both extreme left and neo-conservative social theory collapse the complexity of the issues involved in social policy analysis into the relative simplicity of foreclosed world views. That one side of this classic debate is in the ascendancy is clear (cf., Glazer, 1988).

The so-called 'crisis of the welfare state' has emerged partly as expanding policies of privatization, associated with arguments for social retrenchment, have dominated current debates about the nature of social policy and sought to re-examine the fiscal probity of current levels of welfare provision (Bennett and Johnson, 1980). Demands for social justice, and sustained attacks upon the ability, or even the right, of state authorities to determine appropriate or accurate needs assessments, coincided with the growing importance of monetarist economic policies. These two 'pressures' for change, although they came from either end of the political spectrum, accelerated the development of retrenchment policies. Paradoxi-cally, the emergence of such policies is partly a response to the vociferousness of the debate. The paradox is that at the point where public opinion demonstrates no trust in the willingness of public officials to answer major questions of social equity about welfare provision and needs assessment there is, nevertheless, an associated strand of opinion that still expects that governments should assume responsibility for resolving the dilemmas of equitable provision!

Current theoretical speculation favouring the introduction of contracting draws impetus and justification from beliefs about the superior logic of the market-place and its ability to address the general assumption that there is a fiscal and administrative crisis in the welfare state (cf., Reid, 1972; Esping-Andersen, 1982; Kramer, 1985b; Paul, 1985). These differing assumptions about a welfare state in crisis have restricted any debate about a new theory of social obligation which claims that private and public welfare utilities are interdependent. Consequently, an emphatic radical and egalitarian individualism has supported proposals for a revamped welfare system based on the contracting of social services. Despite the pendulum swing towards neo-conservatism there is an aridity about social analysis premised on the validity of only one of the classic political dualisms – they are no longer satisfactory as explanatory models of the world. There is an equal sterility about the constant demands for rights, encapsulated in alienated or oppressed minority groups, that will not admit of any reciprocal responsibility.

One of the prefiguring assumptions of this social argument is that it is not possible to comprehend the welfare system without recognizing that it is founded on a set of competing political ideas about individuality and community (Weale, 1986: 217). Indeed, as Taylor-Gooby argues, conflict between such self-constituted interest groups is 'likely to be an endemic feature of the welfare state' (1983: 159). Another important aspect of this debate involves the relationship between rights and obligations (cf., Watson, 1980; Morris, 1986). A welfare rights model can only reveal the proliferation of individual or separate claim rights and has no ability to explain, morally, why one set of claims should have preference over others. A similar difficulty arises from the rhetorical certainty of a 'new right' analysis, which has assumed the radical high ground and denied the legitimacy of the state sector. Its protagonists are the 'sharpest critics of existing society, particularly in its political forms. It is the Left which has become trapped in an unusual defence of the state it has helped to build since the war' (Loney and Bocock, 1987: 141).

The rhetoric is also fashioned by ontological questions about different ways of perceiving the world. Any possibility of establishing the grounds for mutual or social obligation must wrestle with how it is that we say we know the world. 'Naming' the world from within the ideological constructs of the classic political dualisms provides no clear guide to the future except to perpetuate separate rationalizations. The endurability of this conflict is one of the few points of agreement between the classic protagonists and, irrespective of the logic of the separate arguments, the persistence of ideological and rhetorical conflict fashions the debate. This political argument is therefore an epistemological question of how social 'knowledge' is created by paradigmatic beliefs, as much as it is a question of beliefs about the political economy. Only recently have we seen substantive efforts to recast this debate in order to establish the possibility of movement beyond the ideological divide (cf., Goodin, 1985b; 1988). Consequently, while attempting to point beyond this dichotomy the ideological aspects of these competing ideas will need to be emphasized.

One of the important questions to be addressed in this debate is whether the concept of crisis is a slogan, used variously by the left and right for separate political purposes, or whether it represents empirical analysis that commands universal respect. Shalev reflects the common assumption that the 'debate cannot be easily settled, particularly since the issues are to a large extent ideological rather than straightforwardly amenable to the tools of positivist social science' (1983b: 47). In this context then it is important to embrace as wide a definition of research as possible, yet we have no research technology which lends itself to the requirements of such objective assessment. There is no clear mechanism by which social planning can be removed from political pressure. Attempts to do so are condemned as irrelevant and there is no commonly acceptable policy research instrument to enable the assessment of conflicting social policies. Precisely because 'the tools for intervention embody values, no simple calculus [formula] for distinguishing means and ends is at hand' (Rein, 1977: 69).

Capitalism is inevitably transformed by the political demands of separate claim rights, sanctioned by a commitment to individualism (cf., Offe, 1982; 1984; Mishra, 1984; 1989; Turner, 1988). The growth of the welfare state was the result of a political response which assessed the relative merits of those who claimed that their separate demands for entitlements were legitimate. The welfare state may be understood as a response to the increasing demands for social and economic equality or as the institutionalization of social rights in a response to the development of civil and political rights. An important consequence of these claim rights was the unplanned growth of such social expenditure. However, because of 'the well-meaning influence of interest-group liberalism little thought was given to the welfare state's capacity to manage its rapidly expanding domain' (Gilbert, 1986: 252). This exponential growth in social expenditure led to a fiscal crisis which also transformed the welfare state. Both left and right agree, for different reasons, that the welfare state and capitalist society are incompatible. Paradoxically, capitalism requires labour as a 'commodity', as a defined group, while the welfare state recognizes individuals as citizens with rights and entitlements. The clash has been inevitable. The welfare state, mandated by tax and bureaucratic regulations, attacks the supremacy of the market – the 'engine' which drives capitalist society. The ability of the capitalist system to finance the welfare state is therefore weakened, which equally thwarts the ability of the welfare state to deliver the social goods that 'legitimate' capitalist society denies (Klein, 1984b: 485).

The concept of crisis thus reflects three differing concerns: fiscal probity; effective delivery of services and outcomes; and the ideological concern about political legitimacy (cf., Baldock, 1989). Mishra analyses the notion of crisis from two conflicting left-wing perspectives, one that argues for the indefensibility of the welfare state and the other which assumes that it is an intrinsic aspect of capitalism. Despite the obvious paradox of these perspectives there are serious concerns about the continuation of the welfare state, irrespective of its auspices. The issue is really one about the feasibility of the welfare state rather than its legitimacy. Too much emphasis on the so-called crisis of legitimacy runs the risk of fuelling the logic of the neo-conservative counterattack that it should be fundamentally changed. Klein, for example, wonders why the concept of legitimacy is used if what it really refers to are the 'unavoidable conflicts of practical politics' (1984b).

Whether it can be argued that there is a deliberateness to the neo-conservative challenge is important. While Mishra's concern that privatization policies have the capacity to unravel the substantive gains that welfare state policies have delivered is valid, the explanation of cutback and retrenchment policies cannot be found solely in an analysis of competitive political economies. Drucker's (1969) assumption of the priority of performance over authority gives a new perspective to this political debate. The antecedents, therefore, for this resurgent neo-conservative view were implicit in the concepts that first argued for the priority of bureaucratic rationality. The very notion of social planning, let alone the collective principles of the welfare state, was suspect. The neo-conservative view embraced a scepticism about social planning, and rational social policy was defined in terms of policy limitation. Emphasis was placed on 'cutting back the role of government and substituting the rationality of the market for the rationality of either policy or politics' (Challis et al., 1988: 12).

It is too narrow a conclusion to argue that the crisis of welfare states involves the power of the neo-conservatives to define the parameters of the debate. Such an argument leads only to the 'safety' of foreclosed ideological perspectives and denies that there is a systemic interrelationship between left and right, that each is involved in defining the other (cf., Spicker, 1988). We have reason to question the continued justifications for such normative conflicts and to search for a more integrative social theory. As Challis et al. elegantly argue, 'the final irony would seem to be that when governments seek to restrict the scope of the public sector, they thereby extend the need for coordination' (1988: 20).

## The Development and Justification of New Social Policies

A range of utilitarian and economic arguments for the privatization of welfare services are intrinsic to the political and social policy imperatives of the 'new right' or neo-conservatism (cf., Burkitt and Davey, 1980; Bosanquet, 1983; Loney, 1986; Loney and Bocock, 1987; Flynn, 1989). These ideas challenge the welfare state protagonists to rework the current paradigm of welfare that emphasizes the primacy of universal claim rights and demands. The nature of these claim rights will be discussed in the following chapter in relation to the argument for a renewed theory of social obligation. It is ironic that one of the side-effects of the privatization and contracting debate, intrinsic to neo-conservative social policy, is that policy analysis is refocused on the validity of the traditional arguments about the welfare state. The initial neo-conservative attack upon the collective and communitarian orientation of the welfare state, which involved variations on a common theme that it hampered individual rights and autonomy, is caught in a complex paradox. The nature of that paradox is revealed in Turner's observation that capitalism

> . . . creates the condition for its own demise and transcendence in that the conditions for socialism grow out of the struggle for genuine rights in capitalism. The anarchy of the market place creates the conditions for the development of the state as that institution which guarantees social contracts and provides an administration within which profits can be realized but the state also becomes an institution necessary for the protection and development of social rights. Capitalism is transformed by a set of institutions which were designed to maintain and protect its continuity. (1986: 142)

Consequently, the neo-conservative challenge to the paternalism of the old welfare paradigm, with its presumed denial of individual autonomy, established the intellectual ground for a welfare rights paradigm. Even though this new paradigm emphasized the rights of groups instead of individuals, the antecedents of that argument are to be found in the neo-conservative disdain of 'welfarism' and a defence of the principle of autonomy in social relations. Any examination of these questions intersects with other significant debates about the relationship of normative theory and social policy (cf., Tulloch, 1978) and sociological argument about individualism, capitalism and dominant ideologies (cf., Turner, 1988). Feminist social policy analysis assumes that government obligation to realize and develop welfare legislation, that sustains the principle of autonomy, 'is precisely what has been missing in social policy as it concerns women' (Sapiro, 1986: 237). Neither the old welfare paradigm with its implicit theory of 'paternalistic' obligation, nor the current welfare rights paradigm about the democratization of welfare, with an implicit anarchism about any obligation beyond that owed to the community, tribe, group, family or network of similarity, can be appealed to if we are to assert the importance of social and mutual obligation. Perhaps the intensity of the debate is fuelled by mutually separate yet unacknowledged realizations that the rigidity of each argument is weakened by the normative assumptions about the true social reality that they each separately defend?

If the 1930s Stock Market crash and subsequent Depression could be said to represent the 'failure of the private sector' then aspects of the revitalized neo-conservative attack on the welfare state, that has precipitated analysis about the 'crisis of the welfare state', also represent the 'failure of the public sector'. Part of the context of this debate involves a consideration of the normative assumptions of a welfare radicalism that argues with sublime assurance for the legitimacy and superiority of 'positive, progressive and politicized' views of the welfare state. Such arguments imply the legitimacy of the demand 'to allow radical service workers to acknowledge and embrace their natural role as social change activists' (Withorn, 1984: x). Disagreeing with the utopian aspects of such radicalism is not to argue for a superior 'realism', but rather to argue for the necessity of both sides of the 'great divide' to accept the ontological adequacy of opposing views. The welfare state is no longer the preserve of the left, and since the 1940s many conservatives have come to accept it. Indeed, the entrance of the new right into the social policy arena establishes the possibility of a unique reconsideration of the ideology and purpose of welfare. The resurgent argument for privatization and purchase of service contracting establishes the neo-conservatives as de facto equal partners in the debate about appropriate welfare policy.

The adoption of social services privatization as a goal and purchase of service contracting as a method are not discrete managerial mechanisms, promoted only to achieve greater administrative efficiency. They also reflect changing political assumptions about the design and implementation of needs assessments. It is these, largely unspecified, assumptions which shape how these social concerns will be identified and addressed. As Johnson has argued, privatization

> . . . does not simply mean the sale of public assets and greater reliance on private enterprise and competitive markets; it also means the transfer of welfare responsibilities from the state to the voluntary and informal sectors. This is partly an ideological issue, concerning the state's

relationship with individual citizens and social groups, and partly a matter of practicalities. (Johnson, 1989: 28)

Arguments for either the full privatization of welfare services, or the implementation of purchase of service contracts, are commonly introduced as if they were solely about the efficient delivery of social services. Such an instrumental explanation hides the fact that these policies have normative political and social relevance. Controversy about the introduction of these social policies embraces political as well as managerial questions about the relative merits and patterns of current levels of social service delivery (cf., Hurl, 1986a; 1986b; Kramer and Grossman, 1987). Their emergence marks a sharp shift in the continuing debate about citizenship responsibilities and obligations. They are not equivalent policies. There is some dovetailing of method, but there are substantial distinctions to be drawn between arguments for either purchase of service contracting or the complete privatization of welfare services.

## Summary

The utopian vision in which mutual citizenship obligations were expected to create universal betterment had, at its base, an internal contradiction. The neo-conservative challenge has exposed the fallacy that welfare state bureaucracies were solely impassive instruments for the social good. When these neo-conservative arguments, however, attempt to pre-empt the social policy debate by asserting that there are simply no other alternatives to their own pattern of social analysis they are also flawed. Nevertheless, this criticism marks a significant shift in social policy debate and any intellectual defence of the welfare state must take these challenges seriously. Defenders of the welfare state must overcome their 'certainty' that the market-place is corrupt and learn to let go a false nostalgia for the old civic contract (cf., Ignatieff, 1984). Only if that can be achieved will there be any viable alternative to market conservatism and the ground laid to reargue the legitimacy of citizenship theory.

The widespread restructuring of the welfare system that the promotion of privatization and purchase of service contracting policies entails is expected to provide not only a substantial review of entitlement for services but also a reconsideration of the relationship between 'providers' and 'consumers'. If welfare services entitlement is to be argued on grounds other than that of citizenship then privatization is not just about the efficient redistribution of services but becomes a more sinister mechanism for attacking those social rights formerly guaranteed by the state (cf.,

King and Waldron, 1988). My purpose is to consider whether there might be grounds for a new theory of social obligation and, if so, what arguments might be proposed in support of that obligation. This investigation will obviously 'stumble' over the entrenched power of the rival ideologies to dominate and condition the current debate. However, knowing that is no reason not to search for an intellectual basis for a welfare paradigm that would enhance social relationships and obligation. If the twin traditional political perspectives are both imprisoned by a rigidity of argument in which any alternative views are rejected out of hand, it is also true that the debate is constrained by the realization 'that human beings tend to use the status quo as a moral reference point . . . one that can never be resolved by an appeal to reason' (Sugden, 1986: 175).

If such analysis starts from the premise that there can never be any resolution then it is that assumption, rather than the separate ideological divisions, which conditions the nature of the debate. Nevertheless, both classic protagonists argue that social and economic policy can now no longer be so easily separated. If social policy analysis can proceed without retreating into false dualisms a new model of social policy might be created in which theories of mutual obligation might again be defensible. While the criticism of welfare state policies is extreme, the fact that the debate has been enjoined in the way that it has suggests that there is a now a possibility of discovering the grounds for a new theory of social obligation which avoids the classic divisions of 'left' and 'right'.

# 2

## Towards a New Theory of Social Obligation

## The language of welfare: why care for the stranger?

> The solutions we find for the future will depend upon the meaning we give to philanthropy, to concern for others, and to the welfare state concept. Do these terms mean, in an open democratic system, wide acceptance that most of us must give to help others, not only voluntarily but through compulsory philanthropy which public, tax financed programs require? Or, do they now mean the competition of various specialized interests each jostling for a share of social welfare? If the former, old concepts of obligation may have to be reinterpreted and re-accepted in modern society. If the latter, what will protect the helpless in the competition?
>
> (Morris, 1988: 61)

Any attempt to propose an integration of views towards a new theory of social obligation must deal with the fundamental 'anxiety' of neo-conservatism 'about personal authenticity in the face of mass consumerism and bureaucracy . . . [and the fear] that bureaucratic regulation (individuation) will undermine the self-regulating individual of the liberal tradition' (Turner, 1988: 62). To argue from a left-wing position for the 'right to be a radical change agent' presupposes an underlying sense of moral superiority and certainty with respect to the direction that social policy should take in establishing equitable patterns of service delivery. To argue from a neo-conservative position against the legitimacy of any form of universal social obligation similarly condemns the social debate to sterility. For its own part the new right argues for the necessity of radical change agents based upon a managerial model of the 'warrior businessman'. It also advocates a concept of particular obligation which is owed to the family, or more loosely to the notion of being a 'concerned and active citizen'. It would be simplistic indeed to suggest that the intensity and complexity of this classic argument could be easily resolved. It will, however, be my intention to outline some of the assumptions that might be made in support of a position that looks beyond the mutual encapsulation of these traditional perspectives in social and political philosophy.

## The Notion of 'Crisis': An Epistemology of 'Welfare'

Excellent surveys and analyses about the 'crisis in welfare' already exist (Bosanquet, 1983; de Kok, 1984; Mishra, 1984; Klein and O'Higgins, 1985; Hill and Bramley, 1986a; Johnson, 1986; Loney, 1986; Munday, 1989). My intention is not to rework these analyses about the political economy of the welfare state. Nor is it to offer yet another comparative analysis of the respective social policy perspectives of left and right. Rather it is to discuss this debate from an epistemological perspective. That is, to consider explanations of a paradigm shift in justifications for welfare and to discover what aspects of this debate might form the basis for a new welfare paradigm (cf., Katznelson, 1986). An epistemological analysis confronts the entrenched normative assumptions of all ideologies with the 'meta-observation' that normative theories are always only sets of beliefs about the world, that they represent symbolic ways to understand the world and not to define it. These belief systems serve to limit what it is possible to discuss. Weale, for example, suggests 'that social thought itself in part constitutes the scope and limits of social action . . . it is at least possible that thinking of welfare, for example, as though it were an unproductive drain on the economy is just the way of making it such' (1986: 198–199). Therefore these ideas of what it is possible to discuss construe the practical world but cannot adequately be said to encompass it. These belief systems embrace symbolic patterns that describe personal 'knowledge' but do not create the grounds for more universal theory-building. Giddens, for example, argues that 'strictly speaking there is no such thing as an ideology: there are only ideological aspects of symbol systems' (1979: 187). Purchase of service contracting policies represents one powerful 'symbol system' that has the power to construe and limit the welfare policy debate.

Social policy analysis, premised only on the inevitability of conflict, cannot easily provide for any theory of integration that would support a theory of obligation. Any argument for the possible integration of the classic 'symbol systems' will require an understanding of how the concept of social obligation is regarded within the normative structures of these separate political ideologies. The concept of a universalist welfare policy is unacceptable to the logic of a neo-conservative perspective. For the neo-conservative theorist the 'harmony of needs is not only undiscoverable but [it is] non-existent' (Challis et al., 1988: 34). It is my contention that no resolution of these 'historic antagonisms', between individual and collective ways of being in the world, is possible unless a new paradigm is evolved based upon a new definition of social obligation. Epistemological analysis provides a different perspective on the rationale for social obligation. Analysis of the reflexiveness of social knowledge suggests that social theory based upon the logic or morality of only one set of beliefs about the world is vacuous. Beliefs can only be completely understood in the light of that which they deny as well as in the clarification and logic of what they affirm. Any substantive new theory of obligation must therefore 'stand in relation' to both these classic political theories of individualism and collectivism. It must, to use the rhetoric of epistemology, adopt a meta-position so that the respective 'symbol systems' can be acknowledged as only part of the whole. Knowledge is therefore about polarities, about that which is denied as well as about that which is asserted. To argue for the truth of only one set of social beliefs 'constructs' the preconditions for dichotomous and dualistic assumptions. Whether obligation is therefore owed to the whole and cannot be assumed to apply only to a part of the whole will be further explored in relation to Goodin's theory of vulnerability (cf., 1985b). Neo-conservative social theory demonstrates an assumption of personal obligation to the 'citizen-friend' and questions that owed to the 'citizen-stranger'. So too, it might be argued, do the social theories of the left and its commitment to the organizing power of separate unions. It may well be the case that individual consciousness balks at any broadly conceived notion of social obligation.

## The 'Welfare Crisis': Convergence of Left and Right

Phrased another way this question is about whether 'social reality' can ever be framed independent of the ideologies that 'name the social world', to recast Freire's assumptions. An assumption of crisis in the welfare state is one of the points at which there is a convergence in the dominant political analysis (Offe, 1982; 1984; Deakin, 1985; Taylor-Gooby, 1986a; Vettenranta, 1986). This convergence has helped to destroy the old welfare paradigm that assumed that the morality and probity of the welfare state was self-evident. It marked the destruction of what Klein (1984b) refers to as 'the hidden hand of social altruism'. The paternalistic concept of altruistic social obligation, manifest in state support for social work intervention, was discredited. This alliance between left and right about the existence of a crisis in the welfare state has restricted social policy analysis to questions of political economy (cf., Gough, 1979). Mishra has argued that the

> . . . neo-conservative counterattack on postwar social welfare has hammered home two things. First, that social welfare is at bottom a question of values – a moral issue – and in this respect there are no guarantees in

history, no immanent laws that spell the 'end of ideology' and carry us effortlessly into higher forms of social organisation . . . . Secondly, and perhaps more significantly, it has reminded us that the consensus of the 1960's *assumed* a harmony between economic and social welfare. It was the disjunction between the two and the apparent threat to the economy posed by social welfare that gave the New Right much of its credibility. Put simply, neo-conservatives claim that to put the economy right social welfare must be retrenched. (1989: 180)

Mishra's assumption that the social welfare debate is essentially an ethical argument about values is valuable but the dilemmas cannot be resolved using only the traditional patterns of moral and individual responsibility derived from either religious or moral codes. It may well be the case that there are 'no immanent laws that spell the end of ideology' but moral arguments easily become normative and reinforce only a specific reification of the process of the debate (Davies, 1977). For example, the use of moral injunctions to support the essential superiority of any particular social theory is automatically dismissed by political opponents who emphasize the specific 'irrationality' of such moral imperatives, and offer the 'obviousness' of their separate sets of moral injunctions. Sugden comments that 'morality cannot be reduced to welfarism . . . our morality is in important respects the morality of spontaneous order; and the morality of spontaneous order is conservative' (1986: 177). Neo-conservatism considers that the welfare state reflects only the interplay of social and political structures forged out of the harsh logic of self-interest, and that it is only tangentially about benevolence and social concern. Katznelson has suggested that the

. . . most analytically powerful of recent policy studies are grounded in choice theory drawn from the parsimonious postulates of neoclassical economics about isolated, self-interested persons who choose rationally between alternatives after computing their costs and benefits. (1986: 312)

This perspective assumes that there is no alternative to conflict and that it represents a greater realism than any perspective based upon respect for collective responsibility. Even the very use of the concept of social policy is suspect because it 'implies a degree of orderliness, even consensus; [that] a way forward has been agreed and delineated' (Challis et al., 1988: 36). Such consensus, it is argued, implies the importance of social planning which has a deleterious effect on the logic of the market-place. Attempts to establish an 'overarching rationality' are rejected as deluded bids to impose order where none can properly exist, except that provided by the 'rationality of the market-place'. The neo-conservative perspective reflects aspects of public choice theory, which views the development of social policy 'in terms of the self-defined interests of competing groups with unequal powers of organization' (Weale, 1986: 216). For this reason it is more profitable to assume that 'true rationality resides in process – the interplay of individual preferences and decisions – not in the imposition of collective strategy' (Challis et al., 1988: 34). This point will be taken up later in a discussion of a renewed justification for welfare based on respecting the status of human vulnerabilities (Goodin, 1988).

## The Grounds for a Theory of Obligation: 'Limited and Precarious'?

The old welfare paradigm depended on an overarching 'super-structure' of normative ideas that justified the welfare state as the practical expression of incontrovertible moral imperatives. These beliefs about the superior political morality of the welfare state supported the growth of an administrative structure which operated on the principle of altruistic obligation. The welfare bureaucracy that followed was entrusted to intervene directly on behalf of the state. The question obviously arises as to why such a social obligation, even if it were possible, should be considered necessary. One obvious reason is that the current paradigm of welfare, and the impetus towards privatization, do not generate any socially cohesive metaphors that one could appeal to in order to establish the grounds for a more equitable or just society. The initial welfare state mandate articulated the political necessity to tamper with the rights of private property in order to create a welfare society, but it did not demonstrate 'how a social contract required for such a project may be negotiated' (Esping-Andersen, 1987: 99). Neither the social analyses of the left nor those of the right command sufficient respect in themselves to indicate how a new paradigm of mutual obligation might be accomplished (cf., Goodin, 1988). Nor does the neo-conservative position have any respect for the concept of explanatory or overarching morality given its disdain for the notion of overarching rationality that was used to justify a social planning perspective (Challis et al., 1988). Suggesting any future directions for social policy is often presumptuous yet the effort to do so is important. As we have seen, the current paradigm of democratized welfare has no implicit or explicit assumptions of obligation beyond that owed to the reference group, which may be a community, tribe, family, organization or self-help group. Ignatieff comments on a different facet of the search for a new theory of social obligation when he suggests that

   . . . this is the truth before which thinking about politics has stalled – the more evident our common needs as a species become, the more brutal becomes the human insistence on the claims of difference. The centripetal forces of need, labour and science which are pulling us together as a species are counter-balanced by centrifugal force, the claims of tribe, race, class, section, region and nation, pulling us apart. (1984: 130–131)

Friedman (1981: 21) suggests that 'the rule of law, the most effective tool ever fashioned by human societies so that their regimes may achieve justice, impartiality, and fairness, is the first casualty' of an approach that focuses on a welfare rights approach sustained and mediated only through bureaucratic administration. This structure of welfare rights is a practical expression of 'interest-group liberalism' in which clients and consumers bargain for services on the basis of their status as 'members' of particular interest groups (Lowi, 1986). These interest groups may have legislatively mandated entitlement or they may equally have gained political power and be pressing for such mandated rights and entitlements. However, as Friedman argues, once the mandate for legally prescribed relationships is shifted away from the legislative and legal arena, and transformed into administrative issues, the result is a 'policy without law'. These administrative decisions, despite statutory guidelines, cannot be generalized beyond the demands and rights of specific cases. Consequently, no validly universal pattern of entitlement, or linking metaphors of social obligation, result from a welfare rights paradigm. Under such a paradigm governments are placed in a perverse paradox in that, while still notionally espousing universalist principles of welfare and citizenship entitlement, the typically administrative pattern of welfare results in the facilitation of particular rights at the expense of the whole. The consequence of this is the perpetuation of precisely the pattern of fragmentation that the policy is designed to alleviate.

## Social Needs: Satisfactions or Interpretations?

Shifting the typical focus of needs defined only as tangible 'social goods' to needs also understood as an interpretation of demand (part of an ideological 'wish-list') raises the question of the essential philosophical nature of the debate. Fraser (1989) has suggested that the assumptions implicit in the rhetoric about needs and the validity of respective claim rights might be better understood if the focus was shifted from 'the distribution of satisfactions' to 'the politics of need interpretation'. She argues that the focus in needs analysis should be shifted from needs to 'discourses about needs'. This is not to assert that all needs are by definition relative, and therefore dismissible, but that the patterned articulation of them under the aegis of a welfare rights model has transformed them into political interpretations about needs. The problem is how to identify, measure and discuss needs apart from their political interpretation. The substance of this argument is that 'needs' will always reflect assumptions about the world. They inevitably involve interpretations as well as objective analysis of political and social disadvantage. Analyses of welfare claim rights in terms of need interpretation challenge those assumptions that attempt to base definitions of needs upon the moral assertion of unique and special entitlement. It is more useful to shift the emphasis from endless ideological repetition towards an evaluation of the function of such prescriptive argumentation. Unless that is done, as Tulloch warns, 'normative theory will remain little more than an impediment to rational thought' (1978: 74).

Viewing needs assessment as 'the politics of need interpretation' shifts the ground from the pessimism of Pearson's 'frame' that social work must inevitably be about the 'ambiguous, moral calculus of need and priority' (1975a: 66). This is not, in any sense, to minimize the actual reality for impoverished people, which is indeed desperate. Nor is it to suggest that social work and allied professions do not work within confused and contradictory public mandates. The point is to argue that there are connections between needs and the politics of their interpretation apart from the empirical reality of actual deprivation. For example, analysis of the structural significance of unemployment, poverty and disadvantage has not yet been politically or socially successful in that variations of the poor law mentality still appear in the debate about requisite social policy. Neither utilitarian nor the moral or religious arguments seem able to resolve the ancient belief that 'relief given to the poor be limited and precarious' (quoted by Goodin, 1982b: 5). The history of social policy reflects a continual oscillation in explanatory arguments together with a rejection of 'grand design' theory. Ideology and ambivalence coincide because part of the fundamental ground of this social analysis is that there is a liveliness in conflict and an inertia in agreement. There is perhaps an in-built social protection in the common democratic assumption that consensus about 'grand design theory' is not possible, which acts to protect democracy from totalitarianism. In the current debate both left and right resort to aspects of totalitarian rhetoric and the imposition of a stalemated consensus. Ignatieff suggests that:

> It is a recurring temptation in political argument to suppose that these conflicts can be resolved in principle, to believe that we can rank human

needs in an order of priority which will avoid dispute. Yet who really knows whether we need freedom more than we need solidarity, or fraternity more than equality? Modern secular humanism is empty if it supposes that the human good is without internal contradiction. These contradictions cannot be resolved in principle, only in practice. (1984: 137)

## Reflexivity: Dualism and Truth?

To establish the grounds for a new theory of social obligation will require an acceptance from both left and right that needs statements and assessments are, as Fraser suggests, about 'the politics of need interpretation'. To do this requires a mutual acknowledgement that there will need to be a reconsideration of the manner in which ideological prescriptions are related to objective and subjective realities (Tulloch, 1978). The difficulty of course is that analysis of needs, together with debate about the nature of political economy, has been one of the classic props to the old left argument about the social destructiveness of capitalism (cf., Gough, 1979; Soper, 1981). Goodin's resolution of this impasse is to point towards a justification for social welfare that 'is couched in terms of the moral duties of the strong to protect the weak' (1988: x). While not arguing with the basic moral premise of this assumption (which Goodin locates as part of a universal morality and not essentially or solely in the arguments for the welfare state) I do not think that any new paradigm of welfare will emerge from moral or philosophical exhortation. The arena of social philosophy is piled high with the respective 'truths' of 'obvious fact'! There may well be a contradiction in the expectation that ideological prescription be evaluated in relationship to objective and subjective reality. To expect this is to demand that normative ideologies cease to be normative and concede the contingency or relativity of their prescriptions. Perhaps the power of beliefs lies not so much in the intrinsic value of particular beliefs but in the fact that they are assumed to be normative. It is, however, important to continue to press for the relativity and contingency that epistemological theory assumes to be intrinsic to all normative prescriptions. Without it we may well be condemned to a perpetual conflict of ideologies.

## 'Private' and 'Public': Rethinking the Dualisms

If new grounds can be established for social obligation our task will be to synthesize these ideological presuppositions with a re-fashioned utilitarianism that will not allow a separation into false alternatives and illusory choices. The question is whether a new theory of social obligation can be developed out of an analysis of the reflexiveness of systems theory and cybernetics. Part of this debate will require a reconsideration of the traditional distinctions that are assumed between the public and the private. Arendt has argued that 'the distinction between private and public coincides with the opposition of necessity and freedom, of futility and permanence, and finally of shame and honor' (1959: 65). The endurability of the classic political argument between left and right about the proper relationship between the categories of public and private is fuelled by these fundamental dualisms which Arendt assumes are essential to social policy analysis. Any new theory of social obligation will need to 'point beyond' these dualisms. It will be necessary to argue that there can be no retreat into an analysis that will not willingly examine the issue that what we assert as the factual basis of our social argument is not fact but essentially a belief. Perhaps there is a more profound humanism and 'morality' in the reflexive posture that 'I believe that my beliefs are beliefs'. Tulloch's conclusion, echoing Gouldner, with which I agree, is that:

> The dissonance with the ideal of objectivity which the pragmatic and moral nature of social administration and social policy produces, cannot be solved by a retreat into the traditional conceptions of a pure sociology . . . . The direction must be towards . . . [a] reflexive sociology, that is, one which will study values and beliefs, and their dialectical relationship with empirical reality. (1978: 74)

As long as the current paradigm of welfare remains focused solely on arbitrary and autonomous claim rights and develops no theory of social obligation the defensive reaction of those with resources against those without will continue. Various arguments for welfare and claim rights based solely on the legitimacy of specific entitlement are divisive. There are, inevitably, systemic connections between the facts of achievement or disadvantage that cannot be explained solely on the grounds of abstracted individualism. A simple ethical posture, arguing that social concern and obligation will only be achieved by the 'remoralization of society' (Davies, 1987), while laudable in intent, is insufficient. The moral/religious imperative that sustained the old welfare paradigm is ineffectual in the current social policy analysis. The utilitarian and economistic imperatives that sustain an argument for privatization are similarly ineffectual. Privatization is proposed either as a new solution or as a welcome return to economic 'sense'. These arguments create the rhetorical 'ground' for assumptions that 'economics' is the paramount reality and that the 'social' is a troublesome fiction. However, arguments for the complete privatization of all former direct state welfare services are socially divisive because they develop no theory of obligation beyond that owed to separate groups or individuals.

## Claim Rights, Needs and Obligations

The old welfare paradigm was able to establish a theory of paternalistic social obligation that created and supported the administrative and political infrastructure of the welfare state. The current welfare rights paradigm has no theory of obligation and has only facilitated the proliferation of need claims. Fraser, for example, argues that needs asserted as legitimate claim rights 'tend to be nested, connected to one another in ramified chains of "in-order-to" relations. Moreover, when these chains are unravelled in the course of political disputes, disagreements usually deepen rather than abate' (1989: 293). They reveal the 'brutal claims for difference' that, Ignatieff (1984) argued, followed on from a welfare rights model that had forgotten its citizenship obligations. Not to do so will condemn social policy innovation to repeated failure. Manning argues that

> . . . much intervention is regressive and ironically leads to 'fatal remedies'. While the typical reaction from the Right is to 'do nothing', and from the Left to 'change everything' . . . the most frequent effect is for policy makers to redouble their efforts at rational problem-solving by taking more variables into account in order to try to control adverse effects . . . . policies based on an understanding of the issues only at the level of appearance will fail. (1987: 21)

Political or administrative responses to an analysis of the respective merits of such welfare claim rights must seek to place these 'nested' 'in-order-to' relations in the context of a new theory of social obligation and needs. Fraser's argument for an analysis of the 'politics of need interpretation' suggests the possibility of an appraisal of social obligation that would, it might be argued, 'objectify' the subjective reality and return the analysis to the practicality of political discourse. The implicit aspect of needs understood as interpretations does provide an answer to Tulloch's question of whether ideological prescription can be related 'to objective and subjective reality' (1978: 74). The proliferation of claim rights in a system of 'democratized welfare' are related not to each other but to the resource provider. The only possible relationship involves an analysis of their respective ability to canvass public opinion or to manoeuvre the welfare bureaucracies. The welfare rights paradigm, while emphasizing the legitimacy of unique claims,

couches the argument for that legitimacy in subjective or ethno-
methodological perspectives. Arguing for uniqueness and difference has weakened the rationalization for paternalistic, expert or
professional analysis, implicit in the old welfare paradigm. Developing opposing sets of normative and explanatory ideas the various
'protagonists' have created a unified belief that obligation must be
owed solely to subsets of the whole.

## The Politicization of Needs and Needs Assessments

Fraser suggests that needs and needs assessments get politicized in
two ways. The first is 'from below', in which 'the initiative resides in
. . . "oppositional" needs-talk; and the process involves the crystal-
lization of new social identities on the part of subordinated persons
and groups'. This coincides with the critical client perspective that is
the substance of the left-wing criticism of the welfare state. The
second is 'from above', in which 'the initiative resides in . . .
"expert" needs discourses, and the process involves "social
problem-solving", institution-building, and professional class formation' (1989: 303). While the self-protective professionalized
aspects of this are intrinsic to the neo-conservative argument, its
support of managerial solutions reflects aspects of 'top down'
problem-solving. Fraser's discussion points to an analysis of what
form of social obligation might be possible, one that neither retreats
into the stale rhetoric of the left for renewed collectivization, nor
adopts the atomized rhetoric of the new right. A thorough analysis
of the debate about privatization and, in particular, purchase of
service contracting will have to lead beyond a debate about needs
interpretation that arises either 'from below' or 'from above'. 'From
above' repeats the mistakes of the past while 'from below' repeats
the mistakes of the present. Fraser contrasts these two ways of
talking about needs with Drucker's (1969) concept of 'reprivatization'. The value of Fraser's analysis is that it points towards a
renewed concept of social obligation that neither depends upon the
rhetoric of collectivization, nor is eviscerated by the rhetoric of the
new right.

## Social Obligation: Dualisms, Purpose and Meaning

As we have seen, any sustainable argument in support of a theory of
social obligation will have to outline how the classic polarized
positions of left and right might be lessened. Paradoxically, the
recursiveness of the argument validates rather than destroys the
other because neither left nor right makes much sense in isolation

from each other. The opponents are locked into a polarized system and it is the systemic nature of this argument that needs further clarification. The first step in analysing the shared premises of these positions will be to indicate how the oppositional nature of the debate actually depends upon a mutual reflexiveness in which the respective ideological claims are interconnected. A theory of obligation can be further developed using the set of dualisms that Arendt (1959) outlined about the respective private and public 'worlds': necessity and freedom, futility and permanence, and shame and honour. These distinctions provide a useful framework with which to explore the possibility of a new theory of social obligation. Much of the substance of the clash between left and right depends on the classic dualism of public/private. Both political philosophies attempt to prove that their ontological view is not only superior but is the only possible one. However, there are systemic connections between the idea of private and public worlds and the 'meaning' of this ontological division resides outside the rigidity of the internal logic of the separate arguments. In simplistic terms welfare policy analysis depends upon a 'both-and' perspective rather than 'either-or'.

Attacking the rigid distinctions between public and private has been one of the major focuses of feminist theory. The idea of a private (or individualized) world set against a public arena of competition is considered to be an artefact of masculine consciousness. The taken-for-granted obviousness of the incompatibility of the public and private is challenged. Social structure and ideology are interrelated in that social organizations and agencies are the factual expressions of beliefs. Acknowledgement of this interconnection of structure and ideology creates the potential for and possibility of major paradigmatic change. Fraser argues that in order to confront the difficult problem of the relationship between structure and ideology

> . . . it will be necessary to clarify the phenomenon of 'public patriarchy' . . . . Long before the emergence of welfare states, governments have defined legally secured arenas of societal action. In so doing, they have at the same time codified corresponding patterns of agency or social roles. Thus, early modern states defined an economic arena and the corresponding role of an economic person capable of entering into contracts. More or less at the same time, they codified the 'private sphere' of the household and the role of the household head with dependents. Somewhat later, governments were led to secure a sphere of political participation and the corresponding role of citizen with (limited) political rights. In each of these cases, the original and paradigmatic subject of the newly codified role was male . . . with the contemporary [development] of the welfare state . . . this type of government defined a new arena

of activity – call it 'the social' – and a new societal role, the welfare client, [and women became] its original and paradigmatic subjects. (1987: 104–106)

If the 'public world' is defined solely as a conflictual competitive and market-driven reality then the 'private world' must be secured as a haven from the hazardous public arena. Feminist theory poses a challenge to the masculine and capitalist assumptions which drive the rhetoric and ideology that supports privacy and individual competition as the norm (Pascall, 1986; Dominelli and McLeod, 1989). The political significance of social policy defined as if it were only an adjunct to the normative economic debate has been discussed (Morris, 1988). The universalist assumptions of the 'queen of social sciences' is revealed in Culyer's conclusion where he states that 'the set of issues upon which economics cannot shed some light is, I conjecture, extremely small' (1983: 202). The rhetoric of the neo-conservatives, based on this presumption about the normativeness of economics, that 'there is no alternative' is exposed both as a hollow argument and as an attempt to constrain the social policy debate to a narrow definition of private obligation. Within this perspective moral obligation belongs solely to the private world of the family or interest group. By definition, the demands of public competition and market alliances reduce social obligation to an analysis of strategic advantage, to relationships between 'players' and 'winners'. Given the pre-eminence of this masculine/capitalist world view there can be few grounds for social obligation and little valid politics of public responsibility.

In the context of the old welfare paradigm a moral and religious imperative for social obligation was translated into support for the profession of social work, an expression of 'public patriarchy' as Fraser describes it. Thus, as Weale (1986) suggests, administrative processes were essentially subjective because welfare policy was an attempt to enact prior moral concerns about access, provision, support and entitlement. The social welfare professions were 'moral guardians' and explicitly or implicitly carried out the generalized moral imperatives about legitimate social services. Within the new welfare rights paradigm economic analysis of the provision of goods and services considers these rights to be subjective claims on public goods. They could be dismissed precisely because they had been exposed as essentially subjective. The proliferation of rights claims had destroyed the basis for assessment and comparison. Paradoxically, in their insistence on difference they had destroyed the capacity of social policy to work on the basis of relativities, that is, on an old model of expert assessment and analysis. The questions are no longer essentially philosophical, about issues of morality or ethics, but are rather about the superior 'morality' of the market which guarantees economic success and will, presumably, also guarantee success in social policy planning. They are about allocative efficiency, restructuring and economic utility (cf., Thurow, 1981) and couch needs assessments within a narrow frame.

Market-based analyses of social policy are never able to explain purpose and meaning, only to describe predisposed choices. At the same time, as Weale argues, it is naive not to acknowledge that the market is constrained by its own internal codes of obligation. To describe the market as completely without moral scruple is to misunderstand the subtlety of these codes, obligations and contracts. Despite these market codes and contractual arrangements the new welfare paradigm provides no unifying metaphor of obligation. It only provides for the administratively strategic allocation of scarce resources and the implicit competitiveness of decentralization and devolution. The feminist critique of a privatized social policy analysis is that the argument cannot be based just on the issues of functional utility but must consider its purpose. This must involve an analysis of the interconnection between public and private and the relatedness of structure and ideology. The neo-conservative assumptions about the pre-eminent reality of the market ignore the question that this 'paramount reality' is paradigmatic and not the unalterable base from which analysis proceeds. The state and the market are different aspects of a systemic political economy. It is a mutual exchange where the state actively defines the system of social protection that shapes the private sector and is in turn influenced by private sector lobbying which seeks to delimit state action. The welfare society is a 'structure of rules and institutions where the state and the market interact as instruments for protecting the members of society against the uncertainties of industrial society' (Rein and White, 1981: 36). The notion of social obligation involves wider aspects of responsibility. The simple but fundamental question is why care for the stranger (cf., Watson, 1980; Morris, 1986)?

## Caring for the Stranger: A Woman's Task and Obligation?

It is possible to argue that the old welfare paradigm of paternalistic obligation reflected a masculine definition of the world. As we have seen, this paternalistic definition reinforced and sustained the social work profession and maintained a particular style of bureaucratic control. In addition, the majority of welfare recipients are female and the social work profession has a high concentration of women (cf., Pascall, 1986). Fraser argues that because 'this beneficiary-social worker-caregiver nexus of roles is constitutive of the social-welfare arena, one might even call the latter a feminized terrain' (1987: 106; Sapiro, 1986). This 'feminized terrain' of social work partly reflects the masculine ascription to women of a nurturant role and an imposition of the obligation to care for the stranger as well as the family. The relatively low social status that social work has achieved is the result of the traditional stigmatization of its clientele, as well as a practical indication of the dominant power of men to define the normative theoretical assumptions and the practical parameters of the profession.

The pejorative rhetoric, that social workers are 'soft', 'politically wet' and have a 'bleeding heart', is aligned with the explicit expectations of the profession that it be caring, responsive, nurturant and supportive. These metaphors and assumptions of practical altruism masked the social control function which the profession equally denied (Bulmer, 1987). Feminist analysis is central to this debate for, in its rejection of any aspect of 'public patriarchy', it reframes the concept of obligation. Social obligation is no longer just the preserve of the traditional social service professions. Feminist social theory argues that social obligation, which the social service and helping professions equated with the 'process' aspects of procedural obligation, cannot be reified into technique. Social obligation is no longer the preserve of a profession, social class or specific gender but becomes at once personal and political. The key questions are what are we obliged to do and why are we obliged to do it? It is to be understood as a mutual recognition of vulnerability, as process rather than technique. This assumption has been philosophically grounded and provides a way in which we might discuss vulnerability as intrinsic to a new theory of obligation that recognizes mutual vulnerability rather than professional obligation. As Goodin argues, an ethical defence of the welfare state can be provided in that

> . . . it is the vulnerability of others, rather than any voluntary act of will on our part, that generates those responsibilities. There are many more people vulnerable to us, individually or especially collectively, than stand in any of the standard special 'relationships' to us . . . we have strictly analogous (and, potentially, equally strong) responsibilities to all those others as well. Aid to vulnerable strangers is thereby justified on the same basis as aid rendered to our own parents or children. (1985b: 782)

Any successful argument for a new theory of social obligation will need to avoid the implicit moral responsibility of the old welfare paradigm. What Goodin is attempting (and perhaps not success-fully) is to outline how social obligation might be recast not as a duty, enjoined by a predetermined moral code, but as a realistic and compassionate recognition of current vulnerability. This seems to me the critical point in the development of any future theory of social obligation. Moral exhortation to follow a set of normative principles is less convincing than how social and personal vulnerabi-lities are recognized and acknowledged. Goodin acknowledges that these responsibilities will be regarded as 'utterly incommensurable' by some, and that there will still be cruel choices in choosing which sets of vulnerable claims require a response and solution. He argues that those nearest to us are more likely to display the vulnerabilities that engage our attention, but that this bias must not be absolute. Goodin concludes these speculations by suggesting that the 'princi-pal challenge facing any defence of the welfare state must surely be to show why protecting these vulnerable people should be a collective rather than an individual responsibility' (1985b: 785). Goodin's answer is that we cannot presume on the good intentions of individuals to respond to these sets of vulnerabilities even in those closest to them. He argues that families and friends will inevitably have 'discretionary control over resources' that ultimately still belong to the vulnerable family member. This realization leads Goodin to the conclusion that:

> Where the subordinate is dependent instead upon the state, however, it is possible to vest that person with a legal entitlement to assistance. Once such laws have been enacted, state officials (unlike families, friends, or private charities) lack any discretion in deciding whether or not to honor claims of needy petitioners. The welfare state, defined as an institution which meets people's basic needs as a matter of right, is therefore a morally necessary adjunct to other more individualistic responses to the problems of vulnerability and dependency in the larger community. (1985b: 785-786)

Despite its pervasiveness the welfare state does not rest upon any absolutely certain ground (cf., Lowi, 1986). The crisis-talk about the welfare state has to do with questions of 'feasibility' rather than its 'legitimacy'. However, while the basic structures of the welfare state are still intact, underestimating the potential for contracting and privatization policies to erode its citizenship provisions is foolish. Goodin argues that 'the welfare state can satisfy the criteria of a morally acceptable dependency relationship' (1985b: 775). This argument pivots on notions of citizenship, rights and obligations and these will need to be considered before returning to the argument for a new theory of social obligation.

## Claim Rights: Formal Dispensation of Social Justice?

Consideration of these questions of rights involves Arendt's first set of dualisms, necessity and freedom. This is well trodden ground! My purpose is to argue that both concepts, while distinct, are in fact the obverse of each other. It will be important to distinguish claims, rights, entitlement and privileges in order to explicate my use of the concept of claim rights. Lowi's definitions are helpful. He has argued that:

> A right will be defined as a claim to a remedy that cannot be denied except by an extraordinary decision-making process . . . . An entitlement becomes a claim to a remedy that cannot be denied except by an extraordinary decision-making process, but one that is specified and formalized in advance. Entitlement is a lower level of right, deniable by a lower level of decision-making process . . . . At the far end of the continuum is a privilege, which is also a claim, but one that can be denied at the discretion of the holder of the remedies or resources. (1986: 216)

The morality of the need for government intervention to preserve citizenship rights and establish social and welfare rights is a theme which runs like a thread throughout social administration and social policy. In considering the concept of rights we must distinguish between legal rights and social rights or, expressed differently, between legal and positive rights, distinct from moral and human rights (Weale, 1983). Legal and positive rights are those which we hold by virtue of some legal code or customary social practice. Human rights are less tangible, being given or denied on the basis of a moral or ethical code. The purpose of establishing a right either in law or in morality and ethics is that having done so we can then argue for a claim that has some intrinsic importance. Establishing a right therefore leads to the validity of a claim against that right, which holds true for both legal and social rights. Such claims require some form of justification as to why that claim is being ignored or unfulfilled.

Legal rights require us to give evidence that certain procedures have been followed. Human rights, however, depend upon the persuasiveness of moral or ethical arguments that certain human rights be recognized. In legal terms we depend upon a code which is clarified and obvious, and to which most people and institutions in a society subscribe. Legal debate is essentially about the clarification of that code. Human or social rights, however, depend, as we have seen, upon moral and ethical codes about which there may well be no consensus. Coded legal rights have an empirical base within which it is easier to establish the concept of 'freedom from' rather than 'freedom to'. This crucial distinction in legal theory has its counterpart in how it is argued that social rights lead to welfare rights. These assumptions in legal theory construe the debate so that it is easier for governments to determine social needs on the principle of 'freedom from' rather than 'freedom to'. This explains why it is easier to establish the ground for an analysis of social policy that accepts the concept of minimum levels of welfare entitlement. The nature of the argument for citizenship rights has changed: instead of being based on the concepts of liberty, or 'freedom from', they have become claim rights. There is, consequently, a distinction to be made between rights that require positive government action and those that require governments not to interfere with the lives of their citizens. There is always a stigma attached to welfare and one reason is that while the case can be made for welfare rights they can never be as autonomous as the legal right to property ownership. Welfare claim rights can establish only the viability of redress of grievance, or disadvantage based on the act of another. The point is that someone else in authority, or some separate administrative system, decides whether or not any individual has justifiable claims to the benefit.

Claim rights are those which have greater command on our attention because they are in response to recognized and procedurally defined vulnerabilities. Part of the substantive argument of the neo-conservatives against the plethora of interest group demands is that these indicate a democratization of rights without commensurate obligations. Lowi argues that defining 'substantive rights procedurally' will provide an opportunity to structure a new justification for the welfare state on the basis of rights and entitlements. This is to create a new theory of social obligation that is a recognition of the reality and universality of vulnerable status and therefore of entitlement. The neo-conservative distrust of a welfare rights approach is that it involved an uncontrolled incrementalism that absorbed more and more resources. Lowi considers that:

> Present welfare-state practices turn out to be trying to have it both ways – by permitting claims to be established by normal interest-group process and then, after the fact, as an effective political strategy, to declare those claims rights. It is a normal part of the political process to protect one's successes by calling them rights, because that automatically sets them above ordinary . . . interest-group processes. This tactic is also used by welfare bureaucrats, who find the vocabulary of rights an effective defense of their own agencies and their own budgets. But if we take the concept of rights and entitlements seriously . . . a very strict limitation or ceiling can be imposed upon the interest-group/bureaucratic defense process. It means that any claim worthy of being called a right or entitlement must have been established by a formalized process well in advance of the dispensation. (1986: 216–217)

In a personal sense, obligations, no matter how laudable, are often accompanied by their obverse, which are resentments. However, the application of systems theory to social policy does suggest that welfare policy that is framed only on the high ground of moral responsibility is flawed. To take such moral stands in order to articulate social obligation is to place oneself outside of a social process that we are inextricably part of. It is the 'meta-position' of moral responsibility that creates the aspect of obligated professionalism. Feminist theory argues that the dispassionate disengagement of the professional is socially and personally destructive in that it is a mechanism for reinforcing the power of the expert at the very point of client vulnerability. While there is a separate world of theoretical debate and speculation involved in these issues, my concern is to highlight the structural difficulties involved in continuing to argue that social obligation is the intrinsic preserve of the social service professions. Public respect for a system of rights and entitlements will be stronger when those rights are seen to be legitimate claims against previously established patterns of dispensation. States obtain 'legitimacy' when financial redistributions are couched in the language of social rights, provided by a respect for citizenship which is protected by the rule of law. Legitimacy is lost and the same states 'suffer backlashes as well as other criticisms, when they devolve largesse onto the citizenry in any manner that approximates patrimonial or premodern gratuitousness' (Friedman, 1981: 23).

### Choice and Personal Freedom: A 'Moral' Market?

The arguments for social obligation and altruism must also respect the hidden aspects of a contrary selfishness and denial of responsibility. The arguments for privacy and the primacy of individualism must also deal with the obverse, which is communitarian, with all the ways that the public may legitimately intrude into the private. Politically, both left and right represent legitimate views of the world but, instead of cancelling each other, they are often in an obverse relationship which suggests their mutual if antagonistic dependence. Mutual respect for legitimate differences may create the conditions for co-operation and social cohesion.

It is important to consider the meaning that neo-conservative social theory gives to obligation and reciprocity. Classic neo-conservatism describes three developmental economic systems. First, a reciprocal type, which is applicable to tribal and 'primitive' societies. Secondly, a redistribution type, which involves the central collection and distribution of resources, based on social and political criteria established by autocratic rulers. Thirdly, the market system, which supersedes all the previous systems. Consequently, one of the neo-conservative assumptions is that the welfare state, with its emphasis on redistributive justice, imposes an economic definition that is retrograde and constrictive. It is, ironically, seen by the neo-conservatives to be an imprisoning 'conservative' idea! Part of the imperative which drives the neo-conservative analysis is, paradoxically, its commitment to social change and development. In some ways the market is a very dynamic process, quick to cast off the old and certain to evaluate the profit potential of the new. For this reason there is an inflexible orientation towards competitiveness that structures a faith in the market's ability to winnow quality out of the inconsequential.

One of the subtle issues that any possible theory of social obligation must confront is how particular concepts of social 'reality' are construed and how certain definitions of social 'knowledge' are established. As Katznelson has argued, public choice theory, which sustains the beliefs about the primacy of the market, regards economics as the arena of 'isolated, self-interested persons' (1986: 312). This 'loneliness' has contributed towards a generally pessimistic view of human nature and public action. A reluctant consensus has emerged 'that the easiest and most risk-free way to run a program is to assume the worst – that people are selfish, lazy, hedonistic, and unchangeable' (Stone, 1983: 593). Public choice theory is, therefore, a powerful adversary to any renewed or revamped theory of welfare obligation. Its metaphors of knowledge have the ability to define the 'known world', especially to construe the world as harsh, uncompromising and competitive. The concept of obligation therefore seems hopelessly romantic, visionary and less intellectually robust than the realism of public choice theory. Arguing for the possibility of a new theory of social obligation will require us to respond to the assumption of 'harshness' in public choice theory. To argue for a 'wet' alternative is so much more difficult than to maintain the superiority of a 'dry' analysis. The rhetoric is important for in its use of language certain meanings are assumed and others are denied. The beliefs that condition the debate are established both by the 'noise' of the public discussion of alternatives and by the 'silences'. Katznelson argues that it is the power of the unspoken, the silences in the social policy debate, which dictate current realities and future possibilities. He quotes from Raymond Williams the trenchant observation that language is not merely expressive but is also selective and that in 'certain social-historical circumstances, there are things which could not be said, and therefore, in any connecting way not thought'. Political agendas are arbitrary because they represent a selection 'from the universe of the possible'. This selection reflects how we limit discourse and construe possibility so that what might be explained is taken for granted as reality. Pejoratively this pivots around the assumption that each protagonist has the 'facts' while the antagonist has only 'beliefs'. However, all political systems have boundaries 'between that which is discussed and disputed and that which is not discussed and disputed' (Katznelson, 1986: 308–309).

Any attempt to take issue with the strength of public choice theory must start with a respect for, and opposition to, the power of its ability to restrict the public debate – to enforce those silences which are constraints on what it is possible to discuss. Arendt has argued that this analysis about public meaning and legitimate social behaviour is constrained by another aspect of 'silence'. This is not the silence which controls the acceptable boundaries of the public debate, but the silence that comes from not being able to talk about the 'good'. Arendt (1959) makes a distinction between wisdom and goodness and suggests that only wisdom can be openly discussed. Whenever goodness, or the good act, is discussed it ceases to be good. It becomes reified into a quality of the actor rather than the act. Arendt suggests that when this occurs goodness is destroyed, that it can be done but never discussed. As she says:

> Only goodness must go into absolute hiding and flee all appearance if it is not to be destroyed . . . . The man, however, who is in love with goodness can never afford to lead a solitary life, and yet his living with others must remain essentially without testimony . . . . good deeds can never keep anyone company; they must be forgotten the moment they are done, because even memory will destroy their quality of being good. Moreover, thinking, because it can be remembered, can crystallize into thought, and thoughts, like all things that owe their existence to remembrance, can be transformed into tangible objects which, like the written page or the printed book, become part of the human artifice. Good works, because they must be forgotten instantly, can never become part of the world; they come and go, leaving no trace. (1959: 67–68)

Many of the problems that the social service professions have discovered in researching and establishing the validity of their work can be attributed to the 'silence' that must accompany the good act. The distinctions that were drawn between the public and private worlds are no longer viable. Arendt, prefiguring the later development of feminist theory, argued that the current conception of government, where the only thing people have in common is their private interests, is contradictory. She assumed that it was this contradiction between private and public which extinguished the difference between the private and public worlds and merged both in the social (1959: 61). Public choice theory depends on the maintenance of a rigid distinction between the public and the private. Nevertheless, in its advocacy of the pre-eminence of the market it redefines that dualism. The essential distinction is no longer between the knowledge of the private and the public but between success and failure. Success is defined as the ability to command sufficient resources to maintain a defended 'private realm'. Such defensive and protective arrangements are attempts to demonstrate that the private is not submerged in the social. The typical contrast is between 'winners and losers', 'players and non-players'. It is possible to see that the power of this harsh view of human nature depends on the ascription of 'honour' to the lonely individual who triumphs, and 'shame' to those who do not succeed. This is yet one more example of how the process of welfare stigmatization is recast so that the 'limited and precarious' welfare balance is maintained. Instead of the moral stigma that the old welfare paradigm assumed we have a new expression of stigmatization based upon market success.

**Summary**

The market is the new 'Grand Inquisitor', the guarantor of the morality of success. The honourableness of individual altruism is ranged against that of the uncertain and bureaucratically suspect altruism of public welfare. This attitude is well expressed by Barry, who argues that 'public beneficence always emerges as the un-intended consequence of private, self-regarding action' (1987: 163). What any defence of the welfare state must argue is not for a renewal of the moral imperative for individuals to care but that it is a practical recognition of mutual vulnerability that leads to a sense of obligation. A renewed exploration of the merits of social obligation is an invitation to consider collective as well as individual responsibility (Sapiro, 1986: 237). As we have seen, the neo-conservative analysis depends upon the assumption that there are rigid distinctions that must be drawn between a public and private world and upon the assumed 'inevitability' of the lonely, competitive individual. As Prezworski puts it, what

> . . . is wrong with methodological individualism is not the postulate that collective actions must be explainable by reference to individual rationality but the substantive ontology of society as a collection of undifferentiated and unrelated individuals. (As quoted by Katznelson, 1986: 319)

The neo-classical argument is suspect because it does not respect that 'social ontology'. Its analysis and assumptions depend upon abstracting from the 'whole'. It is therefore possible to argue that greater respect be accorded those arguments which do not depend upon artificial abstractions from the 'whole'. Personal and social obligations that respect individual vulnerabilities are not ultimately moral demands upon the arbitrary beneficence of individuals but social demands to recognize the legitimacy of such vulnerabilities (Goodin, 1985a; 1988). Katznelson considers that we must

> . . . explore the construction and changeability of the always present division between the domains of political speech and political silence. By making this problem the centrepiece of analysis, we can widen the domain of empirical studies, make a place for counterfactual analysis, and develop a taste for thinking about possible worlds that are not very far away, but seen to be just beyond our grasp. Not only our political science, but our politics could profit from such an imagination. (1986: 325)

The demands for immediate and pragmatic decisions in social policy do not often allow for the relative luxury of speculation about options. More equitable and just policy decisions will result from a more profound analysis of the relativity of our knowledge that we assert to be the truth. Only by rethinking the basis for social policy alternatives will we be able to assess concepts of mutual responsibility and obligation as well as respect the power of the market-driven analysis that has led to the options of privatization and contracting for social services. The next chapter will consider the theoretical debate about the determination of needs – and needs assessment models – and relate these to methods of policy analysis. Only after this discussion can further consideration of the arguments for and against purchase of service contracting and privatization be set in an understandable context.

# 3

## Citizenship and 'Moral Generosity'

## Social needs; privatization and social service contracting

> It is in the name of freedom that experts in need now pronounce on the needs of strangers. Apparently, societies that seek to give everyone the same chance at freedom can only do so at some cost to freedom itself.
>
> (Ignatieff, 1984: 136–137)

All of the arguments about social policy reflect differing and implicit assumptions about the nature of social and community needs and how best to respond to the differing expression of these needs. These 'organizing assumptions' about what is 'real' need have dictated the nature of the welfare state and changing responses to it. Any discussion about the 'crisis of the welfare state' and how this idea of a crisis relates to decisions to contract or privatize the delivery of social services must first consider how concepts of social and community need are defined. Not unexpectedly, many defenders of the progressive social value of welfare states see in the possible contracting of state services a political trojan horse. Those who defend the traditional welfare state argue that these policies have been deliberately promoted to restructure and privatize welfare services (Judge et al., 1983; Lipsky, 1984; Stoesz, 1987). Further, these policy initiatives do represent an objective challenge to those sets of normative political and social beliefs that assumed, however comfortably, that what sustained the welfare state was a political commitment to full employment and universal entitlement (Morris, 1988).

This political commitment has been challenged by the rhetoric promoting government non-intervention, associated with the implementation of these major changes in welfare policy. However, and fundamentally, any suggestion that governments can adopt an essentially non-interventionist position in the determination of social policy is a massive intellectual conceit. In practical terms, a decision not to intervene is inherently a powerful intervention. Nevertheless, the current political dominance of neo-conservatism is evident. Paradoxically, however, there are some interesting implications for a renewed defence of the legitimacy of a welfare approach that arise from the introduction of contracting to the social service arena. Arguments for efficiency and 'quality assurance' in the social services are an acceptance at one level of the legitimacy of social need. Whatever future form the welfare state may take is consequent upon a significant debate that is now joined between those who promote, as viable options, purchase of service contracting and even complete privatization of welfare services and those equally opposed to them. From this debate it is clear that the introduction of these new policies means that the issues cannot be resolved by attempting to re-establish the founding polemic which led to the first welfare state legislation. Beliefs about the moral legitimacy of social needs and the consequent political claims for entitlement based upon citizenship rights have impelled a substantial part of the argument in favour of the welfare state (cf., Soper, 1981; Harris, 1987; Ignatieff, 1989). The rhetorical claims of the neo-conservative challenge to welfare have been sufficiently established to change the ground on which this controversy will be fought. New policy initiatives will have to be developed because it is unlikely that any rhetoric favouring a return to a completely interventionist welfare state could be sustained (Stoesz, 1989: 128). What is not nearly so clear is whether it is yet appropriate for the new right to declare no contest!

In general, policy formulations of social needs are complicated because the term is variously used as a 'descriptive, explanatory or predictive concept' (Clayton, 1983: 231). More subtlety than either a left-wing or right-wing response is required if we are to understand the nature of needs and wants. The assessment and social validation of needs that strive to resolve the dilemma of needs and wants must go beyond one of the two classic political ideologies (Watson, 1983: 509). The inflexibility with which the left assumes the moral high ground in any discussion about needs and citizenship, and automatically rejects any right-wing criticism of the validity of needs and desires, has been disputed. Goodin's (1988) recent attempt to recast social obligation through an analysis of vulnerabilities, discussed previously, significantly challenges the ideologues of both left and right to rethink the validity of citizenship obligations and how they might be used to specify a clearer political base for mutual support.

Underlying all of the respective administrative patterns which dictate managerial options for the delivery of social services are prior political decisions about how social needs are to be identified, assessed and provided. There are insufficient resources available to meet all social needs, and assessments and interpretation of social need becomes a strategic activity, influenced by the vested interests

and professional values of those who formulate welfare programmes. As Parry argues, 'the crisis of the welfare state is precisely
that it has permitted itself to be need-driven rather than resource-
driven' (1985: 290). Thus the administrative options that social
welfare managers use to evaluate appropriate patterns of service
delivery are not the result of needs assessments but rather reflect
these implicit prior assumptions. A comment that runs like a thread
through all social policy discussion of needs is that 'no amount of
data and analysis can disguise the fact that – since they will help
determine who is to get what – needs assessments are essentially
political instruments' (Gates, 1980: 136; Klein, 1984a; 1984b). The
crucial question at the heart of this debate about the identification
and assessment of needs is whether it is ever possible to escape the
symbolism inherent in the needs assessment process. Is it possible

> . . . to transcend the idea that the only possible purpose of needs
> assessment is to make social welfare decision making appear economi-
> cally and administratively rational, not the object of the meandering,
> apparently aimless push and pull of a pluralist, political rationality?
> (Gates, 1980: 137)

While these obvious political and administrative difficulties
intrude into the determination of valid needs assessments, the issue
is complicated further by the dominance of a welfare rights model.
It is relatively fashionable for welfare rights protagonists to talk
about the necessity of meeting 'unmet needs', thus pressuring the
welfare bureaucracies to consider those needs which are not met
through existing programmes. In actual practice, social agencies can
only assess 'partial needs' – those that are met by specific welfare
services but which do not necessarily reflect the intrinsic subjectivity
of needs identification and assessment (Vigilante and Mailick,
1988). It is difficult to set priorities for needs assessment beyond
that which can already be measured and which conforms to existing
policy mechanisms. Our understanding is also clouded because of
the diffuse and interrelated nature of social and health needs.
Furthermore, rapid economic change shapes possible options for
the provision of services based on needs analysis. While the obvious
distress of actual deprivation is often cited in support of moral
arguments about legitimate social needs conceptual difficulties
occur when distinguishing between needs and wants, or needs and
desires (cf., Williams, 1974; Blackham, 1976; Smith, 1980; Soper,
1981; Springborg, 1981; Frieden, 1986; Goodin, 1988). Goodin's
contention that we cannot find reason for the welfare state only in
needs-based justifications because it is not possible to 'find good
grounds for giving even genuine claims of need systematic priority
over desires and wants' seems incontrovertible. As he argues:

Needs-based considerations would provide good grounds for state interventions meeting people's needs to supplant systematically market distributions satisfying people's desires only if there are good grounds for supposing that needs should systematically trump desires. If the latter proposition is indefensible, then so too is the former – or at least the former proposition cannot be defended in terms of the latter, needs-based argument. (1988: 29)

The remainder of this chapter is divided into four main sections. The first discusses a range of issues associated with how needs are defined and determined and by whom! This includes the awkward questions posed by Ignatieff (1984) about the corruption of citizenship by 'moral generosity'. Of equal importance are those neo-conservative arguments that declare that the state systems of welfare have similarly 'corrupted' the 'integrity of the isolated individual'. The second looks more specifically at a range of practical techniques for needs analysis. The third introduces some definitions of the general utility of purchase of service contracting. The final section discusses the issues that arise from the context of the debate: definitions of social agencies; important questions of client status; and policy options.

## The Vexed Concept of Social Needs

Managers of welfare bureaucracies face intractable practical difficulties in knowing precisely what social needs are and how they can be generalized into policy. Nevertheless, because there are no viable alternatives, attempts to validate welfare claims using needs statements and assessments have become part of general political and administrative discourse. The process of determining needs assessments provides a structure that compels welfare managers to clarify the problems and social conditions being addressed by needs analysis as well as the crucial assumptions supporting the strategies that will be used to resolve these social problems (Gates, 1980: 138). Nevertheless, gathering information can become a substitute for policy action as the realization grows that all methods of needs analysis are compromises and that there is an inadequate research base to permit accurate estimations of the number of persons in need. Even if such information and expertise were available needs assessment research processes provide no obvious rules or procedures for determining needs priorities.

However, welfare bureaucrats have translated needs assessments research into precise managerial questions to examine the utility of existing services, to verify social service priorities and to determine budgetary criteria. Needs assessments are undertaken to present coherent policy statements that both illuminate existing patterns of social problems as well as isolating those specific factors that assist or thwart effective service delivery (Siegel et al., 1978: 249). As well as providing a basis for evaluating the network of existing services, needs assessments are used to coordinate programmes between agencies who jointly seek to identify 'at risk' groups. Needs assessments raise other significant questions about whether those needs most frequently reported are an accurate measure of overall need or rather reflect a pattern of political opinion. These questions, taken together, provide a means for politicians and senior social service managers to assign relative weighting to either separate needs assessments or need claims in order to indicate the relative importance of different needs.

What reinforced the power of the traditional welfare paradigm was the assumption that definitions of need, as well as service delivery priorities, were the 'responsibility' of the provider. Social needs, identified from the 'objective' stance of a 'social expert', created relatively clear management patterns for the delivery and administration of social services. Ranking of needs and the determination of priorities were assumed to be part of the professional task and so needs were valid if they were accepted as such by the professionals employed to make such judgements.

With the unfolding of the new welfare paradigm, based more upon 'rights' than 'responsibilities', there is no obvious way to rank the priorities of particular needs. This creates a unique dilemma for the managers of state welfare systems. If the felt or subjectively identified interests of clients (or consumer groups) are a principal consideration in establishing specific managerial decisions about welfare policy and service provision then 'conflict between the demands of a plurality of self-constituted interest groups is likely to be an endemic feature of the welfare state' (Taylor-Gooby, 1983: 150). Managers will have to consider the relative merits of empirical research based on the 'logic' of scientific analysis as well as form opinions about the value of phenomenological research based on respect for subjective experience.

The sharp distinctions between left and right about what constitutes valid social need, once part of the substance of the ideological divide, have blurred. Left-wing analysis has long argued that valid needs assessments must be based on fundamental consumer-orientated definitions of need. These assessments reflect ethical and political commitments to the primacy of citizenship definitions and reject the prominence of the 'social expert' in needs analysis and policy determination. Similarly, neo-conservative criticism of the welfare state has assumed and predicted the bureaucratic incompetence of social service professionals, arguing for the 'need' to return responsibility for needs identification to the consumer. These arguments are a replay of the classic political debate about efficiency and freedom. The problem for social science has been to establish a valid stance from which to observe social needs. With the evolution of a welfare paradigm shift it is no longer possible for definitions of social needs and needs assessment to be based solely on expert analysis relating only to individual social experience. Consequently, one of the most persistent and difficult questions in the administration and planning of welfare services has been how to balance the respective roles of service provision and policy innovation (Hibbard, 1984). It is often argued that these are dichotomous categories and that the adoption of one precludes the other. Both ideological and methodological reasons are used to explain why social planners continue to see provision of services and policy changes separately (cf., Taylor-Gooby, 1981b). Maintaining a practical division between policy analysis and provision separates the state fiscal provider from the consumer or client base, reinforcing the funder/provider split so fundamental to neo-conservative rhetoric. Needs assessments embody values and ethics that cannot be fully encompassed by empirical research which assumes the objectivity of a detached observer and promotes the expert identification of needs. Rein suggests that 'because the tools for intervention embody values, no simple calculus for distinguishing means and ends is at hand' (1977: 69). Current social policy research and analysis has not yet reliably provided legislators with the means to discriminate between various welfare options. It has not expounded a set of research protocols that would provide the norms and standards for policy-makers to evaluate conflicting social policies. Not only is it difficult to determine objective, value-free and statistically sound research but needs assessment and analysis cannot be divorced from the political process which responds more clearly to pressure group lobbying than to social research. Policy statements about social needs

> . . . are normative statements containing implicit value assumptions regarding rights to certain minimum levels of service provision. When dealing with normative statements of this nature, it is important to ask who is making the normative statement. In other words, whose values form the basis of the need judgement. Any model of social need statements should therefore take account of this factor. (Ife, 1980: 97)

If there can be no dispassionately valid way to assess an appropriate balance between public and private spending, then the electorate will act as the 'final arbiter for balancing public needs and private wants' (Frieden, 1986: 29). Not only must we question whether it is possible to divorce needs assessment and analysis from the political process, but we must also consider some of the internal methodological conflicts inherent in needs assessment research. For example, social policies based on the use of needs assessments to influence decisions about resource allocation will stumble over the inability of social policy to determine uniformly acceptable definitions of social need. They will also face other normative difficulties because there is 'an incongruence between the political nature of allocating decisions and rationally collecting needs information' (Rapp, 1982: 49). The practical dilemma for policy managers is that these questions do not remove the need to develop criteria on which they are obliged to make decisions about allocating increasingly scarce resources. Social needs, as well as needs assessments, are often defined within three broad categories: traditional empirical models of expert analysis; qualitative models arising from direct practice; and consumer pressure group models.

### Traditional Empirical Models: The Dispassionate 'Social Expert'

This approach to the definition and understanding of needs and needs assessment, based on a traditional model of identifying need, has clear parallels with the traditional welfare paradigm. It is often referred to as a scientific or medical model, and within it needs are interpreted as intrinsically objective, representing measurable attributes of individuals. The proponents of this approach assume that welfare organizations and agencies are value-free and that they have been created solely to meet social needs more effectively (Armstrong, 1982: 24). Empirical needs assessments are often atheoretical and needs are examined independently of any other theoretical conceptualizations of social need and are not related to any social policy theories concerning the delivery of welfare services. There is little 'observational data on the actual practices involved in the operation of social work and welfare services which purportedly function to meet social need' (Smith, 1980: 64). This neglect leads inevitably to a recursive self-fulfilling analysis with less ability to gauge the importance of welfare clients' subjective assessment of needs. Research serves rather to validate official categories of meaning since needs are solely defined as the properties of the measurements the research is designed to achieve and avoids ethical questions about observer bias that might jeopardize the soundness of the investigation.

*Qualitative or Practice-Grounded Models*
The traditional approach to the definition of need is often contrasted with another, often described as an 'ethno-methodological approach', derived from the work of Berger and Luckmann (1967), who rejected the notion of an empirically verifiable social reality. The central aspect of this argument is that people subjectively create their own social realities; that there is no objective social world that can be measured; and that research into needs assessments must take into account the subjective 'reality' of those being assessed. Thus needs can only be identified within the context of a subjectively constructed world. This perspective has some correspondence with the emergence of a welfare rights paradigm. If the subjectivity or rights of clients or consumer groups are paramount then there can be no generally accepted definition of needs assessment and almost any systematic research technique can be labelled 'needs assessment'. The import of this approach has been to put welfare managers on the defensive. Seeking needs assessments becomes a defensive managerial response to complex and urgent problems of social policy and the findings are often used to confirm already established policy. This pressure to base policy decisions on research findings has meant that aspects of descriptive and aggregate techniques have been too easily borrowed – on the basis of a claim to greater scientificity than the phenomenological approach – from survey research and the findings inappropriately reclassified as needs assessments. Consequently, many needs assessments serve only the political functions of legitimating policy debate since the research data may not be used in actual programme planning. Rather, they are used to discredit alternative forms of needs assessment.

*Consumer Pressure Group Models: 'Similia Similibus Curantur'*
The critical values of this approach are that policy planning ought to involve a constant awareness that needs must be decided by the community through a process of 'empowerment' and not exclusively on the basis of professional expertise. The personal experience of community members, who are involved with community problems and know the issues directly, becomes an intrinsic part of resource allocation. The qualitative model sought to acknowledge that subjectivity implied recognition of difference, while consumer and pressure group models attacked the imbalances in power which are contained in an expert approach to needs analysis. Such an orientation falls within the phenomenological tradition which understands social reality from the vantage point of the person

being studied, in this instance the community members, and requires the use of unstructured needs assessment methods. Consumer pressure groups have focused on needs assessments as a way to fight for the citizenship aspects of the original welfare state's allocation of resources and to challenge welfare bureaucracies to be more managerially 'transparent'. 'Transparency' involves a combination, especially from feminist theory, of various critical viewpoints that emphasizes the demands of welfare client and community-based planning groups for clearer accountability in decision-making. Typically, these orientations regard social welfare research as only part of a wider social movement which assumes that appropriate models of needs assessment must reflect the real issues of local areas. It also assumes that social researchers must see themselves as part of 'an organised movement for social change which is particularly concerned with building organisations and stimulating political debate so as to encourage collective action' (Pringle, 1981: 177; Withorn, 1984).

This attitude echoes the classic position of social administration which never assumed that it was a totally disinterested party in the particular areas of social research that it embraced (cf., Abel-Smith and Titmuss, 1987). Within the context of a welfare rights paradigm, identification of the self-perceived needs of homogeneous self-help groups will require a consultative process and not the application of expert analysis divorced from the subjectivity of the community, group, organization, tribe, family or other similar social sub-grouping. The welfare rights perspective gained strength as clients tried to escape from the dependency of individual isolation by joining self-help groups. These groups, who identified and defined themselves by a set of specific disabilities, issues or ethnic identification, became the means for individuals to clarify their relationship to the state. They formed pressure groups which 'demanded that "rights" be attached to their need for help' (Benton, 1987: 22). Social needs are primarily demands or desires which warrant government intervention because they compel both consumers and providers to see the generally identified 'needs' as important social goods meriting vital service delivery (cf., Nevitt, 1977; Goodin, 1988). This of course raises the vexed question of how to distinguish between needs and wants.

### Definitions of Needs Assessments: Elusive Stances!
While there can be no single or universally accepted approach to the definition and assessment of need, a set of common factors can be identified. These involve implicit research design and implemen-

tation procedures, the availability of information to complete the project and how complex the research instrument needs to be to achieve this. Most needs assessments emphasize the clarification of four primary objectives which determine how the pattern of social needs may be described and, particularly, how practical needs assessments can be procedurally identified and measured. Researchers will need, first, to understand how the political determination of social policy options dictates the establishment of service priorities and, secondly, to assess the source and amount of available funds to meet the social needs being surveyed and to clarify criteria for allocating these funds. Thirdly, they will have to clarify how to evaluate existing patterns of social service provision, and, finally, they will have to determine what managerial procedures will be used to assist relevant social agencies to coordinate their services. Needs assessments involve either a problem to be defined or a review of particular client groups or specific social services. Thus three approaches can be outlined depending on what is the primary focus. Needs assessments can therefore be categorized as either 'community-based, client-oriented, or service-oriented respectively' (Gates, 1980: 100)

A variation on this three-way classification is proposed by Ife who distinguished between population-defined need, caretaker-defined need and inferred need (1980: 100–101). Population-defined needs are community needs assessments based on survey research methods where those being assessed have 'actually made the needs statement'. Caretaker-defined needs refers to discrete reports of groups of professionals, often called key informants surveys. These informants often have a service or caretaking function in respect of a particular community and are therefore concerned with helping to identify and meet the needs of that particular community. Inferred need refers to needs assessment statements and social reviews that administrators, policy analysts or social researchers glean from specific information such as census data, service utilization rates, the personal and family circumstances of clients and their knowledge of or preference for services. Inevitably such needs assessments are made by experts who may have little first-hand experience of the population group whom they happen to be studying. This, it has been suggested, leads to biased research protocols because needs statements are described as the identification of problems but defined only in terms of solutions (Ife, 1980: 97). Martin rejects the three-fold categorization made by Ife and proposes rather the utility of a simple two-fold distinction between consumer and provider in an attempt to resolve the ambiguity that surrounds the debate about definitions of need. While there is a commonsense obviousness to this two-fold classification, needs defined by the consumers will inevitably be different to those defined by service providers. For the consumer the concept of need may embrace an awareness of problems for which there is no adequate service response. When service providers use the term 'need' it is often assumed that they are obliged to respond and seek a remedy for the problem. Specific resources or services appropriate to resolve the problem are identified only by the service provider. Thus judgements about needs assessment are made by those who are in a position to make decisions about the provision of cash or services and it is self-evident that political power lies with those sectors of society able to influence decisions on the use of resources. Clearly, perceptions of social need and the resulting judgements about appropriate policy responses differ if they emanate from those who are in need rather from those empowered to provide solutions (Martin, 1982a: 192). Ideally, definitions of social needs ought to involve both the consumers and providers of services.

## A Survey of Needs: Models, Methods and Policy Analysis

This survey of the social policy literature on needs and needs assessments serves to establish the 'ground' for the previous discussion of a new theory of social obligation which involves a reconsideration of citizenship rights as well as obligations. Political and managerial options for welfare provision depend upon the specific formulation of needs assessments which establishes the basis of the social policy debate. For these reasons, it is important to examine current theoretical conceptions, arguments and speculations about the identification of social needs before analysing the relative merits of contracted social services. The following discussion of social needs is divided into four parts. The first considers Bradshaw's (1972; 1977) arguments in support of his four-fold categorization of needs analysis, as well as the subsequent critical debate which proposed several revisions of Bradshaw's model (Hamilton-Smith, 1975; Thayer, 1977; Clayton, 1983). The second presents an outline and discussion of the major distinctions that can be drawn between empirically and phenomenologically defined needs assessments (Smith, 1980). The third part outlines a range of theoretical assumptions from other writers who have offered alternative models (Siegel et al., 1978; Gates, 1980; Ife, 1980; Martin, 1982a). Siegel et al., for example, suggested that an adequate definition of needs and needs assessment must distinguish between needs identification and needs enumeration. Martin distinguished between provider- or consumer-based definitions of needs, while Ife qualified this argument and developed a model based primarily on the question of who determines that a need exists. Gates proposed, on the conceptual variations thrown up by individual, group or consumption needs, a range of distinctions between client-orientated needs assessments, service-orientated needs assessments and community-based needs assessments. The fourth part considers whether it is possible to overcome the conflict between the rhetoric about needs, fashioned by the relativism of welfare rights, and the possibility of an expert analysis of needs.

*Bradshaw's Need Typology: A Search for a Model?*
Bradshaw's taxonomy (1972) proposed that social analysis ought to be based on the empirical validity of social needs. Theoretical discussion and study of needs assessments owes much to this pioneering work in which he outlined four different categories of need. These are normative, felt, comparative and expressed needs. These distinctions, however, have interestingly restricted the debate about needs. They tended to restrain further analysis because the distinctions themselves have become reified. Thayer succinctly summarizes Bradshaw's four-fold typology:

> Normative need is what the expert or professional perceives to be need in a given situation; felt need is need perceived by the subjects themselves; expressed need, or demand, is felt need turned into action in the form of a request for service; and comparative need is need deduced by the outside observer in circumstances where the individuals not in receipt of a particular service have similar characteristics to others who do receive it. (1977: 298)

For a time the debate was constrained by attempts to verify these 'empirical' categories. However, the categorization did provide a structure for the analysis of different needs where none had previously existed. Bradshaw's typology has also helped to move the debate from the initially pejorative rejection by the neo-conservatives of the legitimacy of social needs to a reappraisal of their central role in social policy analysis and implementation. Consequently, the discussion of needs cannot be blindly rejected on the grounds that it is a thinly veiled call for socialism (Harris and Seldon, 1979). The right is forced, given its own defence of privilege and individualism, to acknowledge the legitimacy of the claim rights of 'interest group liberalism'. While public choice theory rejects the legitimacy of social or communal obligation it cannot logically invalidate the right to private or group assessment of need.

**The Four-fold Typology**    *Normative need* is defined as those needs which a 'social expert', usually a professional welfare administrator or social scientist, designates as valid and specific. In order to establish the fact of normative need, desirable or ideal standards are developed and a comparison made with existing standards. If any individual or group does not meet the desirable standard, then they are presumed to have legitimate needs. It is the comparison of these respective standards and not the assessment of specific claims which defines normative need. Yet because these comparisons are established by the exercise of expert opinion normative needs cannot be assumed to be absolute. They may or may not correspond with social needs established by other analytical methods. This definition is frequently challenged as paternalistic because middle-class norms are implicitly used to assess the needs of working-class clients or groups, or the needs of different cultural and ethnic communities. Another difficulty arises because these norms may well differ from community to community with inevitable conflicts in standards of assessment. Normative standards change over time as a result of both developments in knowledge and the changing values of society and, similarly, normative definitions of needs may well vary according to the value orientations of 'expert' researchers. Opinions differ about the social resources that should be devoted to meeting identified needs and whether any available sets of interventive skills can actually solve the particular problem. There is always the danger that normative value statements will be regarded as statements of empirical evidence and truth. Accurate assessment of social needs therefore can never be made in isolation from the specific research context and the subjective impressions of external experts.

*Felt needs* are defined as those which individuals, groups or communities regard as most compelling and which require urgent attention. Assessments and surveys of social service needs query individuals about whether they feel they need particular services. Inevitably, need is equated with want and subjective desire and it is difficult, when arguing for the legitimacy of felt needs, to determine if needs and wants have been inextricably merged by respondents. Consequently, felt need is, by itself, an inadequate measure of real need because it is limited by individual perception. Clients may not know whether the social service is actually available that might address their felt needs and may, in certain contexts, be reluctant to reveal the full extent of their dependence.

*Expressed needs* are defined as those which explicitly equate need with demand, which is often felt need turned into social action and political advocacy. This definition of need essentially represents the power of certain groups to define their own needs and demand a corresponding service. People do not demand a service unless a need is felt, but on the other hand it is also common for felt need not to be translated into demands. A major difficulty arises since expressed needs are determined by those who are best able to make their needs known. Attempting to generalize from political advocacy can provide no accurate measure of community needs. Those with the greatest needs sometimes have the greatest difficulty in expressing them.

*Comparative measures of need* are derived by analysing the characteristics of those already in receipt of specific social services. Therefore, those with similar characteristics but who are not in receipt of the specific service already granted to others are deemed to be in need. Assessment of comparative need requires a general survey analysis to determine whether there is an equitable distribution of services to meet those needs which have been mandated through statutory legislation. Comparative needs analysis is designed to reveal the gaps that exist between services provided in one area and those that exist in another and these deficiencies are weighted to take account of differences that occur between target-populations.

The attempt to differentiate between different approaches to needs assessment is made more difficult by an apparent contradiction. This arises from the reification of Bradshaw's categories. While social policy theorists agree that it is important to derive clear differences between normative, felt, expressed and comparative needs there is, nevertheless, a constant theme running through the various speculative arguments that these four categories are interconnected (cf., Rein, 1977; Gates, 1980). This contradiction is at the heart of the problem that social science confronts in attempting to categorize and define needs as ineluctable social facts. Notwithstanding this, and perhaps by default, Bradshaw's classification provides a useful way in which to distinguish different approaches to needs assessment. However, the four definitions are not exclusive of the others as each depends upon certain normative criteria. For example, as Thayer argues:

> In the case of felt need it may be a reflection of questions asked or of the respondent's perception of what it is reasonable to expect, which will in turn be influenced by what is available. Expressed need obviously reflects what is available and also, often, the normative criteria controlling access to waiting lists. There will also be a normative element in the selection of relative characteristics to use as comparative criteria. Felt and expressed need are very closely related. (1977: 308)

These four descriptions of need reflect only categories of need or the research criteria used to assess need. They do not adequately describe or take account of the variations in needs perception that occur within particular categories. The confusion arises because of this reification of the original typology in which it is possible to regard Bradshaw's four categories as if they were alternative definitions of need. It is more worthwhile to consider that they represent 'four dimensions' rather than definitions. Normative need will vary according to the unique criteria adopted by the external social expert entrusted to assess these norms. Felt need may vary according to the observer's subjective assessment of how intensely needs were presented, and, similarly, the diverse political and social ways that demands are manifested yields different estimates of expressed need. Comparative need will vary according to which particular areas are considered and the nature of the respective social, demographic or environmental characteristics of these areas. Combining the assessments that can be made using these dimensions it is possible to provide 'an improved but still incomplete picture of that abstract notion which could be called "intrinsic need" ' (Hamilton-Smith, 1975: 36).

There is considerable criticism of the tacit value assumptions revealed by most needs assessment models (cf., Clayton, 1983). That the determination of needs is complicated by questions of implicit value and bias is a common theme but the requirements of administrative 'rationality', nevertheless, demand their use! As I have argued, definitions of need inevitably incorporate the value assumptions of both providers and consumers in the social welfare exchange. Despite the essentially contested nature of the concept of needs it plays an important part in planning the management and distribution of welfare services. The concept has been used as an alternative to establishing services on other principles such as merit or market forces (Clayton, 1983: 216). Current planning and administration in the social services is obviously affected by resource cutbacks and budget rationalizations so that it is no longer possible automatically to satisfy felt and expressed needs (cf., Loney and Bocock, 1987). Ironically, the rhetoric of efficient 'cutback' management often asserts that the proposed changes will make for more efficient and effective satisfaction of needs! As well as the requirement to make clear assessments, consequent upon the competition for scarce resources, welfare administrators and social policy-makers are challenged to make their procedures to assess the relative and competing needs of different groups more 'transparent'.

*Normative Need: The 'Elitism' of Expert Assumptions*   Normative definitions of need are appealing both to social planners, adminis- trators and politicians as well as to social science researchers who attempt to identify community-based needs. They appeal to the social planner because they provide clear goals and are, equally, extremely useful tools for political activists who may press for the resolution of particular community needs. Normative standards of needs assessment derived from research and applied by the social planner or the politician will, obviously, have the sanction of law while those championed by community work radicals and social development activists will not. Clayton (1983) criticized the 'expert' provisions of Bradshaw's categorization of normative need where it is assumed that desirable standards can be mooted and compared with existing standards of service delivery. Attempting to glean comparative standards reflects the rigid assumptions about social uniformity echoed in the old welfare paradigm. Such comparative analysis is hardly applicable within the context of a welfare rights approach which provides little ability or opportunity to determine concepts such as desirable standards of service. Reflecting this, Hamilton-Smith (1975) suggested that there is often little common agreement about normative standards.

Expert assessments of need are influenced by such factors as the demand for the service, political feasibility, and financial and workforce constraints (Clayton, 1983). The basic problem is that the use of specialists to assess need is inevitably tied to the ideology of professional social work intervention and also to bureaucratic styles of management. The decision-making process used in this norma- tive categorization is such that expert assumptions considering eligibility for services on the basis of need are not always made explicit. We do not expect, or require, explicit statements from policy-makers about their own implicit normative standards. It is a common critical theme that policy-makers are reluctant to reveal these standards prior to the development of needs assessment research. There are limits on the extent to which Bradshaw's normative categorization can be used in a community or group context. It is difficult therefore for people to assess the validity of such expert assessments, especially where there is no political 'transparency' about the use of expert judgement. The complication with normative definitions is that information which cannot be made specific to individuals cannot be used. Consequently, data derived from group norms, area comparisons, population forecasts and national estimates of need are not helpful in determining normative need. As Clayton argues, the 'disadvantages of this are obvious, especially since forward planning must take account of demographic trends and estimates of need for groups of people' (1983: 225). Normative definitions of need also reflect an implicit expert presumption that individuals are not necessarily the best appraisers of their own needs. The selective bias of individuals will skew the results and client assessments 'may have to be supplemented, diminished or even rejected' (Clayton, 1983). Such implicit normative standards and assessments are based upon assumptions that remain untested and because of this specific bias these expert but untested standards will often be in conflict with norms established by differing groups. This creates particular problems when these other groups may also be advocating with government for social services in direct conflict with other local agencies (Hamilton-Smith, 1975: 37–38). Normative statements of social need depend upon definitions that ignore specific cultural and gender differences. It is not surprising that social planners, who must obtain normative categorizations of need, may have great difficulty in avoiding criticisms of 'paternalism' and 'institutional racism'.

*Felt Need: Desires, Wants or Wishes – A Subjective Mire*   One of the limitations involved in measuring felt needs is not that they are outrageous but that they are inherently conservative. People want those familiar things to which they are accustomed, or which they perceive to be possible in their situation. The general willingness of people to agree with normative definitions of needs and priorities suggests that they may ignore those factors which contradict the implicit constraints of the initial normative definitions. Measurements or assessments of felt need may be inflated and if 'we are really honest we will admit that being human beings, our own views on most subjects are complex, vague or often ambivalent' (Hamilton-Smith, 1975: 39). However, in spite of these limitations the protocols of public consultation require administrators to ask people what it is that they want. Nevertheless, it is an axiom that expressed or felt need docs not become an authentic indicator of need until it has been legitimated by an expert. Only then does it assume the status of 'approved' need (Clayton, 1983: 221).

Bradshaw's original distinctions between felt and expressed needs are not altogether obvious. While Bradshaw suggests that a felt need is an identified need which is not necessarily translated into action, expressed need is felt need which is translated into service demands. The two types of need are very closely related. As a result of service restrictions people are placed on waiting lists for services which they no longer require. Many waiting lists are out of date and include people whose initial felt needs have changed. Assessment of needs, diagnostically or clinically, does not automatically lead to a viable prescription for their satisfaction and 'one cannot (or should not) point out a need for services without also demonstrating the existence of circumstances which these services are intended to alter' (Thayer, 1977: 308). Factors which influence empirical estimations of prescriptive need include the validity of the information gathered by researchers about need requirements and which services might possibly be introduced to meet that need. As we have seen with normative need, for either individuals or consumer groups, the estimation of felt need inevitably involves subjective judgements by the researcher as well as the client or community group. It is rare therefore for needs assessment research to depend on a single category of need. An obvious limitation is imposed on what criteria can be used to determine empirically verifiable needs when the only measurements used are surveys of felt needs. There are subjective issues inherent in the concept of felt needs and this is reflected in the suggestion that the expression of these needs can only result in a 'wish-list'. It is interesting to relate the identification of needs with obligations and to the arguments for 'user-pays'. These arguments suggest that research should 'ascertain the financial costs respondents are prepared to incur to obtain welfare, just as goods are valued by what price people are prepared to pay for them' (Clayton, 1983: 220; Nevitt, 1977).

*Expressed Need: The 'Public' Face of 'Private' Need*   The development of expressed needs, the actual behaviour of people asking for or demanding a service, provides a further measurable dimension of needs but it too is subject to particular limitations. As with felt needs, the inherent relativity of needs identification as well as the factors of subjective perception are important issues in describing this category of expressed need. Practical ways of gaining knowledge are vital as are the perceptions that the political climate is amenable to pressure, and that change is therefore possible which can in turn create positive motivations (Hamilton-Smith, 1975). Expressed need is comparable to the economists' concept of market-driven demand, but this association of demand theory with Bradshaw's concept of expressed need may well be confusing when assessing needs. Referring to the example of waiting lists for elderly people as an indicator of housing needs, Clayton suggests that these refer to 'only the people who want, have applied for, and can afford the service . . . . The people with the most need may have the greatest difficulty expressing it (1983: 218; Hurl, 1984; 1986a).

*Comparative Need: Social Justice and Expert Opinion*   Understandably, fewer criticisms are directed at attempts to determine needs using a comparative approach. This approach requires social planners to assess the particular services provided to specific communities or groups and then to compare them with those which may not be provided to other comparable groups or communities. Clayton describes this as seeking 'equality between people with similar life circumstances and with territorial justice' (1983: 223). Where these judgements are more difficult to assess it is necessary to 'make weighted comparisons to take account of differences between populations' (Hamilton-Smith, 1975: 41). Weighting is an attempt to standardize service provision, but the actual provision may still not correspond with need. Comparative analysis of the need for service delivery based upon statistical surveys of different communities does not necessarily reflect the demand or the supply of services that may be required. The range of demands that occur within communities is not properly reflected within this particular definition.

*Needs Assessments: Value Dilemmas and Options*   The problems that needs assessment research stumbles over, as we have seen, are usually related to troublesome questions of how values and subjective perceptions of need are to be generalized and compared. This is typical of social science research because social policy is concerned with distinguishing between 'multiple, vague and conflicting goals which are all defined as desirable and necessary' (Rein, 1977). The question is not only how to ascertain what are essential social needs, or how to employ valid assessments of these needs, but how to place these decisions, which are basically judgements, in a context which can also be examined. Bradshaw argued that researchers might clarify separate research methods for each of the four dimensions. This, he argued, would provide policy-makers with a range of detailed information that could be used to inform decisions about evaluations of specific need and to determine priorities for redress.

There is a considerable research literature about desirable standards for the provision of different social services, but even those well tested in empirical research are subject to constant change because knowledge increases and expectations or aspirations are raised by the dominant welfare rights model (cf., Hamilton-Smith, 1975: 37). It is not possible to measure specific needs for any particular service without also considering alternative ways to meet those specific needs. Isolation of one measure of need from another is an arbitrary process and selection of only one measure will require explanation – part of the process of administrative 'transparency'. Some measure of the ability to distinguish needs obliges welfare administrators and social planners to address difficult issues involving the specific merits of different services and their weighting relative to the desired pattern of services. To do this well requires social planners to consider how the social objectives implicit within each service are valued by the wider society. Similarly, for clients distinct from agency structures Bradshaw's categorization does not take into account the problems that occur for policy-makers when they have to assess relative weighting or intensity of needs across populations. Emergence of regional difference makes any evaluation of intensity of need across population and regional groups a dubious exercise. The principle of universality in entitlement is anathema to the political principles promoting the privatization of social services, and governments and social policy-makers are increasingly unwilling to operate needs assessments on the basis of universalist principles. As we have already seen, this creates major problems for those who would defend the primacy of citizenship entitlement allied with certain basic social rights (cf., Ignatieff, 1989). Bradshaw's model does not account for people who may be defined as on the margins of categories of need. As Clayton argues:

> If marginal unmet need is really the focus of attention, either per se or in relation to other groups of people, then perhaps additional or alternative investigatory techniques are necessary. For example, scales or weighting might be developed which attempt to take account of the intensity of need in each category and in their combination. These might prove more useful when all needs cannot be met, as will frequently be the case, for the people with the least overall need will then be dropped from consideration. (1983: 227–228)

Bradshaw's model may well help policy-makers to plan services which are explicitly designed to help people in need, but there is another concern that existing definitions of needs may dictate the types of questions which are asked. Reification of the process of needs analysis and treating dimensions as if they were categories has the potential to condition initial research planning. Inquiries may be so framed that the requirements for a specific service, which already exists, become the definition of the needs to be satisfied. It is these pre-existent definitions which form the basis of the research, and needs assessment becomes an administrative question rather than focusing primarily on the circumstances of the needs as they are actually experienced by the community, or individuals within the community. This has parallels with the way in which social work and allied social service professions were the 'guardians' of social services. In particular, needs were defined by these state employees rather than by the clients. Needs only became 'needs' if they were defined as such. The power of definition lay with the provider of social services. It 'is an essential feature of welfare for profit that profit-seeking providers will meet need if and only if need can be turned into effective demand' (Watson, 1984: 335). Current patterns of welfare administration and social planning reveal the power that service providers exercise, particularly when needs are framed in terms of available services. The typical 'guardian' function of the individual social/service worker, dispensing special needs grants according to tight statutory criteria, has been transformed into an aspect of administrative planning. However, there 'is a danger that service based assessments of need may lead to much ineffectual, inappropriate and wasteful service provision' (Clayton, 1983: 226). Such assessments based upon available social services are too narrow and idiosyncratic. Not only are service-based assessments too specific to be generally useful but much research is atheoretical and subjective in its choice of indicators of need (Hamilton-Smith, 1975; Bebbington and Davies, 1980; Clayton, 1983).

While Bradshaw argued that his model would provide policy-makers with maximum information and engender the minimum number of value judgements, Clayton questioned this assumption on two grounds. First, much valuable data may have to be rejected since the method is 'individual-specific' and it therefore does not provide adequate models for the assessment of community needs (cf., Spicker, 1987). Williams, supporting this viewpoint, argues that 'judgments of "society" play no role in Bradshaw's taxonomy, only those of the individual and the experts' (1974: 64). Secondly, instead of limiting or qualifying the range of value judgements found in needs assessments Bradshaw's model may actually increase them because of the number of different categories involved. Clayton argued that:

> Bradshaw perhaps thought that by making explicit different ways of defining need, value biases would emerge more clearly. This view may be questioned, especially since certain groups have greater power than others to influence perceptions and definitions of need. Experts define normative need but they also play a major role in educating elderly people as to their needs, via the advice they give, the levels of subsidy placed upon different services and specifications of eligibility. Their past decisions and practices strongly influence comparative dimensions of need and their voice is likely to be heard again concerning which of Bradshaw's categories of need should be taken to constitute 'real need' or given priority. (1983: 227)

Effective needs assessment research must take into account two overall problems. The first is that any identification or expression of need is never static. It is not a specific 'product' that can be researched and incorporated into managerial planning models. Needs are dynamic and reflect the realities of continuous social change at a structural level. There is also constant political and social ferment about changing human aspirations, particularly in relation to gender and ethnic issues. Such constant change poses a continuing problem for the social planner and welfare administrator. The task is not only to determine appropriate and valid measures of need, but to establish research procedures that are flexible enough to allow for their continuous monitoring. The second problem, which 'should be self-evident but which is often overlooked, is the essential plurality of human needs' (Hamilton-Smith, 1975: 37). Conflicts occur when attempts are made to reconcile the different needs of consumers, professionals, bureaucrats and politicians. Politicians want mechanisms through which they can convince electorates that their concern is not rhetorical but tangible and consequently their estimation of valid needs will reflect those policies which can demonstrate the tangibility of their concern (Klein, 1977). This is not an entirely cynical process for politicians are placed in a paradoxical position by the community in that they desire services but at no extra cost to the taxpayer, and they wish to determine their own needs while expecting that politicians and social planners will be responsible for the equitable distribution of services!

While it is recognized that there are difficulties in actually assessing what needs are, there is no difficulty in assuming that all people will be conscious of the legitimacy of their particular sets of needs. However, social planners and welfare administrators do not start from any universal assumption that credible but unsatisfied needs exist. The more usual stance is that they wait for some expression of political pressure or community advocacy before accepting the legitimacy of these needs. Only after such persuasion is there an acceptance that credible needs exist and that, morally and politically, governments should act to alleviate these particular needs. It is a truism, but none the less important, that social planners are influenced by the social, political and economic climate within which they operate. They are not completely free to define need on the basis of a predetermined theoretical or research orientation. Factors such as the current administrative patterns and the ideologies of welfare provision embraced by the policies of ruling political parties affect the identification and determination of needs, as well as the general economic state of the country.

These difficulties push researchers and policy-makers back towards those definitions of need and needs assessment which arise out of the empirical tradition. Hamilton-Smith (1975) emphasizes the universal problems of needs assessment researchers who are required to determine categories of measurement despite the total lack of norms regarding any standard definition or understanding of need. Difficulties also occur in establishing appropriate guidelines for research when the policy-makers will make no explicit statements about how they view the problem, and when they will not act in accordance with the demand for transparency. An added difficulty is that by venturing into community needs assessments people are exposed to new knowledge about their social situation. The act of compiling needs information will 'inevitably change their patterns of interest, motivation, aspirations and expectations' (Hamilton-Smith, 1975: 44). It is not surprising therefore that such research is scorned by the client group and disdained by the social administrator. This highlights the major conflict in the theoretical literature between the traditional empirical approach to needs assessments arrived at by 'social experts' and the ethno-methodological approach that respects the subjective assumptions of the community or consumer. Again, the dualism implicit in this debate can be seen to represent the continuing clash between the expert paternalism of the old welfare paradigm and the welfare rights orientation of the new welfare paradigm that encapsulates a democratization of welfare. Despite the criticism of an empirical stance towards needs assessments these attempts to derive analytic models are clearly preferable to those which rely on 'political hunches and intuitions or the vagaries of the policy analysis process' which resist the logic of such models of analysis (Clayton, 1983: 231). However, Clayton cautions that:

> Once we recognise that definitions of need are culturally defined and liable to change over time we move away from the idea that true need can be readily identified if only the right methodology can be found and avoid the common trap of assuming that assessments of need carry their own policy imperatives. There is a large gap between identifying the circumstances of people's lives and deciding that a need exists which the state should alleviate. However, we are not always encouraged to think in this way, for use of a so-called 'value-neutral' scientific approach gives great power to those who define what constitutes need . . . it is possible that a scientific, or technical orientation will be further reinforced by increasing emphasis on the accountability of office holders and the importance of decision making being made open to public scrutiny. It helps to create the illusion that policies are founded on objective facts and not based on values and political considerations about which there may be much disagreement. (1983: 231)

## Empiricism and Phenomenology: 'Experts or Consumers'

One approach to the division between empirical and phenomenological research argues that distinctions between subjective and objective needs assessments depend on whether the focus is on public or private agencies and their particular assessments of need. However, any assumption that public sector officials are more able to conduct an empirical analysis and assessment of social needs is not proven. In an excellent analysis of this issue Smith (1980) argued that major public social policy and welfare enquiries such as those of Seebohm and Kilbrandon in the United Kingdom were flawed because they relied upon expert assessments of needs, encapsulated within what he called the traditional model of needs assessment. Examination of the administrative and consultative process of these reports demonstrated that public officials were confused, unable either to determine an adequate definition of need or to propose reliable procedures to measure need. The planning and research process was constrained by political requirements to contain new policies within existing welfare structures. As a result the officials were not able to develop a conception of need separate from the particular service being investigated, and established a working-principle that needs assessment policy could not be re-drafted in ways that substantially altered the functioning of the current services.

These same constraints apply to the practical day-to-day assessments of social services welfare administrators who, similarly, operate on an assumption that need cannot be separated from the specific existing services. The irony is that it is usually only 'planners and researchers who require officials to consider concepts of "needs" separate from those operative notions' (Smith, 1980: 56). It is the administrators, rather than the front-line social/service workers, who act as the state 'guardians' to control unbridled statements of need. Accordingly, if the clients or community are to play any part in needs assessment and analysis officials ought to hold and define notions of need which are independent of the existing service structures within which they operate. However, as we have seen, because of the difficulty in assessing immediate statements of felt need officials will have to develop sources of information which serve as reliable measures of need clearly distinct from immediate expressed demand. The difficulties in creating a perspective on needs and how they are assessed that is 'outside of' the constraint of specific operative assumptions will become clearer as we consider the range of these assumptions.

**Traditional Notions of Need**   This model unequivocally denies that social need can be associated with any general view of citizenship rights and entitlements. While administrative definitions of need, and changes in the amount of services required to meet those needs, vary, these changes are always considered to be part of a 'sequence of static states' and never as part of a process. To acknowledge need as part of a process would bring an obviously unwanted political demand for the satisfaction of these needs and the resolution of the process through legislative action. These concepts reflect the paternalistic and expert stance of the old welfare paradigm. If need is viewed solely as an unambiguous and objective phenomenon then there will be no substantial recognition of the validity of subjectively perceived needs. Such subjective analyses are always seen as subservient to the central task of exploring 'real objective need'. Proponents of traditional (or 'expert') models of needs definition and assessment disavow the importance of relative contexts and reject any explanation of needs that is not represented as the property of an individual, or at best the property of a collective or interest group (cf., Soper, 1981; Springborg, 1981; Ignatieff, 1989). Consequently, such confidence in the possibility of rational social science research, based on the empiricist tradition, should be analysed as part of an implicit political process.

Traditional welfare policy describes needs in four main ways: first, as an unambiguous and objective phenomenon; secondly, as an attribute of the client or potential client, either individual or community; thirdly, as the property of an individual or group; and, fourthly, as an essentially static phenomenon (Smith, 1980: 66). From a client's perspective needs are related to eligibility for service provision while for managers they direct the regulation of future welfare services. For a range of welfare professionals, social needs represented categories of precise service delivery and a procedure to measure the effectiveness of specific services (Smith, 1980: 65). The argument that needs are objective and can be empirically determined implies that the process of needs assessment is usually considered to be independent of those who are professionally employed either to define or to meet needs. The administrator and the professional practitioner constrain the process of how social needs are determined and assessed.

If need is viewed solely as an attribute of the client or community group then typically it is those who are already clients of the personal social services and welfare organizations who are deemed to be in need. This construes social needs so that they can only be perceived within the narrow frame of agency expertise. Needs become synonymous with agency function, not client status, since they represent agency expectations rather than client experience. What is measured is seldom relevant to actual practice and cannot be used as a sound basis for practice evaluation. Collection of data about actual welfare clients may be relevant to the study of how social need is satisfied but not to the antecedent task of measuring need itself. Need depicted within this traditional model is viewed as if it were 'essentially a static phenomenon' with a universal applicability. Current policy determines legitimate client status and validates certain referral patterns and these are used to ascertain the extent of those defined as having specific sets of needs. Policy-makers also recognize that there are an unspecified number of potential clients who, because they too possess similar characteristics indicative of need, have not requested services but are also eligible for service provision.

**An Alternative Approach: Subjective 'Truth'** The traditional approach is unable to recognize and reflect the 'process aspects' of needs assessments and it does not adequately reflect the reality of how people view and understand their lives. This criticism, which is the core of an ethno-methodological perspective, is vital when considering needs assessments of ethnic minorities. The aggressively monocultural nature of social welfare provision in countries with indigenous populations is such that one must take seriously the notion that social needs be identified through a process which takes clear account of different values and cultural assumptions. For Smith, the 'truth' about social needs does not reside in the ability to measure life empirically but in considered reflection about its phenomenological or subjective basis. There is a disdain for the empirical tradition which had undertaken a search for universal criteria of need which could be used in common by professional practitioners, administrators, clients and researchers alike. This attitude therefore frames needs assessments within a subjective and ontological perspective. Consequently, research analysis that is so inferred does not emphasize statistical and overarching categories of needs analysis, but rather attempts to reveal the subjective meanings that are derived from within the very process of needs assessment and analysis itself. Like Fraser (1989), Smith assumes that needs are essentially 'needs statements' rather than empirically verifiable categories. These assumptions require a somewhat larger agenda.

Social policy analysis is involved in a paradox in that individuals and communities construct a world that they then experience as something other than a product of themselves. Exploration and assessment of need based upon an acknowledgement of its intrinsic subjectivity falls naturally into two parts, that which defines those who are the recipients or clients of the social services and that which defines those who provide them. The clear aim of ethno-methodological enquiry is to turn the process of that social enquiry back upon the 'existential actor' who created it. If we can accept that the social and political 'fabric' is something that we have created, and not an essential given, then it is possible for social needs to be considered as one part of a set of social and political choices. The central feature of this alternative approach to needs assessment is that models of analysis and needs assessment are not independent of the manner in which social service workers routinely authenticate needs. They are intrinsically related to patterns of professional welfare practice. These professional routines exhibit aspects of a socially constructed reality which seeks to 'objectify' subjective needs. The focus is on the context of need, how it is 'situated' and how the 'facts' about welfare needs are socially constructed. This approach suggests that the concept of need means very different things to different 'actors' and draws a distinction between 'topic' (the social construction of needs) and 'resource' (actions to address needs). Need, from a social research perspective, is a topic, for social service professionals it is a resource and for the clients of social services it is an opportunity (Smith, 1980: 68).

**Client and Recipient: The Personal Experience of Dependency**
Little attempt has so far been made to 'validate' the experience of dependency which drives people to seek out social services. In fact the economic or social state of dependency has become part of the pejorative rhetoric of the neo-conservative attack on the welfare state. Yet, given the practical realities of the life-cycle, states of dependency are intrinsically part of that process. Ethno-methodological enquiry into needs assessment is one attempt to ground this analysis in a renewed respect for the practical and inescapable social fact of dependency, of our intrinsic vulnerabilities (cf., Goodin, 1988). This will, at least, require a wider recognition of how social structures condition personal choice and renew debate about whether economic and social independence is always the consequence of an exercise of personal courage and autonomy. However, as we have seen, definitions of needs still represent aspects of a practical political bargain between those who have and those who have not. Socially recognized needs are specific wants articulated by individuals or groups of people, which become politically important once they are acknowledged to warrant intervention and utilize communal resources (cf., Martin, 1982a: 200).

Clarification of the specific norms that condition the actual pattern of the social services is vital because such services are offered to, or imposed upon, clients who may not feel the need for them, particularly the range of statutorily mandated services (Jones et al., 1978; Martin, 1986). Not only do the potential recipients of services vary in their interpretation of their personal situations, but their attitudes and values may appear incomprehensible and even irresponsible to those in authority (cf., Hasenfeld, 1985a; Taylor-Gooby, 1985a; 1985b; 1985c; 1987). It is easy for social welfare administrators to forget that making a request for a social service, or taking some action which registers a desire for assistance, represents a considered judgement by potential consumers. Even when these decisions are made in high distress or panic, applying for such assistance involves knowledge of the range of services and the alternative informal sources of assistance which are actually available. Such knowledge reflects subjective assumptions about identification of needs and therefore needs assessment must reflect the concerns of the consumer. Not so oddly, the costs of being a service recipient may far outweigh the benefits that may be obtained (Martin, 1982a; 1986).

**Provider/Managerial Subjectivity: 'Public Faces in Private Places'**
The ethno-methodological approach implies that the providers of social services are equally involved in subjective appraisal of social needs. There are patterns of subjective assessment that providers of social services depend upon which echo and resonate in the subjective world of the consumers of social services. Martin describes an interesting contradiction. On the one hand administrators of social welfare services and policy researchers can be influenced by inequities of service delivery and a desire to be 'fair or relevant'. However, on the other hand, professional practitioners, ironically, may pay greater respect to the judgements of external experts when determining an appropriate analysis about 'adequate or optimal personal functioning'. Despite commitment to the principles of rational and efficient management senior welfare administrators are influenced 'by current social norms and attitudes, and may be particularly concerned about adverse reactions to proposed services' (Martin, 1986: 195). For example, needs assessments may be established because of strong community pressure on governments, and are often undertaken in situations of considerable conflict.

Where there is high conflict needs assessments may often be used as symbols of rationality, responsibility and rational research, but the actual procedural questions may be determined by subjective responses about the nature of these demands. As Smith argues, 'the most difficult task will be to harness the very limited resources . . . to some questions about the delivery of social services which, for the most part, have already been raised, but which have not yet been adequately answered' (1986: 281). A 'public face' is presented to mask what are essentially 'private' questions about social values. This attempt to respond 'rationally' to ambiguous, competing and even conflictual needs may be one of the underlying reasons why it is easier for policy-makers to revert to the empiricist model of needs assessment and analysis. It is, simply, too problematic to consider the value and possibility of construing some facets of social policy within the subjective frame of the participants as well as of the organizers.

### Bradshaw's Qualifiers!

This section describes aspects of the theoretical assumptions about needs assessment offered by a range of other writers (cf., Siegel et al., 1978; Gates, 1980; Ife, 1980; Martin, 1982a). All of these theorists have attempted to break out of the conceptual constraint that Bradshaw's categorization imposed upon needs assessment research and policy formation. As we have seen, Martin has suggested that distinctions be drawn between provider- or consumer-based definitions of needs. This dualism is important but falls into the trap of all such dualisms in that the analysis can be foreclosed by the oppositional aspect of the debate. Ife has attempted to escape from the question of the clash between the subjective 'truth' of providers and consumers. He proposes a different model based primarily on the importance of determining an answer to the initial question of who ascertains that a need exists. Needs assessments are therefore not categories or dimensions but reflections of practical political and administrative choice. Consequently, Ife has distinguished between population-defined need, 'caretaker'-defined need and inferred need. He has thus been able to expand Martin's dichotomy to include the part that existing social services play in determining need. Gates has developed a different three-fold definition of needs assessment that depends upon how differences between individual, group and consumption needs are identified. Reflecting Ife's analysis Gates makes distinctions between client-orientated needs assessments, service-orientated needs assessments and community-based needs assessments. Siegel et al. have suggested that the complexity of needs analysis, and options for social planners, can be resolved by formulating clear distinctions between needs identification and needs assessment.

**Needs Identification and Needs Enumeration**   In order to establish practical managerial alternatives Gates develops Bradshaw's theme of separate but related needs definitions. He asserts that needs assessment processes can be divided into two categories, both separate but interdependent, involving 'needs identification' and 'needs enumeration'. Needs identification is the process of determining the specific range of social, economic and human conditions that require organized intervention. Needs enumeration is the mechanical procedure of counting the number of persons in need, or determining the nature of specific social services required to alleviate or remedy these needs. However, as Gates argues, while the overall purpose of needs assessments is to find effective administrative mechanisms to determine the allocation of resources, it is possible to identify four distinct ways in which needs assessment may be incorporated into programme decision-making. They are used to establish planning priorities and, when combined with estimations of service delivery, help to determine budgetary requirements. They provide a focus for the evaluation of existing service programmes, as well as for improving coordination between programmes and social agencies (cf., Gates, 1980: 111).

If need and needs assessments are to be included as valid models of social planning and evaluation three crucial questions must be addressed. First, is it valid to assume that there are unique and identifiable needs, or sets of needs, intrinsic to individuals? Secondly, how are these needs specifically identified and, thirdly, how are they measured and included in actual welfare policy? Welfare clients do not 'possess fixed goals, objectives, or policies; rather they possess problems, wants and needs' (Gates, 1980: 101–103). Perception of need is not only an individual question but is vitally dependent upon cultural factors and patterns of group membership. In the current welfare rights context, both ethnic identification and interest group affiliation become critical determining factors in the perception of social needs. Gates distinguishes between two categories of needs, individual or group needs and consumption needs, and proposes that a 'set of causal relationships' is implicit in these two dimensions of need that links particular service provision to either ethnic or group affiliation. Identification of need does not necessarily reflect a commitment to allocate resources to meet such need – there is a structural paradox at work here. While the pattern of social service delivery is responsive to the identification of needs which require intervention, the opposite is also true as existing interventive methods, agencies and service delivery patterns define the actual conditions for intervention. Voluntary social service agencies, and for-profit agencies, will identify as valid needs those which the agency is established to serve (Smith, 1980: 100). The identification and assessment of needs require an understanding of the subjective relationship between those who are defined as needy and those who provide the resources to address that particular definition of needs.

**Client-, Service- and Community-orientated Needs Assessments**
Client-orientated needs assessments promote only the interests of specific sections of a wider community. A specific 'at risk' group, or a subset of a community, is defined, specific problems prevalent within the group are identified and some assessment is made about the level of specific services needed to alleviate these problems. Service-orientated needs assessments are usually conducted by the social service agencies responsible for the provision of particular services. They will be able to identify more precisely the population-at-risk and establish services to respond to the required level of service. Community-based needs assessment approaches, or social surveys, provide a solution to the question of whose actual needs are being served. Within this perspective three conditions are essential if needs assessments are to be useful to social policy administrators. There must be a general political acceptance of the value of state intervention to satisfy certain needs. Only if needs analysis reflects a feasible assessment of what can be provided within existing resources and skills can agencies be expected to contract for service provision. Finally, in order to ensure accountability, needs must reflect states or conditions that are capable of objective definition and measurement (Gates, 1980: 113).

**Needs Identification and Needs Assessment**  Siegel et al., similarly to Gates, distinguish between the processes of needs identification and needs assessment. Needs identification is described as the total health and social service requirements of a community or region, and needs assessment is the estimation of the relative importance of these particular needs. Siegel et al. (1978: 226) argue that on-going regional assessment efforts require models that are practical and capable of being employed on a smaller scale at the community level. It is assumed that this regional assessment activity would provide 'transparent' information for social planners to establish community-based programmes and that needs assessments, conducted regionally, would be less influenced by local political pressure. Several factors constrain isolated needs assessments undertaken independently by community-based agencies, suggesting that comprehensive assessment efforts are neither feasible nor appropriate for such organizations. Concentrating on single regional needs assessment programmes instead of numerous community efforts may conserve limited welfare resources but funding for research may be insufficient to support extensive assessments. The prior allocation of scarce funding to existing social programmes and the agency's need for urgent information may cut short the amount of time available for research. Finally, needs assessments undertaken by community-based agencies often reflect government deadlines as well as revealing the nature of internal community demands pressing for immediate action to resolve urgent social service problems.

Siegel et al. reflect the overwhelming opinion of most of the theoreticians in the field of needs research when claiming that need 'is at best a relative concept and the definition of need depends primarily upon those who undertake the identification and assessment effort' (1978: 216). Despite the fact that information gathered by needs assessments may frequently include objective data, Siegel et al. assume that planning necessarily remains a subjectively human and value-based process. From either a consumer or provider perspective diverse vested interests and disparate values will engender conflicting expectations. As a result,

> . . . the most systematic and objective assessment information must ultimately be filtered through and influenced by the perspectives of those charged with responsibility of translating that information into priorities and program goals. Consequently, the task of translating assessment information about community needs into relevant service programs is not a simple, orderly process, but rather a political task that entails complex decision making involving skills of negotiation and conciliation. It is essential, then, that the program planning process provides a forum for these different perspectives, and that this forum prevents premature domination by particularly vocal viewpoints to the exclusion of others. (1978: 219)

Siegel et al. suggest that social needs are both diffuse and yet interconnected – a point originally established by Bradshaw and a universal theme of other researchers. However, because it is difficult to identify these needs precisely social agencies have problems in determining a ranking of needs. It is therefore hard to institute a logical or empirical assessment of priorities, or to be accurate about what needs can be met effectively by which specific agencies. This dynamic complicates the needs identification process. One consequence of constant social change is that those social needs that initially defined welfare agency objectives and programme structures may have changed or at least lessened when a programme is finally implemented. This is a 'sufficient rationale for an on-going programme of community needs identification that is embedded in an on-going formal planning process' (Siegel, et al. 1978: 220). Developing appropriate and effective programmes to meet identified community needs depends upon other factors which lie outside the issues addressed by community- or consumer-based needs identification efforts. These are the capabilities and interest of staff, the availability of appropriate social service delivery procedures and the provision of adequate funding. In summary, social needs exemplify the dynamic values, culture and collective histories of individuals and communities involved in interpreting constant social change. They are specific and subjective in nature and cannot easily be categorized.

### The Rhetoric and Practicality of 'Needs': Summary and Analysis

The utility and value of needs assessments pivot on the question of whether it is ever possible to escape from the relativist position that the new paradigm of welfare rights implicitly fashions. Fraser, as we have seen, argues that discussion of needs 'functions as a medium for the making and contesting of political claims. It is an idiom in which the political conflict is played out and through which inequalities are symbolically elaborated and challenged' (1989: 291). It can be argued that practical politics and the qualified demands for practical intervention make any question of a distinction between the reality and consciousness of needs unimportant. Manning suggests that reality and consciousness 'are more fruitfully considered as symbiotically or dialectically interconnected, and moreover best revealed or understood through practical activity'. He would rather that the focus be moved from the contrast 'between philosophical interpretation and practical change . . . [to that] between ignorance and the insights that flow from practical intervention' (1987: 20).

Despite this emphasis on informed intervention, the field of needs assessment is likely to remain embroiled in a conflict about social inequality that will oscillate between political 'fact' and symbolic 'understanding'. Once the subjective 'reality' of needs had been accepted into public discourse, one consequence of a welfare rights model of welfare intervention, then the possibility of expert analysis of needs being politically acceptable was lost. Purchase of service contracting and even the privatization of welfare services are managerial policies that implicitly aim to return the discourse about needs to the 'insights that flow from practical intervention'. The proviso in this is that it is no longer the state which intervenes but the contracting agency. There is, therefore, a redefinition of the viability of expert assessment associated with the specific services that the contracting agency can deliver. The political expectations implicit in these policies becomes 'explicit' when we consider how purchasing social services by contract structurally alters the discourse about needs.

The political imperative of consumer-based needs analysis and assessment cannot be gainsaid, yet beyond the proliferation of a range of such needs assessments the implied collective demand must be responded to on the basis of specific criteria that have some administrative transparency. There are arguments to be made that precisely because of their subjective basis needs can be construed as unrealistic or even querulous demands and, as a consequence, the imperative for them can be blunted or even stymied. For this reason further analysis must move beyond the simple dualism of need and demand (Goodin, 1988). Fraser suggests that the rhetoric of needs might be better understood if the conceptual focus were shifted from needs to 'discourses about needs'. As she argues, the focus could be directed to 'the politics of need interpretation' rather than to 'the distribution of satisfactions'. This position is important because it shifts the focus back towards the practicalities of political discourse and generates the possibility for an analysis of obligation that 'objectifies' the subjective reality of needs interpretation. It is not entirely possible to avoid the dichotomy that exists between the expert traditional and the consumer-orientated needs assessment which, as I have argued, parallels the distinction between the old and new welfare paradigms.

## Purchase of Service Contracting: The Search for New Policy Directions

Contracting policies represent a major shift in social welfare philosophy, and in particular how services might be revamped in response to the shift in the welfare paradigm. Despite attempts to distinguish between them purchase of service contracting and privatization are intimately linked and highlight important ideological questions concerning governmental support for voluntary agencies and an increasing role for the private sector in social service provision (Veit, 1987: 1). While contracting is part of the wider social policy frame of privatization, ultimately accountability and responsibility for the delivery of adequate social services remains with governments. This remains so even though the major portion of the delivery of services, including the statutory determination of client or consumer group eligibility, may be undertaken by the agency providing the service (cf., Wedel et al., 1979; Hartley, 1984). Extensive use of contracting cannot be considered as if it were only a part of a set of new 'technical' or administrative policy options (cf., Hurl, 1986a; 1986b). It also represents a major re-drafting of some of the strongest assumptions about altruistic social exchange integral to an understanding of the welfare state. The classic argument for the validity of the public sector as the preferred

supplier of social services was stated by Marshall, who suggested
that the

> . . . responsibility of government in the field of welfare is more
> immediate and compelling than it is, generally speaking, in economic
> affairs. One of the virtues claimed for capitalist private enterprise is that
> it can take risks, and it earns a considerable part of its substantial rewards
> by doing so. But a government cannot allow risk taking in welfare – or
> only minimally. It cannot leave any important part of its overall
> responsibilities in the hand of private agencies unless it takes steps to
> limit risk by regulation, supervision, inspection or safety nets. (1972: 22)

This set of assumptions that Marshall used to justify the presumption that the state ought to be primarily 'responsible' for all the
social service needs of its citizen seems no longer as obvious as it did
when needs assessment was considered the priority of the state-
funded social expert. The current crisis in the welfare state has
grown partly out of apathy towards 'big government' and this
indifference undermines political authority without actually causing
it to collapse. Within this 'troubled environment' privatization and/
or purchase of service contracting appear to be logical developments because the managerial rhetoric which accompanies their
introduction talks of targeted and limited goals. The specific and
limited vision of these arguments is attractive and, as I will argue
later, cannot be summarily dismissed for they have changed and
broadened the arena within which the social policy debate is argued.

The policy literature fails to distinguish between those social
policies which result in purchase of services contracting and those
which result in privatization. The term 'contracting out' is often
used interchangeably with 'privatization' when it ought more
properly to refer to purchase of service contracting (Minogue and
O'Grady, 1985). Welfare privatization can be distinguished from
purchase of service contracting on the obvious ground that the
expectation, implicit in privatization policies, is that the entire social
services and not merely a particular aspect of them ought to be
provided by the private sector. Privatization is used to describe
'almost any attempt to improve public sector performance . . . .
[and] policies designed to improve the operating efficiency of public
sector enterprises through increased exposure to market forces'
(Domberger and Piggott, 1986: 145–146). Privatization is therefore
defined as the 'conduct of operations by the private sector in
functional areas traditionally considered to be in the public domain'
(Florestano and Gordon, 1980: 29). On the other hand, 'contracting
out' or purchase of service contracting indicates the purchase, by
governments, of particular services from private or voluntary
agencies to complete an overall pattern of desired social services.

Typically, contracted services are only one aspect of the overall service provided by the contracting agency (Smith, 1971: 14; Pascal, 1981: 7).

In practice, governmental welfare policies represent two quite separate activities: both the provision and the production of services (Kolderie, 1986: 285). Given the increasing level of political support for the presumed benefits of privatization, it is important to clarify which of these activities is to be emphasized. For example, is the concept of privatization to be mainly associated with the practical aspects of service delivery or should it only apply to those sets of administrative policy decisions necessary to provide services? This distinction between the provision or production of a service is important given that each of these respective managerial activities can be broken down further into several parts, each aspect of which might separately be privatized. This range of possible perspectives creates difficulties in determining accurate definitions of privatization. Kolderie suggests that:

> A service is publicly or socially provided (a) where the decision whether to have it (and the decisions about who shall have it and how much of it) is a political decision, (b) when government arranges for the recipients not to pay directly for the service themselves, and (c) when the government selects the producer that will serve them . . . . [A] service is privately provided (a) where individuals and nongovernmental organisations make their own decisions whether or not to have it, (b) where, if they choose to have it, they pay for it in full out of their own resources, whatever these may be, and (c) where they select the producer themselves. (1986: 286)

Privatization assumes that consumers will pay fees directly to those firms providing the required services. It might be argued then that privatization as a concept can only be applied in those situations where governments relinquish complete responsibility to the private sector for the supply and delivery of a public service. The radical nature of these core assumptions, particularly about privatization but equally well about purchase of service contracting, is based on the application of crucially untested social theory. Emphasizing this point Klein suggests that if the private sector replaces the public sector, there is the 'risk that it may also reproduce its weaknesses: its rigidities, its unresponsiveness and its administrative costs – with the bureaucracy of regulation taking the place of the bureaucracy of management' (1984a: 28). Associated with arguments for privatization of welfare services are those that call for the decentralization and deregulation of social services – the 'trinity of the market' (Lightman, 1987: 310). The central political assumption of privatization is that it involves the active and deliberate transfer of responsibility for welfare from the public to the private realm in order that the 'market can replace government' (Kolderie, 1986: 285; Lundqvist, 1988).

Contracting for the provision of social services embraces different agreements ranging from 'fully negotiated legal documents' to oral agreements. It may be defined in general terms as

> . . . a legally binding agreement between a government contracting agency (with responsibility for serving clients and the resources to serve them) and a contractor (with appropriate service delivery capability) in which the contractor provides care of services to clients of the government contracting agency in exchange for funds or other resources. (Kettner and Martin, 1987: 22; cf., Wedel, 1974)

No clear or consistent definition of contracted service delivery systems has been established. However, three current influences in the social welfare area have contributed to the adoption of contracting agreements. These are increased focus on community care, decentralization of service delivery and political initiatives for regional development in order to make government more locally responsive (Veit, 1987: 4). Trends towards 'deinstitutionalization' of social services have required the development of community-based services which have given impetus to those policies which have sought to revamp the pattern of social services and make them contractual. If contracting to deliver social services does indeed clarify questions of financial planning for social agencies, as Veit suggests, then determining different categories of contractual fiscal relationship and distinguishing between them becomes important.

It is commonly argued (Judge, 1982: 400) that there are four categories of contracts. These are: vendor reimbursement – providing specific services to a known group of clients; proportional reimbursement of costs to designated agencies; significant grants for quasi-contracting; and minor grants to support general community development. Vendor reimbursement, the most frequent and largest contract expenditure, is used to purchase services from a wide range of residential settings and allocate funds to foster families. Vendor reimbursement offers certain practical benefits to agencies because annual payments on previously agreed contract service unit costs are usually consistent. Proportional reimbursement contracts distribute funds to those social agencies which provide services to people with sensory impairment or disability. Contract funding formulas cover already agreed fixed costs regardless of the number of clients served. Proportional reimbursement contracts cover funding of community 'delegate' agencies who contract to provide services to particular groups of clients. Funding is provided as long as these agencies are willing to assume this delegate status and accept total responsibility to provide the particular services that the state requires.

The distinction between quasi-contracting and general community development funding depends on whether these grants enable voluntary agencies to provide more effective services than those provided through the public sector. Quasi-contracting allows governments to establish seeding-grants which can be used to provide financial impetus for the development of new services. Thus substantial grants are allocated with the explicit expectation that particular services will be provided. Under this formula, funding allocations are not associated with either the quality or quantity of service provided and therefore these grants never reflect the actual costs of service provision. Community development grants are self-explanatory and signify an even more explicit political decision to provide specific 'one-off' grants. These grants may be used to distribute funds to a wide range of social and community agencies providing community or neighbourhood advisory services, thus meeting the more particular or idiosyncratic social, recreational and counselling needs of respective communities.

### The Context of the Debate: Agency Definitions, Client Status and Policy Options

The purchase of service contracts poses fresh dilemmas for welfare services with traditional patterns of inter-agency co-operation. Social service contracting and especially the possibility of complete privatization of welfare services will dramatically change the context and social structure of agency operation. These policies create confusion about agency autonomy and structure and obscure the distinctions usually made between 'non-profit' or voluntary social services and those proprietary agencies loosely described as 'for-profit' agencies. The typical pattern of social welfare services involved a mix of state sector agencies with a wide range of voluntary agencies and limited private practice.

### The Non-Profit and Voluntary Agencies: Models, Purposes and Roles

Kramer presented a comprehensive review of these topics in his major 1981 work *Voluntary Agencies in the Welfare State*. He suggests that explanations of either the character, goals or functions of voluntary agencies frequently assume four different organizational roles. The first is a 'vanguard' or trend-setting role where the voluntary agency 'innovates, pioneers, experiments with, and demonstrates' the viability of new programmes, expecting that government will assume direct responsibility for those which are demonstrably effective. Secondly, the voluntary agency assumes an advocacy (or 'improver') role either explicitly criticizing or monitoring the existing spread of social services. Consequently, acting within this role, it acts as a 'gadfly' to pressure governments to 'extend, improve or establish needed services'. The third role is that of 'value guardian' when voluntary agencies vigorously defend their historic right and traditional responsibility to adopt 'voluntaristic, particularistic or sectarian values'. Voluntary agencies emphasize the development of community leadership and actively seek to protect the special interests of social, religious, cultural or other minority groups. Defence of these traditional agency values is echoed in the active promotion of citizen participation in service delivery. The final role is as a 'service provider' in which voluntary agencies provide specific services 'reflecting a public responsibility that government is unable or unwilling to provide' (Kramer, 1985b: 384ff.).

While it is arguable that these four organizational roles are more normative than descriptive, Kramer, nevertheless, contends that the defining characteristics of 'specialization, consumerism, advocacy and service provision' are more frequently pioneered by voluntary than by state sector agencies. A common assumption is that specialization in the particular problems of consumer or client groups frequently defines the concerns of voluntary or non-profit agencies, but, ironically, pioneering or experimentation in new forms of service delivery is often to be found in the state sector agencies. Cross-national comparisons of this argument are difficult to resolve. It may be that while this is true in countries such as Great Britain it does not apply in the USA where the voluntary sector has traditionally been more innovative. Public agencies, often credited with an ability to be innovative (a characteristic that voluntary agencies fear because the state agencies can command more resources), are still not regarded by clients as relevant to their needs. The local, particular or voluntary agencies, despite constriction of resources, are considered more relevant. Clients value the idiosyncratic focus of voluntary agencies in contrast to the more universal scope of government-provided social services (Taylor-Gooby, 1986a). Voluntary agencies, almost by definition, have been set up to service more specific and particular needs than those which are normally serviced by the major government agencies. This reliance on voluntary agencies however is haphazard, less dependent on a sound appraisal of relative merits and based more upon pragmatic interests (Kramer, 1981).

In practice there are four distinct social service contexts which determine relationships between voluntary agencies and governments. Paraphrasing Kramer (1985b), the first is where the voluntary agency is the only or primary provider, its services do not parallel existing governmental services and it may offer radical, innovative or specific services. The second is where the agency complements existing governmental services by providing specialist services. These services can represent the altruism of private benefactors who have significantly endowed specific welfare services. In the third context the voluntary agency supplements or extends state systems by providing an alternative choice of treatment, thereby creating the possibility of direct competition. These agencies often demonstrate how certain treatment theories achieve sufficient intellectual standing to command public support and challenge traditional patterns of intervention followed by the public agencies. The fourth context is where the voluntary agency offers a specific alternative to governmental provision and is directly competitive. It is, therefore, the advocacy functions of the voluntary agencies that may be their most significant distinguishing feature:

> As organisational differences amongst Government, voluntary, and for-profit social service organisations diminish and social services in the Welfare State become more widespread, the historic mission of the voluntary agency to identify and articulate the interests of neglected and undeserved groups takes on even greater importance. In performing this role, voluntary agencies urge improvements in public policy and practice, and criticise as well as defend government services when they are unjustly attacked. Advocacy does not necessarily imply an absence of concern for change among governmental or other interest groups, but is rather a more consistent and legitimate expectation of voluntary agencies. (Kramer, 1985b: 384)

Voluntary agencies are more likely than public agencies to use volunteers in fund-raising, service delivery and policy-making because they emphasize client involvement. The politics of consumerism and the 'transparency' of the bureaucracy underscore the necessity to involve clients in policy-making and reinforce the benefits of self-help or mutual aid associations.

While voluntarism is promoted by governments, voluntary agencies are better placed to attract and use volunteers, who usually seek a greater voice in the administration of the social services. To fulfil the government mandate to provide a network of social services requires that agencies collaborate and that managers seek to rationalize the available resources with other voluntary agencies and service providers. Kramer (1985b) argues that competition between service providers and especially open conflict is infrequent. His argument, however, is not supported by Hurl and Tucker, who suggest that development of social service contracts tends to destroy the former collegiality of the voluntary sector. They propose a different schema with four alternative models to describe welfare systems. These are a market model, a clan model, a quasi-public model and a public model. The analysis assumes that governments must continue to accept political responsibility for both the funding and delivery of services. This would accord with the criterion of distributive justice, promote service delivery standards and ensure accountability for the expenditure of public funds. They suggest that until now scholars have generally ignored a detailed examination of the systems that structure the patterns of social service delivery and avoided these wider ethical issues:

> This lack of attention is a significant oversight for it implies that implementation structures are technical and neutral with regard to outcome . . . . Implementation models are not unbiased mechanisms that accept ends and values, goals and ideologies, as 'inputs', and then work in accordance with known facts to solve problems . . . . [rather they] shape individual and collective activity . . . . [and] can be presumed to have important independent effects for the nature and distribution of social services. (Hurl and Tucker, 1986: 608)

The market model assumes that competition amongst agencies for available resources, including public and private funds, consumers and personnel, is intrinsically valuable. Such a model, argue the public choice theorists, helps to eliminate the duplication of services, identifies programme gaps and improves the efficiency of individual agencies. In addition, social service agencies, operating relatively autonomously and competitively under market conditions, are assumed to be highly flexible, responsive to client need and able to provide high quality services to a heterogeneous population (cf., Anderson et al., 1981; Block, 1987a; Savas, 1982; 1987). It can be argued, however, that the expectations that the market model will efficiently eliminate duplication and fill programme gaps are more rhetorical than practical. Resources are not always allocated equally or equitably. Services are often duplicated and needy clients seek similar services from more than one agency with the consequence that social service funding is overburdened (Burkitt and Davey, 1980; 1984).

The clan model, in contrast to the market model, emphasizes that the establishment and maintenance of a collaborative network between social service agencies is more important than competition. The history of voluntary social service agencies is that they will, 'in the name of efficiency, equity, and the pursuit of broader inter-organizational goals, agree to the formation of over-arching, regulatory bodies, governed by boards with individuals from amongst their own staff or membership' (Hurl and Tucker, 1986: 609). The quasi-public model depends upon an hierarchical arrangement of inter-agency relationships within which governments contract for services to be supplied by non-governmental agencies. When governments apply this model they purchase services according to contract criteria, thus regulating the nature and structure of how agencies allocate resources and deliver services. There is no necessary preference for either the voluntary sector or bias towards 'for-profit' agencies or equally any discrimination against new innovative agencies. However, given public pressure to provide services, government contract negotiators 'have generally reflected a preference for the use of existing services, which for the most part were voluntary' (Hurl and Tucker, 1986: 610). The public model refers to those countries where the public sector has traditionally accepted major responsibility for the direct provision of social services. Public accountability, control and development of the social services were achieved through a statutory bureaucracy, primarily responsible for policy analysis and service delivery.

## The 'For-Profit' Proprietary Agencies and Private Practice

Purchase of service contracting, not unexpectedly, has resulted in a growth of 'for-profit' agencies, as distinct from 'non-profit' or voluntary agencies (cf., Borenzweig, 1981; Reichert, 1982; Wallace, 1982; Grosser and Block, 1983; Epstein, 1988). Combining welfare services and profit expectations raises major issues because it has been widely assumed in social work, as well as by other social service professionals, that profit-seeking by professionals diminishes the quality of care and a commitment to advocate for change (Watson, 1984; Abel-Smith and Titmuss, 1987; Mishra, 1989). Without the efforts of those advocates who pointed towards gaps and deficiencies in the social services it was assumed that 'the prevailing [regressive] economic and political forces guiding the . . . field of service delivery . . . [could] be expected to reproduce themselves' (Rose, 1987: 256). The absence of the profit motive was assumed to be the one major distinctive feature of social welfare programmes (Wilensky and Lebeaux, 1958). Another widespread assumption governing the pattern of agency social services was that the function of welfare services is to provide for a range of needs not provided by market-based organizations. This assumes that the welfare field has been professionally socialized to believe that public, or at least non-profit, agencies provide better services. Market-led 'concepts such as competition and profit have no place in social welfare, where need, rather than ability to pay, is the important factor' (Born, 1983: 114). Some of the justifications for the privatization of the social services and the endorsement of the profit motive are crudely political and refer either to 'the pathologies of bureaucracy' or to the 'inefficiencies of socialism' (Poole, 1983: 119). They reflect the demands of the continuing ideological debate between 'left' and 'right' rather than a proper or useful analysis of the respective agencies. The antibureaucratic bias of neo-conservatism expresses 'a deep-seated social myth whose function is to validate individualism in an era of collectivism' (Goodsell, 1980: 359). Yet it is also true that the relatively 'high sounding' rhetoric about 'unseemly profit' essentially reflects a contrary ideology and a 'refusal' to consider questions about the validity of profit-based service delivery. Private practice is by no means an easy economic option but with the advent of contracting it has facilitated the development of a range of small-scale entrepreneurial agencies.

### The Public or Private Sector: Differences and Distinctions?

To clarify the debate about the purchase of service contracting requires a separate consideration of the traditional relationship between governments and the voluntary 'non-profit' agencies as well as the relationship between governments and the relatively new proprietary 'for-profit' agencies. Non-profit or voluntary agencies encompass both secular and church-based organizations. The for-profit and proprietary agency category describes services provided by profit-orientated organizations as well as by individual private practitioners. While significant differences between public and private sector agencies are often described in the general research literature, less attention is paid to the differences that exist between agencies in the private sector and to the influence that sector has on the formulation of social policy. Much of the discussion is essentially simplistic, focusing only on dualistic distinctions between public and private provision of services. Clear-cut differentiation between private and public social service agencies cannot simply be based on determining respective sources of financial support (Weddell, 1986: 15). Similarly, questions about the most effective delivery of social services cannot be resolved by attempting, simply, to prove that private provision is better than public provision.

The initial rhetoric of the welfare state presumed that distinctions between private and public agencies arose from differences in income sources. These new policies have collapsed such distinctions and the amalgamation of public and private sectors is such that it is often futile to attempt to discriminate one from the other. One of the interesting aspects of this debate is whether the changes in the voluntary sector, occasioned by the purchase of service contracts, sharpen the differences between the non-profit and for-profit agencies and governments or whether these policies create a convergence. Welfare agencies accepting contracts offer more readily identifiable and tangible services than those which typically fall within the residual area of the social services, the traditional arena of public welfare. This simplistic and customary distinction between public and private agencies is no longer useful, but social policy has not yet developed suitable concepts, paradigms or theories adequately to describe this collapse of traditional public and private agency distinctions engendered by the mixed economy of welfare (Kammerman, 1983: 8). The old welfare paradigm, perhaps illusorily, assumed a normative function impossible within a welfare rights model. The arguments for the use of contracting procedures have an internal logic. They place an emphasis on managerial efficiency but cannot be used to establish overarching social policy. Governments cannot easily choose between non-profit and for-profit agencies on the blithe assumption that for-profit agencies are always more efficient and effective in service delivery.

The rhetoric that private agencies will always provide social services more efficiently than the public sector is difficult to assess. Claiming that social welfare programmes are more effectively provided and operated by profit-making agencies is an unexamined belief (Gilbert, 1983: 11). Echoing a contrasting critical opinion, and arguing for divergence, Rice suggests that public welfare agencies differ from the private sector 'because they involve themselves in social action programs which have no particular individual consumer utility' (1975: 390). Agreeing with the notion of divergence but using totally different premises, Hansmann (1980) argues that there are also innate distinctions based upon an analysis of respective legal functions and that it is a common assumption that non-profit agencies were established to alleviate the worst aspects of market provision. For example, the social advantage of non-profit agency services is that the 'discipline of the market is supplemented by the additional protection given the consumer by another broader "contract", the organization's legal commitment to devote its entire earnings to the production of services' (Hansmann, 1980: 844).

There are, therefore, two crucial areas of difference and divergence between private and public agencies. First, for-profit and non-profit agencies demonstrate different organizational purposes.

The private agencies' requirement to maximize shareholder profit distinguishes it from the usual mandate of the non-profit agency. Secondly, the respective financial structures differ because private agencies must borrow capital or generate it from practice and must pay taxes on profits (Collin, 1987). However, tax laws for proprietary agencies may have to change should they assume the increased burden that full-scale privatization (in contrast to contracting for specific services) would place on the for-profit private sector (Morris, 1982a; 1982b). Non-profit agencies, however, accept public donations which are commonly tax deductible. They are usually permitted to reinvest any profit surplus without incurring further tax liability. Consequently, both in their structure and organizational purpose, non-profit agencies are more like trusts than business corporations.

At a structural, managerial level there are other definitions and distinctions to be made between proprietary for-profit and voluntary or non-profit agencies. Both Salamon (1987) and Kramer (1985b; 1985c) highlight the relative neglect of the importance of the non-profit area, particularly in an American context, and suggest that it should almost be considered as a form of 'third-party government'. Denying a structural connection between the non-profit sector and government is part of the dualistic rhetoric of social theory unable to escape the implicit 'logic' of private and public distinctions. Indeed various theories about the origin of welfare states, as well as those analysing the voluntary sector, imply that co-operation between the government and non-profit sector 'could not, and should not exist' (Salamon, 1987: 33). This apparent contradiction highlights the ideological nature of the debate, for it is more common for neo-conservative social policy analysts to deny the significance of this pattern of co-operation, preferring the cruder analytical categories of public and private.

In a clever reversal of the common assumption that proliferation of non-profit agencies reflects the 'failure of the market system', Salamon suggests that we should 'view government as the derivative institution, responding to "voluntary failure", to the inherent limitations of the voluntary or nonprofit sector' (1987: 39). Salamon's theory has a particular cogency in that it is systemic and capable of relating the competing worlds of public and private analysis to a new paradigm which is neither atomistic nor structurally and bureaucratically 'paternalistic'. Both Salamon and Hansmann reflect aspects of a complex debate that will not be resolved by a simplistic denial that there is no systemic interrelationship between governmental and private sectors.

*The Vexed Issue of Client Status within Contracted*
*Services*

One of the major questions relating to client role and status is whether, under contracting arrangements, clients remain clients of the state or whether they become clients of an agency. While this is, at first glance, a philosophical question, perhaps having little moment in the actual delivery of services, clarification of this particular issue is essential for it has far-reaching implications. The historical foundations of the British social service system saw major clashes in philosophical assumptions about just such a question. The Minority Report to the 1905 Royal Commission on the revision of the Victorian Poor Laws clarified for a generation that there should be no discrimination between the deserving and undeserving poor (Moroney, 1983). There was an explicit rejection of the notion of a two-tiered welfare system where deserving clients would be cared for by the private sector and those deemed undeserving by the public sector. Over time this pattern, it might be argued, has nevertheless developed and there is the possibility that questions about deserving and undeserving poor will re-emerge in the guise of what services might more appropriately be contracted out.

Veit (1987), in a unique argument, has demonstrated that contracting may in fact be seen as an alternative to either state or totally private services. This particular assertion builds from the assumption that with the introduction of contracting the client remains a client of the state and is not a client of the agency. The argument rests on several facts. First, that agencies sign legally binding contracts agreeing to undertake specific services according to governmental priorities. Secondly, purchase of service contracting implies that consumers remain clients of governments while served by a government contractor. Thirdly, the fact that government workers are more involved with contract negotiation monitoring and evaluation does not mean that the clients of contract agency workers cease to be government clients (Veit, 1987: 15). Greater use of contracting procedures is not an opportunity for the state to divest itself of its legislative mandate but is rather an opportunity to introduce an administrative system whereby market-place rationality and the spread of voluntary agencies may be used to balance out the respective roles of state and private sector in providing an overall pattern of social services. Most funding mechanisms, whether they be block grants, base level funding, capitation grants, salary subsidies or building subsidies, imply that the client is a client of the agency.

When an agency is almost totally funded by the state, this particular issue is more difficult to resolve. Whatever the source of their funds, voluntary agencies are seen to provide services in such a way that clients are clients of that particular agency and not clients of the state. Taylor-Gooby (1986a) has demonstrated that under certain conditions it may still be argued that the state provides more efficient services. Nevertheless, his extensive research shows that clients believe that they get a better service from voluntary agencies, even when it may be argued on other grounds that the service they receive is in some senses 'inferior'. The public sector cannot, therefore, resolve some of the problems that are addressed by the more particular and idiosyncratic nature of the private or voluntary agency.

## Summary and Conclusion

The introduction of extensive purchase of service contracting has set the scene for a different pattern of relationships between the state and the private agencies. This policy shift reflects the rejection of previous monolithic systems of state-based institutional care, but we can be sure that complete rejection of such institutions makes no more sense than their former unilateral acceptance. The evidence which would allow us to make such assessments is not available. Policy-makers will need to understand better those sets of circumstances in which it can be argued that contracting is in the public interest (Dorwart et al., 1986: 878). Purchase of service contracting is both an administrative mechanism for addressing the particular issues of the social legitimacy of the state involved in direct social services and an attempt to borrow from the managerial ethos of private enterprise (and entrepreneurial development) systems of cost-benefit analysis and management by objectives. There is a set of important and vital policy questions which arises out of the establishment of these policies. Managers will have to determine what and whose needs are to be met and to select agencies to meet those needs. They will also have to specify the contract, which will include clarification of acceptable budgetary arrangements, the nature of the preferred monitoring and evaluation mechanisms, and the managerial system which will need to be instituted in order to achieve these overall aims. Managers will equally have to decide the beneficial outcomes that these contracting mechanisms will provide.

The range of arguments for and against purchase of service contracting lends credence to the suggestion that the introduction of these policies has the potential to create a 'strengthened partnership between the private and public sectors' resulting in an increased availability as well as refinement in the provision and delivery of specific high quality services (Weddell, 1986: 26). There is general agreement in the current literature that clients value more highly those agency structures which may be seen to be more intrinsically related to them either ethnically, culturally, religiously, locally or in respect of gender. Allowing for both the practical and ideological issues that are implicit in the debates about the nature of the 'political economy', it is likely that governments will not be able to resolve all of the issues involved in social policy. Ultimately welfare policy options pivot on the question of 'who gets what'. Whether these questions are 'about the political allocation of economically scarce resources on some criteria of social fairness' remains to be seen. Purchase of service contracting and particularly the privatization of welfare services give governments a policy instrument with which 'to make retrenchments at the expense of the politically weakest sections of the population, rather than to concentrate resources on the most vulnerable and deprived' (Klein, 1984a: 29). The next chapter will consider the theoretical debate about purchase of service contracting as well as the issues that surround the complete privatization of welfare services.

# 4

## The Purchase of Service Contracting Debate

## Citizen 'friends' and welfare 'strangers'

> . . . as in all serious conflicts, there is much to be said for both sides – for the insistence on a radical and egalitarian individualism, and for the defense of complex institutions and social bonds, incorporating authority and, if you will, superstition, as an unexamined but accepted element. But if the first side wins out, as it is doing, the hope that social policy will assist in creating more harmonious relations, better-working social institutions, broadly accepted as the decent and right way to order society, cannot be realized.
>
> (Glazer, 1988: 155)

When the administrative concept of purchase of service contracting was first introduced into the discussion about the efficient management of the social services its advocates did, as Glazer suggests, represent one side of a renewed public debate about the function of the welfare state and its relationship to the corporate or managerial state. The current mix of economic policies that are used to justify the restructuring of state-owned industries within welfare states have also been drawn on to justify policies that seek to restrict the power of public sector bureaucracies (Minford, 1987). This bias against state commercial bureaucracies has prompted substantial theoretical and practical reviews of the purpose and design of public welfare and the supporting bureaucracies. Neo-conservative social theory argues for major changes to be made in the customary patterns of political and social support for the welfare state, specifically focusing on the promotion of social policies that favour either the complete privatization or, less threateningly, the contracting of social services.

The promotion of social services contracting has introduced a new element into the old debate between 'private enterprise' and 'state socialism'. For some considerable time social policy discussions have been preoccupied with questions about whether the welfare state should be maintained under its original auspices or whether it should be redrafted, fuelling, as we have seen, the continuing polemic that the welfare state is in 'crisis'. Policy initiatives such as the contracting or privatization of social services reflect this new climate of opinion that aims to redraft both the structure and the vision of a welfare society. They are not just technical managerial issues and cannot simply be seen as procedures for efficient service delivery. Those who make further attempts to argue for the legitimacy of social policy based upon a welfare tradition are obliged to rethink the initial imperatives for the welfare state. This requires a willingness to re-evaluate the benefits of government social intervention as well as the current promotion of contracted services. In order to understand how we might create the conditions for such a re-evaluation this chapter examines the major arguments in the contemporary literature for and against purchase of service contracting and the privatization of social services. The range of issues that are canvassed in the current debate about these new polices will be examined in five sections. The first provides a general overview of the range of arguments in favour of contracting and the impetus towards privatization, as well as the corresponding contrary arguments. Three subsequent sections survey the range of arguments for and against purchase of service contracting particularly as it affects governments, social service agencies and clients. The first of these considers the potential political and strategic advantages and disadvantages for governments implicit in the establishment of these policies. The second considers the impact of these policies on the voluntary sector, specifically the arguments about the relative merits of proprietary or 'for-profit' agencies and voluntary or 'non-profit' agencies. The third section surveys a range of arguments about the respective advantages and disadvantages for the consumers and clients of social services faced with the imposition of a contract welfare system. A final section provides a more general summary and analysis of the debate.

## The Ideology of Social Service Contracting

As we have seen, political rhetoric about 'the crisis of welfare states' has often been used to support revisionist arguments that seek to create a new welfare policy environment. The intention of this rhetoric is to present the private sector as the 'answer' to the deficiencies that are presumed to be the inevitable consequence when governments act as the sole or major supplier of welfare services. Excessive government regulation and public sector welfare systems are believed to be the basic cause of social and economic problems and, accordingly, cannot be used to cure them (Gibelman, 1983: 101; Savas, 1982; 1987; Linowes, 1988). However, this survey of the various social policy arguments highlights the necessity to develop an analysis that does not retreat into false dualisms. It is not possible simply to reject the validity of establishing a system of contracted social services on the dubious grounds that its administrative structure applies market principles to the arena of social welfare.

Those advocating contracted social services argue that success requires the specification of specific contracts and support for competition in service provision. It also requires opportunities to be made for new agencies to tender for existing contracts, the establishment of 'competitively determined fixed price contracts' and the provision of clear incentives for cost-effective service delivery (McCready, 1986: 256; Gibelman and Demone, 1983; Savas, 1987). The achievement of effective social service contracting, applying these particular managerial tasks, requires the establishment of new administrative structures. Consequently, the underlying logic of these new administrative policies draws heavily upon the prevailing philosophies of the market-place. It is suggested, for example, that even where the private sector is regulated, and its profits are therefore curtailed, empirical economic evidence reveals that a regulated private sector is more efficient than any counterpart in the public sector (Bennett and Johnson, 1980: 393). Typically, these arguments about obvious market efficiencies depend more on the assumption of such efficiencies in the private sector, and of their absence in the public sector. Empirical research has not, as yet, established the validity of these rhetorical arguments, which is not to deny their potential truth but simply to affirm that substantive work has still to be done to prove their validity.

While the arguments against the practical usefulness of purchase of service contracting on a macro-level seem substantive, there are significant reasons to argue for its benefits at a micro-level (cf., Gronbjerg, 1983; Weddell, 1986). While there is clear support in a mixed economy for a blend of public and privately contracted services at this micro-level, issues still arise about the application of these policies. The rhetoric of 'welfare-crisis' has been used to justify changes to levels of income maintenance and reduce overall access to services. For example, current arguments endorsing purchase of service contracting at the micro-level have been used at a macro-political level to reverse general trends toward welfare state support (Heclo, 1981; 1986). The use of contracted services imposes obligations on subordinate groups and low-status people that continue to bind them to the institutions that are simultaneously diluting their benefits and influence (Lipsky, 1984: 21). The living standards of the low income sector have also reduced because taxation policies have enhanced the gap between rich and poor (Gronbjerg, 1983; Lipsky, 1984; Block, 1987a; 1987b). These policies may entail a 'redistribution of public funds from the poor to the middle classes though this may not be seen by all governments as a disadvantage' (Graycar, 1983a: 388). The apparent loss of public welfare benefits does not mean that the needs cease to exist. On the contrary, while these needs are no longer met by public programmes, increased demands fall on the private sector for emergency assistance and services. This is particularly relevant to countries whose social policies are dependent on the future development of bicultural and multicultural welfare systems.

The distinctive characteristic of private social welfare systems to recognize and respect individual difference is particularly significant for such pluralistic societies in which indigenous ethnicity and religious beliefs are salient features. Purchasing welfare services from governments based on gender, regional, ethnic or racially distinct patterns offers these community groups a way to maintain their distinct differences (Gronbjerg, 1983; McCready, 1986; Weddell, 1986; Veit, 1987). Providing social services by contract also gives governments an important opportunity to assist indigenous and ethnic groups to acquire an independent but integrated economic base. Increasing awareness of the political and welfare claims of differing ethnic groups reinforces the observation that there has indeed been a shift from the old welfare paradigm based upon religious and political codes of obligation to a new paradigm based upon the legitimacy of claim rights. The urgency and moral imperative of these ethnic and, in particular, indigenous ethnic claim rights have accompanied successive reviews of the welfare state (Mishra, 1984; Jayasuriya, 1987; Williams, 1987). Indeed, George and Wilding argue that racial 'conflicts are perhaps the most prominent as well as the most threatening to social stability in many advanced countries' (1985: 133). The paradigm shift from paternalistic obligation to welfare rights has not only provided an opportunity for a recognition of these rights but has also helped to focus and even form them. The claims seek economic redress through new administrative mechanisms that are antithetical to the normal pattern of legislatively mandated individual welfare entitlement. Appropriate ethnic social policy requires not only a reconsideration of the basis for entitlement but also the decentralization of a bureaucratic and centrist welfare system and devolution to tribal authorities. A range of agreements will have to be developed with indigenous and ethnic groups about how they might develop some 'form of private agency' to fulfil the purposes of administrative contracting.

Arguments about specificity and relevance are usually tied to those about flexibility. Indeed, one of the prime advantages commonly proposed for the use of a contractual approach to the delivery of welfare services is that new or innovative services can be established more quickly by the private sector because it has the capacity to respond rapidly and specifically to local problems or needs. Purchase of service contracting can allow governments to emphasize the importance of specifically idiosyncratic approaches in the delivery of services. All of the presumed benefits about the application of these new policies to the delivery of ethnic social services also apply to local or community-based services. Agencies providing such innovative services can operate on a small scale. They are able to respond more deftly to needs and can be creative in developing unique service solutions. It is becoming clear that governments neither can nor should do everything (Pascal, 1981). The fiscal capacity of modern governments simply does not allow them to meet the full demand for compensatory services. Particular demands for health care, education and quality of life constitute a 'bottomless pit' where there is always more that could be done, and even though governments provide services to cater for basic needs citizenship rights are likely to be violated or weakened (cf., Lipsky, 1984; Hurl, 1984; 1986a; Abramovitz, 1986). Finally, a private welfare system may be significant in the mature welfare state since it can provide a limited and specific, but highly valued, sense of participation, where personal worth and involvement are achieved distinct from the explicitly public welfare sector (cf., Kramer, 1985c; Salamon, 1987).

### The Case against Purchase of Service Contracting
Decisions to implement extensive purchase of service contract arrangements represent, in part, the dominance of those political and ideological assumptions that argue for a balance between the provision of private social welfare and direct state involvement in the supply of social services. As we have seen, the validity of this balance depends upon general acceptance of the principle that the private sector can provide services more efficiently than the public sector (Reichert, 1982). While private agencies are believed to be more efficient and effective than either the public sector or the voluntary non-profit agencies,

. . . there are broader concerns of the social market that the pursuit of profit does not enhance. The pursuit of profit, for example, engenders little compassion for the economic circumstances of others and hardly cultivates the idea of individual sacrifice for the common good. Stringent concerns for economic efficiency give short shrift to interests in the adequacy of social provisions. Thus, welfare for profit poses a delicate issue for the mixed economy of welfare. The delivery of social services may to some extent benefit from the inclusion of profit oriented activity.

But if such activity is not embraced selectively and with great discretion, it may eventually undermine the values and distort the communal character of the social market. (Gilbert, 1983: 73)

Despite the fact that it is a commonplace argument among the protagonists of social service privatization and contracting that the voluntary agency can deliver the same services more cheaply than the statutory public sector there is no reliable evidence to support this assumption (Judge and Smith, 1983: 217). Certainly, there is no consistent or unambiguous rationale to support the contracting of social services nor even enough evidence that specific services can be provided more cheaply. However, Judge and Smith report that voluntary or even for-profit agencies can provide cheaper service delivery than the public sector when the determining factor is the scale of the agency operation (1983: 219). While smaller voluntary agencies certainly enjoy a cost advantage this is not so for larger agencies, who are 'probably more expensive than local authority units of a similar scale' (Knapp and Missiakoulis, 1982: 335).

Throughout much of the literature there is general agreement that current research is not yet of sufficient quality and standard to argue conclusively for or against the usefulness of revamping the administration of social services through the use of widespread contract agreements (Rein, 1977; 1983; Judge and Smith, 1983; Veit, 1987). Weddell suggests that

. . . assumptions about privatisation rest on a number of untested hypotheses and programmatic dilemmas. Evidence to support the notion that private resources will make up for losses in government funding is not encouraging. In the short run, the result of privatisation may in fact be a serious weakening of both private voluntary and public sector efforts and reductions in service provision to those in greatest need – namely low income and disadvantaged clientele. (1986: 24)

Comparative research across the whole social service sector is difficult because reliable information can be generated neither about the actual distribution of social services nor about what 'percentage of GDP . . . goes in social services, on the amounts which pass through government and non-government hands, on the numbers of people served in toto, and in each sector' (Graycar, 1983a: 388). This common 'complaint' about the lack of verifiable research is also described by Kramer (1983: 422), who suggests that while it might be preferable to assess the value of contracting out social services from the client's standpoint there is, as yet, no reliable research that could indicate what difference it might make to clients if social services were provided directly by the state or through contracts. Not only has such research not been done but the consumer preference surveys which elicit client interests are often synonymous with those favoured by specific governments. While much of the research literature is inconclusive some reasonable impressions can be made that the 'impact of government funds on controlling voluntary organisations is actually much less than is commonly believed' (Kramer, 1985b: 380).

Despite 'the ubiquitous softness of the human services' Kramer argues that there is a sufficient research base to develop an analysis about the relative organizational costs and benefits for both governments and voluntary agencies, but only if the client's or consumer's perspective is excluded and the relative merits of contracted services are discussed on purely administrative grounds. Lowery, for example, argues that contracting may lead to lower costs but render 'poorer quality in service production' (1982: 517). As we have seen, arguments in support of contracting tend not to debate the issue of client or consumer service but to embrace a type of rhetoric that reflects the unanswerable logic of their assumptions. This is equally true of the arguments against these policy experiments. Neither research nor any contrary public opinion is as important as an internal logic that reflects an ideological persuasiveness. The strengths imputed to the private sector are founded on perception rather than hard data and it is an intuitive belief in the benefits not careful deliberation that has directed the protagonists for a contracted service delivery. Policy-makers, social service administrators and social policy theorists still argue for the benefits of contracting social services, even while accepting that there is a dearth of research that would fully support such conclusions (Gibelman, 1983: 104; Judge and Smith, 1983: 231)! Commenting on the number of ironies connected with the advocacy of these new welfare policies Minogue and O'Grady conclude that:

> It is held to introduce into the world of bureaucratic self-aggrandizement the neutral and curative properties of market criteria; yet its introduction requires a degree of political intensity which few local authorities are capable of, and many would not welcome. It is linked with themes of free choice and local responsiveness, but its success depends on rigid specifications of consumer requirements and on centralized evaluation procedures. It is supposed to be even-handed in its workings: yet it is effective primarily in areas where conditions of pay and security of employment are already low. And it is ventured as a panacea for all bureaucratic ills, whereas the conditions where it is feasible severely limit the scope of its application. (1985: 89)

Other arguments against purchase of service contracting concentrate not on the obvious problems of inadequate research but on the implications that such policies have on traditional patterns of accountability for service provision. These arguments arise from within the intellectual tradition that assumed that public service was an ethical activity. Part of the typical justification for this ethical defence of the public service was the presumption that only the public service offered reliable guarantees of political and public accountability. This tradition suggests, as we have seen, that privatization or contracted service policies remove public responsibility for the provision of services and diminish traditional patterns of political accountability (cf., Watson, 1980; 1983; Ashford, 1986; Abel-Smith and Titmuss, 1987; Harris, 1987). These policies are seen as an administrative device to maintain a myth about the virtues of minimal government while actually whittling away at the basis of private autonomy (Brilliant, 1973: 394). This will have major repercussions because public social services have already overtaken private philanthropy and the private sector is merged into all aspects of publicly mandated programmes. As a result of this 'partnership' the dominant themes of private welfare have shifted from particular client needs to general quality of life issues. This process reflects aspects of the transition from the old welfare paradigm, with an obligation on those who had to give, to the new welfare paradigm, where the obligation is on the claim rights of those who are excluded, for whatever reason, from access to employment, resources or opportunities. Increased public provision required the development of complex supporting bureaucracies for both public and private sector social services. While private philanthropy was wrestling with increasing organizational complexity it was complicated by the growth of a professional approach to the provision of social services which found more ready support for innovative theoretical practice in privately established agencies. Finally, the new managerial demands associated with the use of public funding, as well as general public attitudes towards social services, 'imposed universalistic standards on private philanthropy' (Gronbjerg, 1982: 2). All the implicit problems of discretionary administrative power, undecided in the management of public welfare bureaucracies, are increased when state welfare decisions are given to private groups and individuals (Manser, 1974; Weddell, 1986).

The relevance of the excessive discretionary power of public sector agencies may well be exaggerated in order to promote these new policy directions. The current neo-conservative reaction has found new impetus for an old quarrel rather than discovering essentially new grounds. Gronbjerg, for example, takes issue with the assumption that the public welfare bureaucracies had ever assumed such prominence, particularly in the United States where there has always been a profound ambiguity and controversy surrounding state welfare services (1982: 1). She argues that private philanthropy, while often subsumed into public welfare arrangements, has nevertheless exercised a powerful brake on governmental intervention. While such profound ambiguity represents a particularly American cast to the debate nowhere has the welfare state achieved complete acceptance. The advantages of private flexibility and discretion, pledged by welfare privatization and a system of contracted services, may come at the expense of citizens' rights. The dilemma is that if protection of constitutional rights is to be guaranteed during the introduction of these new policies governments will be obliged to 'restrict the discretion permitted to private agencies. In the end privatization and protection of civil liberties may prove to be mutually exclusive goals' (Sullivan, 1987: 466).

One of the key political aspects of constitutional democracies is that public service officials must be held accountable for all their decisions. Their first line of accountability is to the elected officials and then through these officials to the general public. When previous public responsibilities for the direct provision of welfare services are allocated to private agencies through service contracting there is an inevitable loss of political accountability (Moe, 1987: 457). Dilemmas surrounding conflicts of interest appear when assumptions are made that what is good for a particular private organization is necessarily good for the country (Weddell, 1986). When the case for full privatization is argued most purchase of service contract agreements are usually made with the well-established and financially solvent non-profit agencies. Consequently, financial support is granted more readily to the larger and more fiscally independent agencies. One of the less obvious disadvantages of a contractual system is that it provides private employees with opportunities to receive the benefits of public service without having to pay for the costs. It is also possible that governments can be 'captured by contractors' and that in order to avoid this governments must develop a skilled managerial team that can effectively contract, monitor and evaluate private sector social services (Moe, 1987: 458).

In summary, the disadvantages are that voluntary and for-profit social services will become too fiscally dependent on the state provider and their autonomy will be jeopardized by this dependence. Despite extensive monitoring arrangements private agencies will not be especially accountable for their services. Increasing numbers of competing service providers, and a focus on the 'benefits' of managed social services, collapse all of the previously separate professional, clinical and practical assumptions about how specific social needs are to be addressed and further constrains coherent social policy. Gronbjerg argues that:

. . . the overall picture is one of gloom for the private welfare system, at least in the short run – added responsibilities, frustrated claims of entitlement, and diminished resources. At a time when the possibility exists of creating an important, contributory role for private welfare in the welfare state, it may be incapable of meeting the challenge. More important, its very existence may allow for a dismantling of the welfare state to go effectively unchallenged. Without a strong welfare state, citizenship rights will be seriously weakened. At least those welfare states that managed to kill off their private welfare systems earlier have no replacements waiting reluctantly in the wings to assume responsibilities or to attempt to meet entitlement claims. (1983: 789)

## Social Service Contracting: Options for Governments

One of the pre-eminent themes in neo-conservative social theory is that contracting has the potential to reduce the overall burden on government of the fiscal costs involved in the direct provision of social services (Volland, 1980; De Hoog, 1984; Terrell and Kramer, 1984; Kettner and Martin, 1986). These arguments for cost effectiveness are usually linked with classic market theories which suggest that contracting will lead to the delivery of better quality services. This is because open competition among suppliers is expected to produce better service performances due to a direct monetary incentive. Contracting out of social services, it is argued, allows for greater attention to be focused on the more important economic and political functions of the public sector (cf., Wedel et al., 1979; Wedel and Katz, 1980). It is argued not only that administrative costs can be lessened, but that contracts provide more efficient and better quality social services than those similarly delivered by public employees. Where the delivery of specialized services is the predominant factor, and also where aspects of local distribution and political accommodation of ethnic or gender differences are involved, contracts may ensure a better array of services. Establishing a contract policy environment is thus an attractive and useful political mechanism to distance executive authority from the conflicts that inevitably occur when the state is the major provider of direct social services.

More practically, four arguments are typically used to justify the cost effectiveness of contracted social services. First, contracting eliminates waste because the true costs involved in the provision of a wide range of social services will be revealed in the process of competitive contract tendering which also demonstrates policy support for the 'profit motive'. This is electorally astute in those countries where neo-conservative or public choice theories are dominant. Government policy can then intersect with popular beliefs that the private sector can deliver more effective and efficient social services and reduce overall government administrative responsibility. Depending on private sector and non-profit agencies to distribute needed services means that governments can offer popular services without the burdens of high start-up costs or the unwanted problems of too much public accountability.

Secondly, 'economies of scale' will result from the reduction in establishment and overhead costs, inherent in the public sector. All budget variables are assumed to be less under private sector service provision and these cost savings allow the private sector to be more innovative in the provision of particular services. Thirdly, contracting provides governments with an opportunity to determine the direction of welfare policy and its administration, unencumbered by the controls imposed by a conventional bureaucracy. With increasing economic constraints on central budgets, contracted social services provide a convenient means to extend limited fiscal resources encumbered by civil service regulations. They are, currently, politically acceptable mechanisms for the neo-conservative state to bypass the imposition of politically damaging legislation such as rigid administrative and budgetary regulations, public sector freezes on the hiring of personnel or the demands imposed by the maintenance of public service salary standards. It also allows the state to avoid high personnel costs, primarily by bypassing the power of state service unions, who inevitably confront the public sector provision of direct services.

Governments, fourthly, derive renewed normative benefits by continuing to support the voluntary non-profit sector through extensive use of contract mechanisms since these policies provide an oblique way to control the direction of welfare policy. These policy instruments give governments 'an opportunity to coopt and gain the political support of the community constituency dependent on government for a substantial part of their budgets' (Kramer, 1983: 423). Services can be both initiated more easily and terminated more rapidly under a contract formula. However, the better endowed and established agencies pose a managerial dilemma for governments because they can survive even though the demand for their services has diminished. Consequently, a major advantage to governments is that agencies which depend upon contracted funds demonstrate a 'significant degree of flexibility resulting from the relative ease with which [such] agencies can form and disband and the closeness of governing boards to the field of action' (Salamon, 1987: 44).

These new welfare policies therefore provide 'secondary gains' for governments since the creation of a pattern of contracted social services provides indirect ways to influence the service standards and delivery patterns of the voluntary sector. They may be less concerned about efficient service delivery and use these agencies to champion 'other important social values, such as group and individual freedom, diversity, a sense of community, civic activism and charity' (Salamon, 1987: 44). The use not only of fiscal supply systems but also of monitoring and assessment procedures gives governments the potential to integrate voluntary agency programmes into a more coordinated community pattern that adheres to the government's overall social policy design. These normative political and structural considerations determine typical social roles for both the voluntary non-profit and private for-profit agencies. The procedural aspects of monitoring and evaluation create a climate that conditions the nature of the welfare debate. Adherence to the monitoring clauses of contracts becomes, therefore, an opportunity to exercise political influence. These expectations create new sets of normative standards in that agencies who do not fulfil the contract criteria will have less claim on the 'public purse'. It is the implicit aspects of these policies which serve a political purpose in helping to define the boundaries and administrative mechanisms considered appropriate in the social services arena.

The range of questions that arise about the application of funding procedures do not represent technical or solely administrative issues. These funding mechanisms are at the heart of the social policy debate concerning an appropriate policy structure to identify needs and to deliver social services. Monitoring of contracts is often more concerned with issues of fiscal accountability than with programme effectiveness; greater emphasis may be placed on financial details than actual service reporting and the latter may be restricted to outputs rather than outcomes (cf., Poertner and Rapp, 1985; Hurl, 1986a). This is particularly so in relatively small countries where there is public pressure for the democratization of the more rigid aspects of fiscal accountability. The contracting agency's management of fiscal accountability procedures is complicated, not only because these requirements substantially increase administrative demands on voluntary agencies, already hard-pressed, but also because the purchase of contracts operates within a competitive context.

Given the ability that large voluntary agencies have to sway public opinion the allocation of contracts provides governments with a legitimate opportunity for patronage. Since previously autonomous agencies now have to accommodate themselves to governmental demands they have become more responsive to pressure for consumer participation (Kramer, 1983). Social service contracts accordingly provide governments with more flexibility in the provision of specific or targeted social services (cf., Volland, 1980; Gronbjerg, 1982). They also provide greater opportunity for governments to use administrative personnel to oversee and monitor the effects of short-term experimental projects. Governments can therefore recognize areas of specific new need without automatically, and immediately, having to address the issue of comparative entitlement. Experimental programmes can be introduced into the private sector without governments having to respond to an automatic demand for universal provision. Social service contracting, it is argued, provides an acceptable political means to avoid these constraints so that any marginal or specialized social services not part of a government's political agenda can be contracted out (cf., Gronbjerg, 1982; 1983). Not only, it is argued, does the application of contract formulas facilitate the development of an efficient social service, but the creation of flexible service provision also enhances the use of community volunteers who particularly contribute to the work of non-profit agencies. Volunteers are more easily obtained, supervised, supported and administered under the auspices of a voluntary agency. The use of volunteers by the private agencies has often facilitated the establishment of different and experimental patterns of service delivery, or even new innovative branch agencies, in areas where new social needs are identified, before governments are able to develop alternate or adjunct services (Salamon, 1987). The application of these implicit political beliefs to the provision of social services requires governments to argue that the private sector can deliver these services more efficiently than the public sector. Much of this argument refers to economic and managerial efficiencies obtained in areas other than the social services; it is reductionist and depends upon an unjustified extrapolation from the private commercial sector. There are hidden costs for both the provider of funds and the supplier of services that are not readily revealed by an emphasis only on the practical utility of contracted services.

## Disadvantages for Governments

The contention that private systems of social welfare are inequitable is based on the assumption that one of the prime functions of state and public sector social services is to compensate for and redress some of the imbalances and inequities that exist in a typical welfare democracy. This perspective obviously assumes that the private welfare system is unable to act as a compensatory social device and that the creation of a more equitable and just society will always require the state to be directly involved in the provision of services.

This is particularly the case where the provision of such services is a publicly acknowledged compensation for and redress of inequality. An important aspect of the criticism of private welfare provision is the observation that while costing formulas can be better administered under private provision, such arrangements cannot be formed into cohesive policy. Purchase of service contracting therefore poses additional difficulties for governments in creating and implementing coherent public welfare policy (Brilliant, 1973; Sharkansky, 1980; De Hoog, 1984). It is suggested, for example, that the constant political problem of forging public sector accountability will only be intensified when private and non-profit agencies take over the bulk of public sector welfare provision:

> . . . in many services it is usually more difficult to hold contractors responsible to the needs of citizens, legislators and managers. In addition, the creation and implementation of coherent public policy may become a more formidable task with the extensive use of outside suppliers . . . . Planning for and co-ordinating a multitude of discrete activities of outside service agents may only add to the already confusing, overlapping, and contradictory divisions within government itself. (De Hoog, 1985: 431)

Four important considerations will concern governments about possible difficulties in joint partnership arrangements with voluntary agencies; financial accountability, equity in service provision, diversity of services and public accountability for selected service priorities (Salamon, 1987: 45). Financially, it is not possible to expect the voluntary sector alone to generate the widespread level of support necessary to sustain complex patterns of existing social services. Political sensitivity and ethical issues involving the range of social services, demands for political accountability and equity in how they are distributed confirm that governments are better able to finance needed services and ensure equitable distribution. Private or charitable financial support may or may not be available when the need for it is most pressing, and voluntary agencies, with limited fiscal resources, may not be able quickly to establish agencies in different areas to meet emergent need. However, as we have seen, this is contradicted by those who argue that such flexibility does indeed exist in the private sector and is explicitly not found in the public arena (cf., Volland, 1980; Gronbjerg, 1982). As I have described earlier, arguments that the private sector agencies can establish services more quickly are an extrapolation from the entrepreneurial aspect of the private commercial sector. The commercial viability of private sector agencies, even when supported by contract formulas, still requires different sets of managerial decisions in the evaluation of specific programmes than those appropriate to the public sector with a more clear and explicit political mandate to satisfy certain social needs.

Advocating complete welfare privatization, or the adoption of contracting, may not ultimately assist the state to remove what are often pejoratively described as the overweening or inefficient aspects of centralized social planning. Merging public and private welfare activities obscures the degree of implicit government interference with the private sector. The laudable rhetoric about community autonomy and local authority, highlighted in various schemes that argue for decentralized and devolved social services, is not necessarily reflected in the ways that they are implemented. Fiscal problems are created for governments since the costs of a full commitment to monitoring and assessment procedures, as well as the establishment of practical and workable systems of accountability, might well outweigh the costs of direct service provision. For example, the costs 'required to monitor hundreds of service providers are sufficiently high that governments are often discouraged from active performance' (Hurl, 1986b: 9). There are, as we have seen, huge problems in trying to measure the efficiency of welfare programmes. Adoption of fee-for-service contracts actually gives governments less power over agency budgets than do block grants and subsidies which can be withdrawn more readily. Voluntary agencies usually have other sources of funds, not subject to government investigation, and the potential fears of governmental control through the draconian use of efficiency and accountability procedures are exaggerated because they are often not carefully administered (Kramer, 1985b: 380; Hurl, 1984).

Any consideration of the value of public welfare services must acknowledge that one of their benefits is the maintenance of some form of administrative equity, that they serve to create a degree of procedural fairness regarding access to social services. However, these concerns are expensive and always 'difficult to incorporate into an economist's analysis of performance' (Klein, 1984a: 16). Purchase of service contracting creates two sets of problems for governments. There are major difficulties involved in, first, establishing and managing systems of accountability and, secondly, formulating and providing coherent social policy because privately contracted welfare service systems are either fragmented and inadequate or clustered and wastefully competitive.

**Accountable to Whom and Monitoring What?**  The supervision of service delivery standards through the judicious use of appropriate systems of monitoring and accountability of voluntary non-profit and for-profit social agencies creates a specific set of issues. The smaller and/or newer community-based social agencies have restricted abilities and opportunities to manage contract procedures. Their goals are often idiosyncratic and specific and rarely conform to the typical pattern of managerial expertise found in the private sector. Many have inadequate bureaucratic systems as well as inappropriate accounting systems and they do not use the categories and criteria of private sector management to measure effective service provision. Administrative outputs such as the number of interviews are substituted for effective outcomes, and service delivery, evaluation, uniform accounting and information systems are lacking because the social services, generally, have difficulty in specifying accurate results. Certain agency processes and procedures are more easily assessed than others and these factors become the focus for governmental appraisal of effective agency management. However, 'under-regulation and little monitoring are much more frequent because government agencies rarely have sufficient staff to oversee a contractor's performance' (Kramer, 1983: 423–424).

The issues, for governments, stemming from inadequate monitoring and the lack of sophisticated managerial skills in social agencies are compounded because the state is often extraordinarily dependent on private agencies or the voluntary sector for the provision of services, and certain voluntary agencies may obtain a monopoly over particular services (cf., Hurl, 1984; Poole, 1985). These agencies may also make agreements amongst themselves not to compete with one another and to avoid the intention of contracted services, thus 'survival and expansion . . . [have been] obtained at the expense of service quality' (Frankfather, 1981: 143). In addition, where there may be no alternative resources governments may be forced to maintain clients in defaulting agencies. Even after having agreed to contract monitoring terms and conditions, governments might be unable to adhere to the initial standards of the contract. Defaulting agencies may have to be used despite the fact that the contracting authorities had determined, when routinely applying the contracted monitoring mechanisms, that these agencies were not providing a proper standard of service and therefore stood in technical breach of contract (Hurl, 1986a: 509). This is one of the crucial problems of contracted social services because establishing distinct contract specifications is administratively complex and monitoring procedures are often difficult to institute and maintain as well as being expensive (Pack, 1987; Sappington and Stiglitz, 1987).

These problems are sometimes ignored by commentators who

suggest that one of the benefits of contracting for governments is the ease with which funds might be cut to private for-profit welfare agencies which do not meet government requirements (McCready, 1986: 254). Again this is an argument extrapolated from the private sector which cannot be blindly translated to the provision of social services. The mandating power of governments to withdraw support for defaulting contractors is only workable in principle. The reality is less simple because specific client services are not readily understood as product categories. The 'managerial goals' of agencies have usually been presented as the provision of services and not the supply of a 'product'. Another related issue is the control that the private sector has in determining areas of service. Questions inevitably arise about the equitable distribution of services because voluntary agencies tend to apply specialist or selective criteria in their intake policies so that there is an in-built tendency that 'the less troublesome and/or middle class clients are served by voluntary agencies, under contract' (Kramer, 1983: 424). The poorer and more difficult cases are defaulted onto the residual public sector by the private sector, especially where 'state services are the services of last resort' (Graycar, 1983a: 388). There is some suggestion, though, that funding formulas could be established that would not bias private agencies against needy and difficult clients (McCready, 1986). The current blending of private and public delivery of services impels the private sector to focus more on those areas of client service where demonstrable success or positive client feedback is assured. Professional demands for efficient and successful intervention create an undesirable outcome in that these demands lead to a neglect of the more severe cases, particularly where such services are likely to become more expensive. There is no evidence that can yet verify the assertion that it makes a tangible difference to clients whether services are provided by the government or whether they are contracted out (cf., Graycar, 1982; 1983a; 1983b; Kramer, 1983).

Private agencies do not necessarily act to fill those gaps in services that may occur when the public sector withdraws from the provision of services and establishes a pattern of contracting with the voluntary and private sector. The argument that private agencies will duplicate those services withdrawn from the public sector is not sustainable, particularly when emergency assistance is required. There may well be irreconcilable conflicts between the profit requirements of private sector agencies and the legitimate service expectations of clients because the relevant private network will not expand to compensate for simultaneous reductions in many public services (Sosin, 1984: 22). There is an equally compelling and contrasting argument that all social agencies, both public and private, 'face internal and external constraints that severely limit the extent to which they can respond to social problems' (Poole, 1985: 404).

**Fragmentation of Services: Policy Planning Dilemmas** The second major detriment for governments is that the implementation of these new welfare policies reinforces the fragmentation that was a troublesome aspect of the traditional pattern of social service delivery. Wide variation in the voluntary or private nature of social service provision under contracting arrangements limits the opportunities for coordination and makes it more difficult to establish coherent patterns. The complex proliferation of decentralized services has reinforced the problems isolated agencies have in maintaining consistent communication and coordination. They have resisted a 'succession of legislative mandates requiring more planning, coordination, and service integration' (Kramer, 1983: 424). Similar criticisms are developed by Weddell, who claims that:

> Despite the growth of public social services and national level guidelines over the past two decades, several lingering problems have continued to plague the designers of social service systems [fragmentation, lack of co-ordination and service duplication] . . . . When privatization occurs, marketplace processes are set into motion which will very likely exacerbate the problems with even further fragmentation, waste through the duplication and competition, and service gaps – especially for low income and disadvantaged individuals and families. (1986: 24)

These micro-level problems are often described by social service managers required to operate within a contracting environment. A recent survey of some managers of government social service agencies reported the following disadvantages, weighted in terms of major concerns (Terrell and Kramer, 1984). The predominant concern was lack of accountability, which, while it included questions about fiscal accountability, also involved typical problems about programme design and expectations. Managers were concerned about how to ensure the adequate provision and monitoring of services for which they had no specific control. The second most important concern was a host of issues related to inadequate management such as insufficient budgeting and financial accounting skills. Specific staffing concerns were identified, particularly about staff who were employed without proper qualifications, where supervision was inadequate and key elements of the programme were not sufficiently advertised. Finally, community pressures on the contract provider were ranked as the last significant issue that the implementation of contracting procedures would involve. Further, there was little concern expressed about wider ethical issues of equitable service delivery. Governments therefore abandoned any pretence at cohesive policy planning as managers rated the demands of community pressure and lobbying equally with agency merit in arranging contracts (Terrell and Kramer, 1984: 36).

Disadvantages arising from such fragmentation are compounded because of the tendency, already discussed, for the private sector to concentrate its services on clients or consumer groups where it believes there is a greater chance of success (Kolderie, 1986). Some of the most obvious difficulties arise because 'the commonly used per diem rate provides an incentive to prolong service while a flat fee may encourage ending the service prematurely' (Weddell, 1986: 24–25). The availability of contracts also creates a potential for 'price wars' as agencies submit competitive bids which could lead to inferior services. Given the management skills already available to them large private social service agencies can corner the market by underbidding the smaller agency and then subsequently artificially inflating costs (cf., Reamer, 1983). It is also probable that the network of mutual support that the voluntary sector has previously enjoyed will be placed under severe strain by systems of competitive tendering. The former processes of cooperation that marked the relationships between agencies will be much harder to sustain in a system of competitive contracting. Upholding an argument about the benefits of purchase of service contracting at a macro-level is particularly difficult. Weddell's conclusion is sustained: 'it would appear a formidable challenge to achieve a stronger national posture of social service integration with comprehensive and professionally adequate services available through privatization alone' (1986: 25).

Another aspect of the argument justifying the preservation of the state sector, and in particular the involvement of social workers in direct provision of social services on behalf of the state, is that agencies operating under purchase of service contracting arrangements are too parochial. It is argued that generally only governments are able to have a complete overview of the skills and resources required to meet the needs assessments of significant sectors of the population. A related argument is that only governments are likely to have the authority to plan effectively (cf., Hurl, 1984; 1986a; 1986b). It is asserted that governments, through the statutory sector, have had the potential to establish comprehensive and integrated systems of care. Only the state can organize the network of professional services and relate them to other professionals and volunteers available from the voluntary and proprietary agencies (Austin, 1984). The role of the public sector professional in creating networks is crucial. As we have seen, the smaller agencies are less able, for fiscal and staffing reasons, to undertake the development of networks of welfare resources.

## Contracting – Options for Voluntary Agencies

Purchase of service contracting offers immediate fiscal advantages to voluntary agencies struggling to maintain services on limited budgets, although at a cost to their autonomy. Government contract funding is a more reliable source of income than private fund-raising. Prior to this voluntary agencies were dependent on private fund-raising and other less predictably secure public funding appeals. This contract funding allows agencies to apply their traditional income sources to the more distinctive or idiosyncratic social services which they pioneered. They are therefore able to maintain the independent and specific client focus that has separated them from public sector agencies, which are usually mandated to serve wider client constituencies. Not only are voluntary agencies freed to focus on service to their particular clientele but specific contracts may involve their traditional client constituency and so contract funding can be used to enlarge the scope of their unique activities.

Contract funding also allows voluntary agencies greater scope to develop a network of volunteers (Kramer, 1983). When public sector agencies have sought to establish a network of volunteers they have usually met with an indifferent response. Traditionally, non-profit agencies, able to address specific religious, cultural and ethnic service needs, attract more specific volunteer support. Providing some of their services with volunteers gives agency directors more flexible responses towards changing client need. As well as creating effective networks of volunteers non-profit agencies provide these volunteers with more creative work. Typically, non-profit agencies operate on a smaller scale which provides a greater opportunity for services to be fashioned to unique or specific client needs (Salamon, 1987: 44). Equally, because these agencies have greater access to private charitable resources, as well as a viable network of volunteers, they can enhance the quality of specific services. Accepting publicly provided contracts allows the private or voluntary agency to reinforce general public perceptions of the value and importance of their services and increases their ability to 'leverage public dollars' (Salamon, 1987). Participation in contracting arrangements also provides the private agency with an oppor-

tunity to have a greater influence on governmental decision-making
and to advocate specific policies intrinsic to the work of the agency.

### Disadvantages for Voluntary Agencies

There are three main types of disadvantages for the voluntary
agency in accepting service contracts. There are those that relate to
fiscal issues, which emphasize the dangers of an excessive bureaucracy that applies government monitoring and accounting procedures. There are others that involve questions about agency
autonomy, threatened because of excessive reliance on governmental support. Finally, there are those that alter the voluntary
agencies' traditional role of client advocacy, which is threatened and
perhaps weakened by the pursuit of available government contract
funding (Salamon, 1987: 43).

**Fiscal Disadvantages**  Inevitable administrative delays in the
transfer of contract funds creates a disjunction between the exact
costs incurred by social agencies and the actual rate of governmental
return. Typically, both private and voluntary agencies must wait
and absorb these deficits and are not able to claim the full cost of
recovery, which acts as an indirect subsidy to governments
(Kramer, 1983: 424). The important task of balancing these budgetary requirements suggests that the more bureaucratically sophisticated agencies, or those which focus on more socially acceptable
causes, will be more able to prosper under these particular arrangements. This is an even more vital issue to those more innovative
agencies which provide services on the margins of social acceptability. An additional fiscal disadvantage for the voluntary sector
involves the demand for greater sophistication in budgeting. This is
particularly troublesome to the innovative community agency with
depleted or scarce resources. The budgetary demands associated
with service contracts may mean that excessive resources are
diverted away from the goals of direct service provision. Increased
staff resources are required to oversee the more complicated
guidelines associated with contract monitoring and reporting. These
management and agency structural upkeep tasks are 'special
burdens on small agencies because they force them to become more
formalistic, thus initiating the attributes desired' (Kramer, 1983:
425).

The relative uncertainty of income supply creates other difficulties for agencies whose finances depend on the acceptance of
contracts. Monies may be delayed because of administrative
problems for the public provider, or severed if legislative and
political change cuts the level of funding allocated to that area of

service. One of the cruel aftermaths of government welfare cutbacks and the application of contracting formulas is a dramatic decrease in financial support for social services. These policies have altered or reduced specific fee-for-service schedules that the public sector had used to reimburse private agencies acting as adjuncts to the state sector. Similarly, these policies have changed how grants are allocated; some have been abolished and others decreased. Ironically, private agencies are facing an increasing demand for services while there is a simultaneous reduction in the overall amount of available welfare funding (cf., Gronbjerg, 1983). Arguing against the position that contracting reduces government costs, Weddell (1986) suggests that conventional cost-orientated contracts may require agencies to increase costs or compromise the quality of services. The compensatory or redistributive aspects of state-based social services, particularly income maintenance programmes, will be compromised by privatization or contracting policies. High levels of unemployment, inflation and general economic stagnation reduce the amount of discretionary income available for philanthropic donation, and the increased use of volunteers will not lessen the problems that confront voluntary agencies dealing with income-maintenance issues and client emergencies. These negative aspects of contract accounting constrain the smaller and more innovative agencies and increase management problems. If these agencies rely more on government funding and neglect their traditional sources of private contributions they will eventually confront a fiscal crisis. Governments will be forced, for other considerations, to make projected reductions in social service spending (Richter and Ozawa, 1983: 31; Kramer, 1985b: 378).

**Loss of Autonomy of Private Sector Agencies?** Participation in contracting arrangements will inevitably mean that voluntary agencies not only run the risk of losing the capacity to be innovative but may also forfeit rights to client exclusivity (cf., Manser, 1974; Lipsky, 1984; Gronbjerg, 1983; Warren, 1987). Private and voluntary agencies, typically, have been able to experiment with new social service delivery methods without those sets of bureaucratic and legal constraints so inhibiting for public agencies (Richter and Ozawa, 1983: 36). As contracted private agency services become more universally available they lose the distinctive character which marked their establishment. Contracting requires that external systems of accountability be introduced into those subtle and practical aspects of agency life where voluntary agencies have previously had considerable freedom. Procedural changes are introduced with contract monitoring proposals that mean that these agencies are now subject to various policy restrictions that relate to client eligibility and service delivery. It was both the selection of clients and the actual procedures of how services were to be provided which previously symbolized the autonomy of voluntary agencies. When private or voluntary agencies become 'public service providers' they become adjuncts rather than viable alternatives to government services and offer only an illusory choice (Kramer, 1983: 425). Accepting contract finance results in a 'blurring of the distinctions between the public and voluntary sectors, each doing what it does best' (Wedel and Katz, 1980; Gibelman, 1981: 28; 1983). The voluntary sector will inexorably be drawn into the public arena if it relies on contracting as the major source of finance. Agencies will seek to follow government trends in order to secure contract finance and consequently the 'world of social welfare, both public and voluntary, . . . [will become] more unitary and less independently varied' (Rice, 1975: 394). This is perhaps part of the sequence of unintended consequences of privatization that Drucker did not foresee when he argued that institutions should 'do what they are best equipped to do' (1969: 22). It may not be possible to continue to regard agencies as private and voluntary once their survival is subject to public funding. Rather than viewing such agencies as private it might be more realistic to consider them as privately administered public agencies. Lourie suggests that it

. . . is possible to argue that even without the direct use of public funds, voluntary agencies enjoy tax exemptions which render them tax supported. If they did not have the advantages of tax reduction and other benefits, that tax money would be coming into the public coffers and would be available for other expenditures. Hence, private agencies are really quasi-public agencies, even without directly provided public funds. (1978: 20)

An interestingly different and even contrary viewpoint suggests that the current range of social services are not related to the need for them. Sosin (1984) argues that private agencies act not to complement public agencies but to compete with them. He asserts there can be no statistically significant relationship between public welfare expenditure patterns and the extent of private welfare networks. In fact, extensive private service networks usually exist in tandem with large public welfare systems rather than in isolation from them. The greater the degree of community poverty the less well organized are the networks of public and private services. Clearly, how extensive the private network might be is associated more with the pattern and spread of existing services than with the level of need for them (Sosin, 1984: 18–20). This research suggests that when community resources are greater a more comprehensive private network of social services will be supported. This, of course, is the opposite of the needs-based prediction that agency networks will be more common when needs are greatest.

The pattern of mutual rivalry will continue because both public and private social services depend on an ideology that supports the provision of services and expects that competitive variations between private and public agencies will persist despite dramatic use of public funds by non-profit agencies (Sosin, 1984: 18). However, because private agencies do not actually fill the gaps in public services it cannot be presumed that the independence of the voluntary sector will be diminished. Official eligibility requirements mark the major distinctions between public and private agencies and there will always be a separation between private and public agencies because of the discernible differences in how clients are served (Jansson, 1979). Public agencies tend to provide services to defined geographical areas and their clients are generally poorer, more representative of minority groups and particular ethnic minorities. While public agency managers are more involved in the provision of services to politically important areas of the population such as ethnic minorities they are often disillusioned with the outcome of those services (Jansson, 1979: 365–366). Public agencies are statutorily obliged to take clients who fall within service criteria while private agencies rely more upon referrals and their ability to establish service criteria which the public agency is not free to do.

**The Loss of an 'Advocacy' Function?**  Another consequence of accepting service contracts is that voluntary agencies may lose their traditional position of free advocacy. This is a distinctive role which, prior to the development of contracting proposals, had been the historic preserve of voluntary agencies. Voluntary social agencies are caught in a major dilemma. On the one hand, increasing services to a broader range of their specific clients by accepting government contracts is very attractive. On the other, these gains may be at the expense of the religious, sectarian, ethnic or minority values which especially characterize their historic concerns. One consequence of accepting contract finance, as Kramer argues, is that the 'distinctive advocacy functions of a voluntary agency can be . . . restricted to the advocacy of self-interests through continuous lobbying for higher rates and fewer regulations' (1983: 425). The more that these agencies come to depend on government money 'the less involved and the less effective they become in legislative advocacy in social action' (Richter and Ozawa, 1983: 29). While they gain service flexibility they can weaken their position as independent advocates for their traditional clients. Paradoxically, it may be the case that the private welfare system may violate wider social and political rights, while at the same time reaffirming that membership in basic 'primordial groups' is an essential value. The key aspect of this criticism is that the voluntary agency's ability to undertake legislative advocacy and to promote community social action in support of its clientele is likely to be diminished according to the ratio of the amount of funding received (Manser, 1974). However, Richter and Ozawa's study showed that this conclusion of Manser's, which has dominated the case against purchase of service contracting for almost ten years, was not necessarily true. In some circumstances private agency directors thought that contracting for use of government welfare funding dramatically increased their involvement in legislative advocacy and social action because it broadened their network of contacts (Richter and Ozawa, 1983: 32). Nevertheless, the former independence of these agencies is weakened by the inevitable control of their 'purse-strings' that governments achieve through contract service proposals.

The private provision of social services and the use of contracts similarly present an 'unresolved dilemma' for the social work profession, whose members have generally had an historic commitment to support 'client well-being' by advocating more equitable social legislation and societal change. Deep divisions exist in the social work literature about the legitimacy of private practice, echoing aspects of the classic debate between left and right about welfare policy (Borenzweig, 1981; Abramovitz and Epstein, 1983; Abramovitz, 1986; Weddell, 1986). There is little acceptance that social work's advocacy goals could be achieved through the private provision of services. On the contrary, it is argued that private for-profit agencies reflect the primary needs of private enterprise for profits and expansion. Privatization will destroy the historical mission of the social work profession towards redistributive justice for clients because only those who can afford it will use social workers in private practice. Changes to the roles and structure of professional activity, contemplated under the auspices of purchase of service contracts, will have far-reaching implications for the social work profession. As has been argued previously, the development of these contracting procedures has been built upon the 'principle that the well-being of the public is primarily a responsibility of individuals, families, and the communities in which they live' (Reamer, 1983: 452). This reflects, in summary form, the arguments that comprise the basis of the neo-conservative challenge to the continued legitimacy of the welfare interventions of the state. Consequently, with the introduction of purchase of service contracting, social work will have increasing difficulty in maintaining its publicly supported role. The former activist aspects of this role will be denied and it will be forced to adopt residual roles. As Stoesz comments:

> . . . the focus of social welfare will be changed from the public weal to discrete individual problems . . . . communities are not expected to provide services to everyone as a matter of social right; rather, services are provided as a matter of market-expressed individual demand . . . . In this way the mission of social welfare is altered. The purpose of social welfare, from the neo-conservative view, is not to change the social structure, properly understood as political activity, but to solve individual problems, a restorative activity. This change of the role of social welfare can be institutionalized by systematically rewarding private entrepreneurs who respond to discrete problems. (1981: 404)

Privatization and purchase of service contracting will accelerate a movement away from institutional and structural analysis or advocate and social broker roles to those that favour residual social services (Graycar, 1982; 1983a; Reamer, 1983). Purchase of service contracting, with all the attendant changes to the role of social workers in government departments of social welfare, may well diminish support for the 'welfare advocacy' roles that the profession has traditionally exercised (cf., Abramovitz and Epstein, 1983; Withorn, 1984; Kutchins and Kutchins, 1987; Mishra, 1989). Despite these cautions the actual political power that social work has to restrict these developments is minimal. Where social work abandons full commitment to public sector services, or is required to relinquish advocate roles, it is likely that 'the banner of professionalism and public human service agencies may well be carried by the management disciplines with a major emphasis on self-support, efficiency and utilitarianism' (Kettner and Martin, 1985a: 10).

Implementation of purchase of service contracting diminishes the importance of the social work profession and enhances a new managerial 'class'. One effect of the worldwide trend to cut back the welfare state has been that the boundaries between the established welfare sector professionals have been blurred. As we have seen, the welfare bureaucracies, almost by definition, are assumed to be inefficient and wasteful, and social service practitioners who migrate up a career ladder to administrative posts are said to lack the aspects of managerial skill necessary for the running of complex social services. Privatization and purchase of service contracting have brought this new generation of service managers into areas of decision-making that were the traditional preserve of trained staff. Issues of assessment, accountability and monitoring are no longer decided only by professionally trained staff (cf., Ghere, 1981). Privatization and contracting will also dramatically change the supportive and networking community aspect of public agency practice. Social work has provided an important network function in creating informal, voluntary and statutory care practices, especially as they affect those who are young, elderly and/or disabled. These networks will be seriously weakened if the service demands of contracted practice question the financial utility of time spent on the development and maintenance of welfare and community networks. Certainly it is the potential loss of services to these specific groups that forms the substance of the criticism against private practice (cf., Borenzweig, 1981; Reichert, 1982; Lewis, 1989). As I have argued earlier, there is a strange paradox at work in that the very vital ethic of community autonomy is proposed by the neo-conservatives as a rationale for privatized and contracted services. Almost wistfully, some believe that 'the resulting inequalities of the free market can only create resistance to privatization and increase pressure for an expanded welfare state' (Abramovitz, 1986: 262). That remains to be seen!

**Contracts and Conflicts – New Options for Clients?**

Generally, notwithstanding the concerns that have already been identified, these new systems of social welfare administration enhance the capacity of voluntary agencies to promote flexible and responsive services and to deliver more effective services than the government agencies (Terrell and Kramer, 1984; McCready, 1986; Weddell, 1986). Client groups who consider themselves marginal to the prevailing ideologies of the political process can influence the provision of services through private or contract-based agencies that respect difference. By reinforcing the popularity and access of neighbourhood-based, ethnic-sponsored organizations, governments can more effectively serve a greater range of clients and consumer groups. This enables 'alienated' individual clients and consumer groups to achieve a partial sense of citizenship through participation in service delivery from a private agency. Client dissatisfaction results from a disjunction between the implicit function of 'social control' which they expect from all agencies which are established and maintained on a state basis and their need of them. It may well be that the state, while providing quite excellent and expert direct services, is nevertheless not expected by many clients to provide a meaningful service because of this structured perception of alienation (Timms and Mayer, 1971; Reid and Gundlach, 1983; Taylor-Gooby, 1986a). Pejorative public assumptions about 'the welfare' have become part of the vernacular. The relationship between the subjective 'construction of the problem to be solved and the "fit" of the agency's service to this construction also seems related to consumer satisfaction' (Reid and Gundlach, 1983: 39).

*Client Attitudes – Support for Contracted Services*
Client satisfaction, in certain respects, depends on the subjective assessment by both client and worker of the nature of their relationship. Typically, reports of client satisfaction are characterized by clarity of problem definition and mutual agreement on goals. Satisfied clients view workers as trustworthy and believe that they understand their problems and somehow '[lessen] their shame' (Timms and Mayer, 1971). Reported feelings of alienation and general expressions of anger with respect to the public provision of services do not occur so often among client surveys of voluntary or private agencies (Taylor-Gooby, 1986a). These positive responses have some relationship to the size of the agency as well to its private nature. People tend to relate more easily to agencies that offer particular or specific services, or to those which are based in the community, than to those established by state provision. It is the private voluntaristic nature of the exchange that more obviously characterizes contracts between clients and smaller private agencies which explains this factor. Clients indicate that these agencies provide a sense of participation and belonging, in marked contrast to state-organized services (Timms and Mayer, 1971; Parry et al., 1979). That many governmental services are often under-used reflects factors such as geographical inaccessibility and the absence of appropriate cultural and psychological matching between agencies and clients (Terrell and Kramer, 1984: 36).

Conflict between perceived feelings and attitudes towards state welfare and private provisions of welfare typify client reactions to social services. Explanations for the supposed decline in support for state welfare fall into two categories. On the one hand, clients often report psychological and practical coercion by state service providers and criticize their lack of freedom in the use of a service. On the other hand, they assume that the consumers of private sector services are autonomous and free from these typical patterns of coercion in the public sector (Taylor-Gooby, 1986a). These two arguments are seen to be the mainspring of public opinion. It is the perceived quality of the state service that is important. As Taylor-Gooby reflects:

> Ideology contrasts with preference. The data suggest that the knell of welfare consensus may be sounded somewhat prematurely: the popular-

ity of state welfare spending is higher than it has been in the last six years. Satisfaction is generally high. Where satisfaction is low, the problem is understood mainly as the outcome of inadequate resources – the central feature of attitudes to pensions. However, state welfare is seen as inferior to private alternatives – again, chiefly in areas that directly reflect spending. How are these facts to be combined into an explanation of support for the welfare state? . . . . It may well be the case that perceptions of resource difference have no relationship to support because the view that the state sector is under resourced is as compatible with the desire to escape from it as it is with the desire that it should be improved. (1986a: 240–243)

Client satisfaction is related to three variables: relevance, impact and gratification. Clients will report satisfaction to the extent that the service provided corresponds to their own perception of their social needs. Satisfaction is also vitally related to client perception that the initial problem has been reduced and that the 'impact' of the presenting problem has become less of a personal issue. Similarly, personal issues such as the extent to which the process of being helped increased their sense of self-esteem, personal power and integrity are related to reported satisfaction (Goodsell, 1980: 354; Gilbert, 1984a). Respect for social services is related to the relative weighting of power and dependence since clients who are able to be proactive and pressure for resources to be applied to specific needs are more likely to rate positively their encounters with social service personnel (Hasenfeld, 1985a: 633). One explanation for the unexpected positive ratings, higher than the professionals expected, is that they reflect the tendency of clients to rationalize their agency participation positively as a defence against the loss of self-esteem consequent on seeking services in the first place (Scheirer, 1979; Stipak, 1979; Martin, 1986). A different analysis of the reasons for the relatively high positive client support is proposed by Taylor-Gooby (1986a). He outlines the paradox that public sector clients, who might be expected to reject the introduction of social services contracting because of their traditional hostility to the private sector, nevertheless see some justification and argument in support of them. While there was a perception that the state sector contained unlimited resources, clients nevertheless perceived them to be inadequate. No such assumptions surround private agencies, at least not to the same degree that they surround the state when it is the sole provider of social services. How intimately related these questions are to the factors of efficiency and effectiveness in the provision of social services is only part of the question. They reflect important ideological issues with respect to leadership and the power of people's expectations. It is important to clients to have access to services provided by people who are seen to have expertise with respect to the particular problem for which they are seeking help. The same holds true even when the service required involves something which might properly be seen as the responsibility of the state.

Privatized services are supported by many consumers because they perceive that the people providing the service are high status professionals. Client satisfaction is therefore related to how these extraordinary paradoxes about competence, expertise and quality of services could be resolved within a privatized structure divorced from state provision. Part of an answer to the contradiction may result from the higher status of those who provide such services, such as the medical profession, which may well lead people to minimize their experiences of oppressive treatment by these high status professionals (Taylor-Gooby, 1986a). A negative evaluation of the service might result in a loss of needed services which leads to the emergence of a 'halo-effect'. They might regard the exercise of such power as legitimate or they may be apprehensive about influencing their entitlement to services (Hasenfeld, 1985a). The explanation for such paradoxes may have more to do with an underlying justification for the ideological effectiveness of voluntary agencies, which are smaller and therefore more personal than the state sector. The crucial determinant may well be size.

While there may be a clear acceptance that the state is the financial provider, or even the originator of services, there is still enormous respect and preference for agencies that can be seen as personal, idiosyncratic, locally based or culturally relevant. It is much easier for groups of people, whether they be ethnically different, demonstrate a regional difference or exemplify a religious or even gender difference, to relate to social services which they see as specifically and solely set up to meet their particular needs. Such supportive perceptions about the specific or idiosyncratic nature of social services do not apply when these services are provided under the auspices of the state sector. Efficiency and effectiveness in the delivery and provision of public social services are not key determinants of the relevance for clients. In the end the subjective and enduring power of ideologies and assumptions may be one of the most persuasive reasons for supporting moves towards a contracting approach to the delivery of social services. Such reasons supersede and even override the dominant questions of efficiency and effectiveness.

If it is 'our agency' which establishes and maintains specifically relevant social services then clients clearly perceive that more benefits are available to them through such agencies. Issues of identity, meaning and purpose, reflected in the support for specific and idiosyncratic agencies, may be more important than generalized or universalist services provided through state bureaucracies. These 'perceptions' are held even though such evaluations may not be substantiated by formal research. For people who are disenfranchised from the political or economic mainstream, provision of services through a private or voluntary agency may provide a partial experience of citizenship which will always be denied them through the 'faceless' state services. For those who perceive themselves to be alienated from the mainstream of community life, the pathway towards the exercise of full citizenship rights may well lie through participation in a small agency which delivers services which they perceive as 'theirs'!

### Disadvantages for Clients and Consumers

There is an enduring problem in arriving at measures of effectiveness with respect to the efficiency of social welfare programmes delivered by either the private or the public sector. No matter how sophisticated are the 'statistical manipulations . . . accompanying client surveys, the translation of consumer satisfaction ratings into judgements of social welfare programme performance is an exercise of dubious validity' (Gilbert, 1984a: 67). The major reason for this is the difficulty in determining empirical measures of effectiveness. How do we measure the existential or epistemological 'meanings' that people will ascribe to the services that they see as intrinsic to their personal or social well-being? Quality of life issues cannot be generalized (cf., Ignatieff, 1984; 1989). Even people receiving the same services may perceive them differently. However, Duke and Edgell (1987: 280) query the assumption that client attitudes to welfare depend upon either class, sector or partisanship. Rather, they suggest that client acceptance of these new contract policies accords with original national welfare distribution patterns.

The wide range of questions involved in using client satisfaction ratings as part of an evaluation of a programme has been well discussed (cf., Stipak, 1979; Bosanquet, 1984a; 1984b; Hasenfeld, 1985a; Martin, 1986; Taylor-Gooby, 1986a; 1987; Duke and Edgell, 1987; Papadakis and Taylor-Gooby, 1987). Using client satisfaction as an index for evaluation in the personal social services can be problematic (Shaw, 1984). Client opinion needs to be based on relatively informed consideration of the range of possible alternatives and must take into consideration changing knowledge and expectations (Hurl, 1986a). In an interesting analysis Hasenfeld (1985a) suggests that social policy researchers must recognize that satisfaction with a service may often co-exist with criticism of it. Client verdicts about satisfactory outcomes are influenced by the frame of reference within which they are reached. It is important to note that judgements about the satisfaction of social service needs should be clearly distinguished from judgements about the success or otherwise of welfare services. However, Bush and Gordon (1978) suggest that the inherent bias and subjectivity of client information can be balanced by other evaluations. They consider that clients can be 'thoughtful witnesses' of social service programmes as they have had the time and reason to think about effective services and generally can discuss fundamental strengths and weaknesses. Bush and Gordon also point out that research indicates that casework notes are more efficiently maintained when the particular services are contracted and attract matching funding, while the records of other similar but non-contracted work remain incomplete. Official records can be balanced and checked against clients' perceptions and the data quantified to enable the identification of trends. Bush and Gordon also suggest that what is defined as the problem by funding agencies and social welfare organizations ought to be measured against the personal evaluations of those experiencing the problem!

As might be expected, there is much argument that full privatization of social services and purchase of service contracting will inevitably mean a retrenchment in the services offered to clients. It is a common assumption that any weakening of the non-profit sector by privatization or purchase of service contracting will result 'in cutbacks in the supply of just and caring human services provided to the most vulnerable and needy' (Lewis, 1989: 13). Epstein (1988), in an exhaustive study, demonstrated that the voluntary sector refused to 'champion the claims of unserved groups'. These agencies were constrained by their specific service ideology, the client population that typified their social mandate for voluntary donation and purchase of service contracts. Epstein is convinced that

> the claims of the unserved must first be legitimated politically and socially . . . . current social welfare policy expresses preferences for voluntary and minimalist responses to social distress. The national mood seems to reject a more "universal" welfare state. (1988: 121)

Not only will these policies mean cutbacks in services but clients will suffer because they also create a two-tiered system in which the poorer and most needy clients will be less well provided for. The private non-profit sector agencies are less able than the public agencies to deliver essential services. Under the destabilizing conditions of economic recession private agencies are more likely to accept government retrenchment in welfare provision and accede to financial cuts in service programmes (Randall and Wilson, 1989: 17; Morris, 1982a: 338). There is, as we have seen previously, a

statistically significant relationship between those patterns of administrative financial support that sustained private agencies and the
problems and services they were willing to provide (Sosin, 1987: 26).

Together, these arguments contribute to a general assumption
that the privatization or contracting of service delivery to the
voluntary sector will result in cutbacks to the level of services.
Criticism of the market provision of social services insists that the
usual conditions of market competition very rarely apply when it
comes to the provision of social services. The assumption that
genuine competition can apply in the provision of social service
contracts is not borne out in practice. The practical realities of social
service delivery do not easily allow governments to apply the
monitoring clauses which would normally see them cancel existing
contracts because of non-compliance. The reliability of client
attitudinal surveys is questioned by those who argue against the
introduction of these policies. Clients themselves cannot be presumed to be 'free agents' in the choice of services. They tend to seek
out services when they are involved in some major personal crisis
and consequently may have problems in understanding or assessing
the merits of various counselling styles or the level of care they
need. There is thus a 'halo-effect' involved in the degree to which
clients estimate that agency services are beneficial (Dorwart et al.,
1986: 877). Welfare clients and consumers of social services

. . . can be locked into transactions for which exit is not a viable option:
they may not know whether or not they can get better service elsewhere;
it may be therapeutically inadvisable to cease counselling or to remove a
child or elderly person from a residential setting; [but] there may be no
other facilities immediately available and accessible. (Hurl, 1986a: 508)

There is reason to doubt the reliability of the common assumption
that innovation is more likely to occur in the private sector, which is
part of the rhetoric supporting the introduction of contracted
services (Kramer, 1979). In fact Tucker argues that 'private auspice
does not contribute to innovative activity in the delivery of social
services' (1980: 44). One of the conclusions to be drawn from
research about client attitudes to welfare services suggests that
policy-makers should be cautious about using such survey data to
measure government performance because there may well be no
necessary connection between client satisfaction and the actual
service provided by governments (Stipak, 1979: 441). The rhetorical
assumption, used to bolster arguments for contracted social
services, that greater innovation of service delivery and interventive
theory is to be found in the private sector is a truism. The common
assumption that public sector agencies are by definition less creative
or responsive than the private sector is not proven by research

(Hasenfeld, 1985a; Taylor-Gooby, 1986a). While it is often rein-forced as the dominant conclusion of client-satisfaction research, based on statistical attitudinal surveys, this is because the clientele of gender, ethnic or locally specific agencies believe that these specific agencies provide more effective services.

Client attitudinal research about the importance of these private agency services does not necessarily mean that the public sector is automatically less innovative. Within the private sector it is possible to discern different attitudes towards clients of for-profit and non-profit agencies that suggest that privatization or contracting of services will not necessarily be in the clients' best interests. How-ever, because of their belief that the provision of private welfare services ought not to be a matter of entitlement but must be subject to the decision of providers, the advocates of privatization cannot easily argue for the integrative aspect of these policies. For example, one research report suggested that there were 'certain subtle, though measurable differences in viewpoint held by proprie-tary as compared to non-profit spokespersons of institutionalized geriatric care' but that non-profit agencies showed less hesitation than the proprietary agencies in promoting agency and service community relationships (Kaye et al., 1984: 17). The authors argued that while neither private nor public agencies demonstrated much concern about geriatric 'patient representation in long-term care facilities' the non-profit agencies were more willing than the proprietary agencies to accept the intrusion of an ombudsman as a patient advocate.

The major argument that privatization provides governments with an opportunity to influence the pattern of welfare services and to insist upon an overall integration that will efficiently deliver services to clients is flawed. Relatively few social services can be provided by specific or time-limited contracts because the services provided by most agencies depend upon previous commitments and mandates (Hurl, 1986a). The political and social imperatives of established welfare systems are likely to make it difficult and perhaps even impossible for a structure of private welfare to deliver integrated social services (Gronbjerg, 1983; Kramer, 1985b; 1985c; Weddell, 1986). These assumptions are based upon observations that comprehensive and regularly issued data on private sector service delivery patterns, in contrast to the public sector, are lacking. As there are no reliable standards of data collection across the private sector, specific agency information cannot be combined in order to furnish overall perspectives. Accountability procedures are complicated by the relative difficulty of transferring funds between the various government agencies, and this is particularly true with 'revenue sharing funds and other unrestricted bloc grants' (Gronbjerg, 1983: 775). It is also difficult to distinguish between public and private agencies, particularly when they perform similar types of services. Clients may move independently between agencies or be subject to transfer. Financial networks have been established to transfer funds between public and private agencies when both are involved in the delivery of similar services. The result is that when 'public welfare programmes hold the purse strings, private welfare agencies may be viewed as extensions of public welfare or as instruments for carrying out government mandates' (Gronbjerg, 1983: 778). However, despite the rhetorical argument that the private sector agencies can provide a more effective and cheaper range of services a 'strategy of rolling back responsibility for welfare to the informal sector of care raises problems both of social equity (i.e., the distribution of burdens) and of social feasibility' (Klein, 1984a: 25).

Despite the fact that the use of service contracts requires the use of detailed accountability and monitoring procedures, they are less stringently applied in practice because they are expensive and complex, with the result that there is a potential for such review systems to be compromised. Current evaluation processes are inadequately applied and because 'social service technology is highly indeterminate' it is difficult to define explicit service objectives or to evaluate the performance of service providers (Hurl, 1986a). In addition, social policies administered by public social welfare agencies are subject to mandatory public review but private agencies determine their own policies and are not subject to the same rigorous public scrutiny. They are able, therefore, to place themselves outside of political or popular control, although, as has been argued, purchase of service contracting attempts to redress this (Kramer, 1983). Though the notion persists that the fiscal provider has greater power to influence the direction of social policy because of public sector accountability this remains an elusive objective. Frankfather argued in an extensive case study that private systems of social services embrace

> . . . the rhetoric and appearance of innovation to satisfy entrepreneurial ambitions. Obscure service coordination mechanisms, unmeasurable objectives, high coverage/low impact services, a strong cash-flow position, and control of information prove to be successful strategies for capturing demonstration grant funds. As a result, lower-quality services and exaggerated policy implications are exchanged for organizational expansion and new prestige. (1981: 129)

These general criticisms continue and extend the debate that private welfare efforts have increasingly focused on quality of life issues, rather than on the provision of basic needs (cf., Kramer, 1985b; Weddell, 1986). Contracting social services to voluntary agencies will not guarantee equitable provision to those whose needs are most pressing since the survival 'needs' of the agencies take precedence over service quality (Frankfather, 1981, 143; Gibelman, 1981: 28). These criticisms fuel the critical assumption that privatization will inevitably create a two-tiered system of social welfare (Klein, 1984a). The monitoring procedures built into contracts should include an analysis of agency service patterns to ascertain whether members of impoverished or minority groups are discouraged from using the agency's services. This investigation should also include some analysis of how specific agencies seek to provide services to those persons who do not normally use the agency's services. Agency discouragement of clients may be inadvertent but intake procedures nevertheless reflect obvious patterns of inclusion and exclusion. This process of client selection is sometimes referred to as 'creaming', where the private agencies often do the more simple work while the more residual or difficult work is left to the state sector (Brown et al., 1985: 248; Jansson, 1979; Gibelman, 1981; Kolderie, 1986).

This alters the traditional pattern of government distribution of welfare resources in favour of the private sector. It also weakens the strategic power of claimants and union groups who have usually relied on public sector agencies to resist inequality in the distribution of social services. Clients who obtain services from agencies in which there is a clear separation of the service function from the provision of financial assistance are forced to look for income maintenance services from the public sector agencies. Public sector welfare clients are less likely, therefore, to receive comprehensive financial assistance from voluntary or for-profit agencies (McDonald and Piliavin, 1981: 634). Separation of function between the public and private agencies, the major element of a two-tiered system of welfare, is achieved at the expense of an integrated service provision. There is, however, some confusion and disagreement in the literature about whether the introduction of contracting does in fact create such a two-tiered system. Gronbjerg argues that:

> Private welfare tends to be relatively unresponsive to 'unpopular' needs such as those of low status minority groups and of those (e.g., criminals) considered responsible for their own predicaments. As a result there tends to develop a queue system in which private welfare agencies appropriate the more attractive, more treatable clients, leaving those with the more serious problems to public agencies. Such a pattern will almost inevitably result in private welfare agencies providing services of higher quality or services to higher status clients in public agencies,

simply because private agencies can select their clients. In practice, then, equality of services and often entitlements will be difficult to maintain in a system that relies exclusively or significantly on the private provision of welfare benefits. (1983: 780)

In some senses, these arguments are contradictory. On the one hand, it is assumed that voluntary agencies will inevitably lose their exclusivity and uniqueness when the realities of contract administration require these agencies to take on a wider range of clientele than they might otherwise have been expected to do. On the other hand, it is asserted that problems arise through a two-tiered system of provision of social welfare. The contradictory nature of the debate simply serves to highlight the paucity of reliable research that could settle the argument and, because these disagreements are essentially ideological, there is a lack of willingness amongst the various protagonists to examine the normative and prescriptive nature of their respective arguments.

**Summary and Analysis of the Debate**

Purchase of service contracting represents for welfare policy the revival of former liberal definitions of the nation state, a predominant characteristic of which was a high degree of private responsibility for the production and delivery of social services. However, these policies will not achieve the complete redrafting of the 'corporate welfare state' that some would argue represents the way ahead for western liberal democracies (Mishra, 1984). The practical criticisms that surround social service contracting are substantial, yet it is apparent that decisions to implement these new welfare policies are not primarily based on empirical research about efficiency or effectiveness but on overwhelming ideological assumptions (cf., Terrell, 1987). Evaluation of policy options with respect to the introduction of contracted service agreements will, in the end, depend upon a political analysis of the relative importance of the public interest in pursuing such an option. These policies represent a fundamental ideological cleavage because their effect is to adapt social welfare services to the needs of private capital. They are part of the neo-conservative effort to shrink the welfare state and represent a form of 'revamped residualism' (Mishra, 1984; Duke and Edgell, 1987: 279). These political assumptions emphasize public sector efficiency and productivity and seek not only to revise all levels of public education so that they more closely parallel the needs of private employers but also to relate social welfare programmes to the changing needs of the market. While advocacy of contracting policies is founded on arguments for procedural and managerial efficiency these social policy decisions are further sustained by particular philosophical orientations which determine, in a restrained fiscal climate, the political decisions about how social services are to be delivered. There is a real danger that former public commitments to minimum standards of living, citizenship rights and community support are being attacked by an orientation towards privatization of social services. Neo-conservative criticisms about the overbearing nature of public welfare are misplaced

> . . . they are based on illusory or inadequately defined expectations of the impact of welfare spending on inequality. Transfer incomes are markedly more egalitarian than income that is distributed through the market, but the market – and employment in particular – is still the major determinant of inequality. A substantial reduction in inequality therefore requires a reduction in the role of the market or a reduction of inequalities within it. During the recession in the United Kingdom, the role of the market has diminished, but its inequalities have grown. Income transfers have significantly stunted this growth. (O'Higgins, 1985: 303)

The most likely possibility is that public social welfare will be overtaken by a process of incremental privatization. Governments will steadily relinquish responsibility for the direct provision of social services, and the less politically damaging will be cut entirely. User-pays charges will be introduced, competition between social services will be promoted and the balance between private and public sector interests will be shaped by pragmatic policies (Weddell, 1986: 25–26). Private social service agencies will continue to penetrate the social market, and the attractions of private practice will continue to lure some social work professionals into the private sector. Governments will, of course, provide the financing for social welfare, but the production and delivery of these services and benefits will continue to be delegated to the private sector through contracts or the provision of benefits in the form of vouchers redeemable on the economic market (Kramer, 1983; Weddell, 1986).

Many voluntary non-profit agencies were initially established in order to deliver specific services, or to emphasize particular needs that the state was either not mandated to provide, or had no interest in providing. Needs and services which do not have the ability to create political pressure for their support can be ignored by the state but may well be able to attract random private patronage and endowment. Nevertheless, while this has established a pattern whereby voluntary non-profit agencies are associated with meeting more particular or idiosyncratic needs they have had greater difficulties than the public sector in supporting a diverse range of services. While both private and public sector agencies gain strength from mutual involvement there is a mutual recognition about the problems of competition and the duplication of services because the voluntary and private non-profit agencies can never be relied upon to be the sole provider of services. They were not established to respond to the ethical issues that relate to diversity and equality of access, and are less likely than the public sector to have their actual procedures subject to rigorous public scrutiny. Private voluntary agencies, while representative of specific client interests, have sometimes been charged with intruding into the personal, religious or moral preferences of clients during service delivery and with dominating particular service areas (Salamon, 1987). A central tenet of democratic welfare societies was that priorities about the pattern and distribution of social services should be set by publicly accountable agencies, and that there could be no justifiable reason for complete dependence on private sector initiatives.

These reflections highlight the separate problems governments have when determining overall social policies to deal with unique issues. Despite the argument that social service contracts provide governments with an opportunity to integrate the provision of social policies, initially through budgetary control and later through control of how the private sector delivers services, a more powerful case can be made for the position that if a system of social service delivery relies only on private provision then it will inevitably become idiosyncratic and inequitable. Equally, reliance on the efficiencies of managerial expertise in the social services removes the focus from client service to different patterns of accountability, more cued to the structural survival of the agency. The current eclipse of the 'service ideal' by the efficient and self-evident superiority of the managerial process is not easily sustained. Gronbjerg suggests that:

> In the case of both private and public policies, elite interests may dominate the debate and the final outcome, but public policies are subject to public review and debate on adherence to national goals and standards. The policies of private agencies are not [subject to the same review] . . . . The emphasis on professionalism, protection of civil service jobs, and concern over employment and wage levels in the welfare state makes it unlikely that a private welfare system can provide compensatory services with genuine opportunities for voluntary services in close cooperation with a strong public welfare system. Thus some of the central characteristics of the welfare system will make it difficult for the private welfare system to perform its potential positive functions. (1983: 782–786)

Beliefs about the prime importance of the public sector in ensuring equitable and diverse services are built upon assumptions that the economic surplus of a country is better distributed through public welfare systems. These beliefs also assume that it is not feasible to rely on the voluntary sector to allocate services equitably, nor could it efficiently collect public contributions to maintain these resources. Public entitlements to services are not recognized under a private welfare system which is dependent on the access limitations inherent in contracted services. Not only is the provision of benefits likely to be distributed inequitably but private systems of welfare make it more difficult to make an effective appeal against unfavourable practice decisions. The current paradigm of welfare which emphasizes claim rights has no explanatory metaphor or ethic of obligation. It may, as Turner (1986) describes, create the conditions for a re-examination of the need for the state to ensure the equitable distribution of services. However, as a strategy for 'dismantling' the welfare state, privatization is yet to make substantive inroads because the non-profit sector is unable to provide for an equitable distribution of services (cf., Harris, 1987; Salamon, 1987; Morris, 1988).

Complete privatization of social welfare would establish unwanted market forces that would exacerbate and perpetuate service gaps and problems of fragmentation as well as continuing to waste resources through duplication and competition. The in-built bias of private agencies, concentrating on consumer or client groups where there is a high likelihood of success, will mean that they will neglect the more severe cases where services become more expensive and harder to deliver. While the growth of public social services has not solved major problems such as the fragmentation of services, or lack of coordination and duplication of services, these factors increase when these new social service policies are introduced. Privatization policies will increase the decentralization of social services and emphasize competition between public, non-profit and for-profit providers of service. While there are recurring demands for community empowerment, the removal of excessive bureaucracies and 'reprivatization', little viable research has yet determined

> . . . what difference it makes whether government, a voluntary agency, a self-help or neighborhood group, or a for-profit organisation provides a service . . . . similar service delivery system dysfunctions – such as lack of access, coherence, continuity, and co-ordination – are found in most advanced welfare states, regardless of their mixture of public and private providers of service. (Kramer, 1985b: 382–383)

This survey of the advantages and disadvantages of purchase of service contracting reveals substantive arguments against the validity of any 'macro-level' implementation of these policies (Weddell,

1986). Their effectiveness at the 'micro-level' of service delivery, however, merits consideration. Notwithstanding these conclusions the political pressure grows for the adoption of this wider political alternative. This is in spite of all the arguments that conclude that on 'balance it would appear a formidable challenge to achieve a stronger national posture of social service integration with comprehensive and professionally adequate services available through privatization alone' (Weddell, 1986: 24).

A particular advantage of contracting at the 'micro-level' is that the overall costing of social services on the basis of service units can highlight issues of accountability and efficiency, particularly when used to develop specific rather than general patterns of service delivery. Contracting has the added advantage that the monitoring procedures, written into contract negotiations, have the potential to promote assessment standards and assess qualitative and quantitative outcomes. Nevertheless, the actual administration of such systems is complex and costly and, in practice, these contract monitoring provisions are often not adequately administered (Hurl, 1984; Hurl and Tucker, 1986). Governments cannot easily cancel contracted services when there are demonstrable failures in the contract agreements. There are often not enough agencies competing for contracts such that the failure of one service provider might mean that others were waiting to take up the opportunities. Another benefit of the introduction of these policies at the micro-level is that the location of smaller private agencies nearer the workplace or community, which is a typical pattern of private sector social service provision, complements the more traditional public social service agency settings and makes social services more accessible to people in need. Clients and consumers will avail themselves of services when the option of a discreet private office visit is available, and these services will attract more clients because confidentiality is protected (cf., Stipak, 1979; Bosanquet, 1984b; Martin, 1986; Papadakis and Taylor-Gooby, 1986).

Review of all the competing arguments confirms that a mix of private and public sector involvement in the provision and delivery of social services would offer some tangible benefits. Social service contracts can complement natural helping networks which seek an active involvement in targeted or idiosyncratic welfare provision. Public attitudes to welfare suggest that there is a desire for a more diverse mix of social services and an expectation that governments alone will no longer formulate social policy. As governments also retreat from direct social service intervention comprehensive provision of services might more effectively be given by a range of service providers, including non-profit, for-profit and government agencies

(McCready, 1986: 255). Some social service clients feel more comfortable knowing that they can go to private or voluntary agencies for services, in contrast to going to 'the welfare' (Taylor-Gooby, 1986a; Weddell, 1986). Voluntary, non-profit agencies have the potential to develop innovative service delivery systems, and can respond flexibly to limited community needs for specialized services. Similarly, the systematic and greater use of volunteers by voluntary agencies develops important concepts of citizenship obligation, both in the delivery of services and in increasing the general public awareness of the importance of such social services to the community. While arguments about the greater flexibility of the voluntary non-profit and private for-profit agencies are valid they refer more to the actual provision of services, to their ability to reflect and respond to specific issues, than to the speed with which services might be established. In that respect the state sector has more resources to develop needed services quickly. Whether justified or not, there is a perception that the private sector has the capacity to provide social services in such a way that 'clients', whether they be communities, groups or individuals, will deal more efficiently and effectively with their particular needs and issues.

The provision of private welfare services is not solely dependent on either a rational or moral argument for entitlement, but is subject to political decision. While it can be argued that the private sector has no real interest in questions of social justice and equity not all of the difficulties that privatization and contracting imply for the social services can be located in an analysis only of the relationship between public and private sector agencies (cf., Poole, 1985). Much of this criticism about the public provision of social services reflects an assumption that hierarchical and bureaucratic models of administration are less effective in the provision of social services. Policies of devolution, attempts to administer services in a culturally appropriate manner and supportive responses to the differing requirements of innovative agencies mark some of the reasons to consider the value of these new policies of contract service delivery. The development and administration of a contracted system of services within social welfare has fundamentally changed the nature of the relationship between the government and the non-profit private sector. Decisions on future social policy will continue to be made, as they have often been made in the past, on the basis of political considerations. If the introduction of these policies were to be based solely upon arguments for efficiency with respect to client service delivery, and assumptions about what it is that clients particularly want, then that would ignore the results of all those client surveys that contradict this.

Considering all the evidence, the left-wing argument that a private welfare system cannot, under any circumstances, deliver any appropriate services is not tenable. Private sector services can, if only for those societies in which regional, ethnic or racial identities are important (particularly where ethnic minorities are indigenous), fulfil important integrative functions by granting political acknowledgement and purpose to such group organizations (Gronbjerg, 1983: 774). Yet the cautions must not be lost sight of, for once moves are made to establish social services substantially in the private sector, through administration of service contracts, then it is often possible to see the steady emergence of inequities (Morgan and England, 1988). Ignatieff's paradox, that 'societies that seek to give everyone the same chance at freedom can only do so at some cost to freedom itself' (1984: 136), is at the heart of the contentious issue of the proper relationship between the state and the voluntary non-profit agencies as well as the private for-profit agencies. These questions are examined next in relationship to the dramatic management restructuring required if these policies are to be fully implemented.

# 5

## Privatization – Contracting and Management
## Policy experiments: options for welfare management

> . . . in the last resort, policy options for welfare revolve around the question of who gets what. They are about the political allocation of economically scarce resources on some criteria of social fairness . . . . the underlying policy bias will be to make retrenchments at the expense of the politically weakest sections of the population, rather than to concentrate resources on the most vulnerable and deprived.
>
> (Klein, 1984a: 29)

Corporate and state sector restructuring has established a policy climate which has compelled state welfare bureaucracies to redraft welfare policy legislation and to refashion the fundamental structures of welfare services. This climate of opinion has exposed the comfortable 'hegemonies' of the state welfare bureaucracies to an awkward reassessment of their purpose and function. None of the previous patterns of welfare management, associated with the old welfare paradigm when a certain 'magisterial' style prevailed, are currently viable. That paradigm reinforced a pattern of social legislation that established the statutory procedures for welfare entitlement. Social services had been imbued with a quality of timelessness and objectivity and social legislation was removed from the 'public awkwardness' of political choice and conflicts about aims and objectives (cf., Abel-Smith and Titmuss, 1987).

These bureaucratic patterns, established when social welfare reflected a more monolithic, paternalistic and authoritarian organization, are ineffectual (cf., Moroney, 1977; Gates, 1980; Klein and O'Higgins, 1985). Pawlak et al. suggest that there 'is some evidence that people in power view social workers as politically active, but not politically influential' (1983: 9). The traditional welfare bureaucracies, geared to non-market models, frustrated the development of the new administrative structures designed to manage purchase of service contracts. They acted as buffers between the political expectations of respective governments and the actual agencies providing the services. Consequently, neo-conservative social theorists have condemned welfare management for maintaining, as they believe, a dependent and lacklustre citizenry (Anderson et al., 1981; Bosanquet, 1983; Savas, 1987). These general attacks on a 'malign' welfare bureaucracy represent a drastic revaluation of the political concept of social obligation and citizenship. The provision of universal benefits represented the practical answer that welfare states gave to previous crucial policy questions about the respect that would be paid to the stranger seeking services (Ignatieff, 1984; Morris, 1986). The new policy environment suggests that the citizen-stranger who seeks social services is to be accorded a lesser status than the citizen-friend!

Arguments for the social cohesiveness of a redistributive social policy, so eloquently expressed by theorists such as Titmuss, echo wistfully in a harsher monetarist and market-orientated environment. This is not to reject the humanity or the social logic of these arguments but to recognize that, at least for the moment, the integrative function of the former arguments for the welfare state has little current political appeal. The political consensus between patterns of legislated responsibility and professionalized altruism that marked the establishment of welfare states is no longer sustainable. The administrative processes of needs assessment and service allocation do not just concern the distribution of social services and outcomes but reflect important implicit assumptions about social philosophy. Paradoxically, the business and managerial culture of 'management by objectives' has coincided with the emergence of a welfare rights approach to service delivery. Both of these apparent ideological 'enemies' have rejected the paternalistic and professional style of the traditional welfare bureaucracies.

The administrative process in welfare bureaucracies seems eventually to stagnate through the unrelenting pressure of community demand and expectation. Any resolution of this 'stagnation of purpose' must involve an appraisal of the concept of managerial 'transparency' and the usefulness of adopting a strategy of policy experimentation. Realistic evaluation of what needs can be met within tight budgetary restrictions must also be clearly delineated. The social stigmatization of 'welfare dependency' has engendered a political alienation in those who are the typical recipients of public welfare services. The democratization of welfare, reflecting a move away from expert assessment and monitoring towards decentralized social planning, highlights the importance of those management practices that recognize difference rather than similarity. The old professional metaphor of disinterested expertise is no longer sustainable. Appropriate needs assessments will increasingly demand management styles and skills that reflect and respect difference. Managing for difference and uncertainty, instead of universal prescription, must also take into account appropriate policy responses towards gender difference and the delivery of services to women. The structure of the old welfare consensus which established a managerial style based upon the inherent power and authority of the bureaucracy is no longer applicable. This suggests that a more flexible and experimental style of management is required rather than an inflexible bureaucratic style that operates prescriptively (cf., Mayntz, 1983).

The introduction of social services contracting cannot be dismissed as if it were just the invention of public choice theorists who explicitly seek to dismantle the welfare state. It is no longer possible to administer social welfare programmes from a stance of 'knowledgeable and unquestioning' expertise. Managers are required to develop polices that redraft the bureaucratic structures of a former state altruism which inherently resisted the innovativeness of market solutions. Major staffing reviews of government welfare bureaucracies have removed defenders of the 'old order' and those who remain have 'insufficient technical expertise to resist pressure from private sector lobbies' (Biggs, 1987: 243). However, welfare management can never be explained by focusing only on the tasks involved. New and experimental policies are required that stress the value of targeted and specific project funding in order to address the practical question of what policies might work to reduce patterns of cyclical and entrenched dependency. These policies acknowledge the performance gap between identified social need and service provision and accept that public welfare bureaucracies cannot prevail over the inherent structural defects of society. They have been charged with too great a political responsibility and, despite their best efforts, these structural defects create unrealistic expectations about which needs can be solved. The traditional bureaucracies, awash with unused policy reviews, and lacking faith to experiment with new policies and services, have provided no adequate ways to build support in their client constituency (Stone, 1983: 595).

Managerial options involve aspects of either policy formulation, programme development or the implementation of policies (Ghere, 1981; Gurin, 1978). Some difficult questions may be resolved by opting for the latter focus. However, even if this option is selected it is still not possible to avoid a major quandary that confounds social services managers. They are still expected to develop policies that will reconcile the welfare bureaucracy's mutual social responsibility to 'curing' and 'caring'. The oscillation in role between advocacy and support has been an important feature of the development of welfare policy (cf., Sosin and Caulum, 1983). Graycar states that:

> There are ideological arguments about why intervention takes place at all, and about the location of the appropriate base for care. In some systems, it is held that the family ought to provide social care and support, and to the extent that it is not able to do so, people in need should go without. In such cases when formal structures are reluctantly brought into play some role, the formal, and ultimate statutory provision is likely to be residual. If it is held that the state has an obligation to its citizens to provide a basic infrastructure, and opportunities for life chances, then the relationship between formal and informal is very different. The formal sector has an innovative and preventative role to play and it complements family activities. In reality prevention and innovation rarely occurs, and although there has occasionally been some rhetoric to indicate it is desirable, what actually happens is that residual statutory services prevail. The role of professionals balances between managing and delivering residual services in something like trying to create and plan preventive services. (1983a: 386)

If the fundamental preoccupation of the administrator is with the content of administration, then the process of management can be likened to imposing an empirical conceptual framework upon a subjective 'laundry list', or 'wish-list', of community needs and expectations. It will have no analytical impact and will reflect only the contingent responses of a harried bureaucracy. A realistic consideration of the public accountability of welfare managers requires an acceptance, free of ideological overlay, of the typical 'conflicts, contradictions, and uncertainties' of welfare management (Stone, 1983: 595).

The main trends in social services management, revealed in the implementation of these new policies, are a greater emphasis on organizational effectiveness and on the strict evaluation policies necessary to assess contracted services. These initiatives emphasize the competency of direct social service workers and the selection of appropriate procedures to measure client satisfaction (cf., Sarri, 1982). These administrative skills reflect only the technical aspects of the management of social services. Welfare bureaucracies have also been charged with the 'extra' normative dimension that they, almost in isolation from other government ministries, will solve intransigent social problems. Systems of state welfare provision therefore reflect political decisions about altruistic concerns, in particular ethical and philosophical questions about the 'proper' balance between selfishness and obligation. Welfare administrators, operating within this new managerial ethos, deal constantly with the twin policy questions of how to assess the exact nature of social needs and what resources will be allocated to them. The selection of appropriate patterns for public and private social services inevitably imposes certain political and social constraints on the satisfaction of identified needs. The current economic climate, dominated by arguments for restructuring state sector bureaucracies, 'has simply strengthened the case for recognising . . . [that all governments are opportunists], and incorporating the inevitability of opportunism into the way we think about social policy' (Klein and O'Higgins, 1985: 229). The management of welfare policy development is never value-free (Terrell and Kramer, 1984; Kettner and Martin, 1985a; 1985b; 1986; 1987)! The practical dilemmas of policy analysis and social needs assessments can no longer be discussed without reference to the impact that the concept of 'transparency' has had on the style and processes of current welfare managers (cf., Dunleavy, 1982).

**Managerial Issues: 'Transparency' – Rhetoric or Fact?**

Interestingly, the 'new right' has used aspects of the rhetoric of the 'old left' that favoured community autonomy and decision-making to promote the administrative options of welfare privatization and the contracting out of social services. Consequently, public 'transparency' about these implicit beliefs and assumptions and the prospect of social justice and equity have meshed with the development of a welfare rights paradigm to challenge the normative power of the traditional welfare bureaucracies. The demand for transparency in welfare policy echoes those commercial managerial traditions which have insisted that accountability is not possible without clear goal specification (cf., Hoshino, 1973; Hartley, 1984). These major shifts in the style of private sector management have influenced the design and implementation of new public policies necessary to manage change in de-regulating economies. These new management patterns require specific clarification of the overall purposes of social welfare, as well as clear assurance of how 'meaning and definitions' will be construed by the practical procedures used to identify and meet need.

In order to address these perennial questions social welfare bureaucracies have adopted the business methods of management by objectives and output measurement. One of the most important issues revealed by the application of these management approaches to social services is how difficult it is to maintain consistent objectives while allowing for the choice and opportunity to select methods which can achieve those objectives. A management by objectives approach, or quality assurance, provides a different and more accessible 'framework of purposefulness' which seeks to prevent the needed experimentation from being random, inconsistent and sometimes destructive. Clear objectives, both long and short term, create this framework of purposefulness and provide a structure within which to analyse 'opportunistic' options. Both aspects are important in providing the flexibility and adaptability essential for the management of uncertainty. Irrespective of the issues about the desirability or possibility of privatization all agencies responsible for the provision and delivery of welfare services will need to adopt 'the critical efficiency-generating characteristics of small owner-managed enterprises' (Judge and Knapp, 1985: 149). These characteristics are the decentralization of managerial responsibility, particularly in relation to the deployment of resources, the importance of comprehensive cost-benefit analysis and appropriate incentive reimbursement mechanisms.

The more conflictual aspects of the social control function that various welfare professions have exercised demand more open accountability. Managers will not only have to specify the goals of social policy but they will also have to clarify the processes of how they are determined. While there can be no argument that the efficient delivery of social services is necessary, it is the manner in which concepts of efficiency are defined which has changed. In the context of the 'old welfare paradigm', fundamental questions about the assessment of social needs were resolved by direct state intervention. The old managerial style emphasized careful and painstaking adherence to established ways of conducting the delivery of services. Social workers and social service personnel were the 'gatekeepers' to social resources and operated under the mandate of statutorily provided services. Most welfare bureaucracies developed complex codes and manuals that left little room for discretion, although the literature of social work is replete with various aspects of how these manuals were subverted in actual practice (cf., Pearson, 1975a; 1975b). There was very little debate about the nature of the services to be delivered, only about their effective distribution, based upon initial funding criteria. Consequently, managers could avoid the more difficult ethical issues about equitable access, deny their implicit 'social control' function and adopt a protective mantle of technical expertise. An expert stance is required in order to make judgements about needs identification, service delivery patterns and whether such needs should be decided on the basis of descriptive, diagnostic or prescriptive information. Nevertheless, managers must deal with precise and unambiguous criticisms of that expert stance. Managers, attempting to sort out the ambiguous moral equation which links need and priority, will need to adopt an experimental stance (Gurin, 1978: 306). Information that is able to be generated from needs assessments may not answer some of the fundamental questions involved in equitable resource allocation, but an administrative stance that moves away from the maintenance of centralized control towards one that will risk experimentation is more likely to be successful.

## Managerial Issues: Discovering an Experimental Style

The apparent intransigence of serious social problems has underscored the need for experimentation (Moroney, 1977: 131). Faced with the implementation of new social policies administrators have developed a managerial style that is more strategic, one that is more concerned to negotiate the boundaries between agencies and the state sector rather than focusing on the content of care within existing agencies. Confronted with a gradual transition towards the wider use of contracts in delivering services these bureaucracies have, as we have seen, responded defensively to successive reviews which have revamped traditional support for direct service provision. Recognizing the key aspects of the often inconclusive and relativistic problems of policy analysis takes social service managers to the heart of the problem about establishing viable social policy (cf., Gurin, 1978: 306). Further debate must take place about the relative merits of targeted rather than universal funding and more flexible programmes be developed to allocate resources to programmes that emphasize regional, ethnic or gender differences. Efforts can no longer be devoted to understanding only long-term policy objectives. Managers must also examine the validity and usefulness of short-lived, self-liquidating social programmes. Funding will need to be committed to social welfare programmes with the clear expectation that this may be short term, that it reflects commitments to seeding innovative schemes to see if they are viable and transferable. This shift in managerial style dictates a redefinition of what is meant by the concept of social policies. The application of a corporate model to welfare bureaucracies distorts and skews the actual process of administrative decision-making. Further efforts must be made to understand 'how the dead hand of bureaucracy' cripples the best efforts of senior managers to achieve their stated 'mission goals'. Managers will need to construct policy and services experimentally and persuade their 'traditional constituency' that these new policies represent a search for adaptable and creative solutions. As Klein and O'Higgins have noted:

> In the past, there has been a tendency to define social policies in terms of specific instruments: the programmes and services of what is known as the welfare state. But if we define social policies in terms of a particular

set of objectives or desired outcomes (the promotion of equity in health status or the maintenance of minimum incomes, for example), we then have far greater freedom to use whatever instruments may be indicated . . . in any given situation. (1985: 228)

## Managerial Issues: The Identification of Needs and Patterns of Service Delivery

The authority to identify and define needs is the key to determining which needs are met, by whom and in what ways. The translation of social service needs into practical policy options is one of the central political questions involved in welfare management because the choices reflect clear political preferences (Ferris, 1986: 294). Selection of needs assessment models depends on an analysis of who identifies which needs are to be served, and who decides what pattern of service delivery is to be instituted. The analysis and identification of needs will therefore reflect a continuum of needs assessment ranging from those that have been accorded political status (needs consensus decided through 'expert' policy analysis), to those that are yet to be accepted as an important part of policy planning (needs difference produced by client or community identification of needs). Managers can more clearly identify their policy objectives by understanding the political process that determines the pattern of the relationship between needs identification and service delivery. There are interlocking aspects in an analysis of these two questions which cannot be divorced from each other; a decision in one area will have an effect in the other. Within the new paradigm of welfare rights governments are caught on the horns of a dilemma, namely that needs research almost always reveals some degree of unmet needs which generates its own impetus and demands for solutions. Needs assessment research is therefore expensive to undertake, and its results are equally costly to implement, because it usually identifies these patterns of unmet needs. Irrespective of the chosen research method, ethical issues arise for most researchers, who argue that prior commitments are necessary about how agency resources will be re-allocated once the needs, identified by the particular research technique, are identified (Olson, 1980: 126). There is a growing ethnic 'voice' claiming that needs assessments and other forms of research that do not result in effective action are pernicious (Jayasuriya, 1985; 1987). Siegel et al., for example, argue that if governments offer no prior 'commitment to planning or restructuring programmes in accordance with those needs identified, no useful purpose is served by an assessment effort' (1978: 225).

The actual management of contracted social services is dependent on administrative decisions about whether social welfare clients are clients of the state or clients of the contracted agency. The question of client status and the recognition of that status through citizenship entitlement is important. When social services are purchased through contract procedures the clients of such contracted services are clients of the state and not clients of a particular agency. Contracting does not remove the state from direct responsibility for the financial provision and monitoring of social services (Veit, 1987). When public funds are involved the quality of service delivery and the assessment of effective outcomes remain a government responsibility. If this expectation is accepted, and clients are still seen to be clients of the state rather than clients of the agency, then the needs assessment will demand more sophisticated systems of monitoring and evaluation. Most systems of accountability in contracted services

. . . have largely been concerned with accounting for dollars spent and numbers of clients served. There has been insufficient attention to monitoring client outcomes and little thought to establishing performance standards. There has been little attention to developing techniques for translating data collected into improved program performance. Part of the problem is political: More rigorous accountability is resisted. Another part of the problem is technical: Methods for monitoring the performance of purchased services in an effective and efficient manner have not been adequately developed. (Poertner and Rapp, 1985: 57)

How social needs are actually assessed is critical, including questions about whether they are to be determined on a regional, local or national basis. Equally, the former legislative framework which sustained systems of welfare based upon individual entitlement will need to be rethought if adequate attention is to be accorded various groups who seek citizenship status in their own right. There is an inherent structural conflict of aims and objectives between a managerial or corporate culture and the client culture; and particularly with respect to social service delivery (cf., Murray, 1975; Abel-Smith and Titmuss, 1987). The specific relevance of needs assessments to tribal authorities or other ethnic groups, religious groups and gender-separate agencies, or those that relate to some specific disability, will also need to be addressed. Arriving at a definition and perception of social 'problems' and 'needs' always involves a degree of subjectivity. There is a constant cycle of reflexive understanding so that not only does social change engender problems 'but already existing situations may also become newly defined as a challenge for political problem-solving' (Mayntz, 1983: 137). Commitment to a professional ethos inevitably encourages the formation of attitudes and agency practices which may run counter to client needs. Professionals will usually prefer to undertake interesting rather than mundane tasks, prestigious tasks and obligations will be chosen before those thought to be ordinary and the 'fashionable' will win out over the 'unfashionable' (Weale, 1985a: 156).

The use of more sophisticated managerial procedures to evaluate social needs assists governments to determine which services to purchase from the private sector. They clarify the service goals and expected costs, describe desired outcomes and furnish more sophisticated comparisons between agencies. Appropriate policy options for differential needs assessments can, using Bradshaw's (1977) classification of needs, distinguish between normative and comparative needs, as well as felt and expressed needs. Each of these categories can be used as separate models to describe specific administrative policies. Normative needs are those which are defined by authorities, experts or opinion leaders, while felt needs are those experienced and identified by the community or group concerned. Expressed needs are felt needs turned into action through community and political service demands, while comparative needs are those inferred from an analysis of social indicators such as demographic characteristics and the study of patterns and levels of service provision (Ife, 1980: 95). These ideas are summarized in Figure 5.1.

*Box A* represents the old monolithic pattern where the state acts in a paternalistic way to identify community needs. The responsibility for the administrative decisions about what particular forms of service delivery are to be used to meet those needs lies almost exclusively within the welfare bureaucracy. From this perspective social workers and social service personnel are considered by policy planners and management to be state servants operating almost entirely within the statutorily established welfare bureaucracies. *Box B* indicates a set of managerial assumptions where needs are primarily identified by the community. The state continues to fund the direct provision of social services, but the impetus for change and movement within the social services lies with the community workers. Some of them may be directly paid by the state, while others may well be financed by the groups for whom they act as advocates. *Box C* represents a system of management where the state identifies needs on the basis of policy analysis. Targeted change efforts are closely related to sets of political pressures and specific needs that arouse public opinion. They also include previous institutional responses to particular needs, market-led social

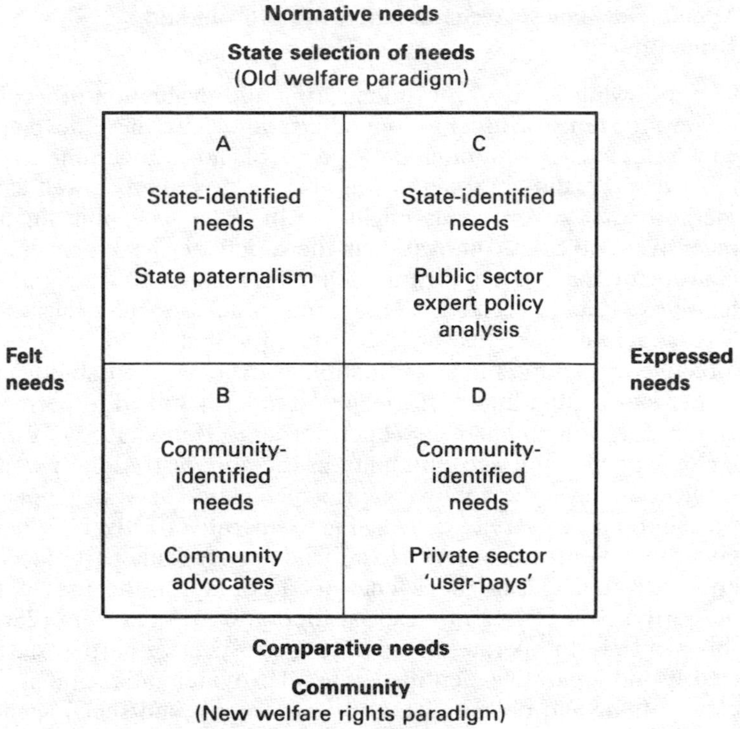

Normative needs

State selection of needs
(Old welfare paradigm)

| | |
|---|---|
| **A**<br><br>State-identified<br>needs<br><br>State paternalism | **C**<br><br>State-identified<br>needs<br><br>Public sector<br>expert policy<br>analysis |
| **B**<br><br>Community-<br>identified<br>needs<br><br>Community<br>advocates | **D**<br><br>Community-<br>identified<br>needs<br><br>Private sector<br>'user-pays' |

Felt needs *(left axis)* · Expressed needs *(right axis)*

Comparative needs

Community
(New welfare rights paradigm)

Figure 5.1 *Patterns of Welfare in Relation to Needs*

policy analysis and moves away from specific and direct responsibility for service provision. In this context there is a mix of private and public service delivery patterns. *Box D* refers to that situation in which the community identifies needs and attempts to solve certain targeted needs through the mechanisms of private 'for-profit' and private non-profit service delivery. In this particular context, the state employs a minimum number of social workers in the delivery of direct services. Service delivery patterns are clearly targeted and selective. The main management questions relating to needs identification and allocation of resources are reflected in movement along the axes. Movement along a continuum from A to B represents the current pressure towards increased client- and community-based responsibility for identifying and meeting needs. Movement between boxes C and D represents management of the devolutionary arguments which endorse the use of carefully negotiated purchase of service contract arrangements.

## Managerial Issues: Accountability, Monitoring and Evaluation

The following discussion of monitoring and evaluation procedures reviews systems of fiscal accountability and how these develop or constrain agency autonomy. Aspects of how governments can reward successful contractors will also be described as well as the methods that governments might use in order to exploit financial incentives and create innovation in the supply of social services. The concept of managerial accountability in welfare policy signifies a legislative duty to account for the terms of a contracted transaction. The separate elements of accountability include organizational effectiveness, programme evaluation, worker accountability, consumer satisfaction and performance standards linked to corrective action for non-compliance (Poertner and Rapp, 1985). Precise technical aspects of accountability in the administration of welfare services involve the following principal elements which must be present for social service contracting to operate effectively. Where a government entrusts or lends to a social agency some part of its own authority it may call the agency to account for the use of that authority. Neo-conservative social theory argues that, in order for this principle to operate effectively, the respective parties must be clearly and separately identified as fiscal provider and recipient. The expectations and obligations that governments and social agencies have of each other, particularly the procedures through which that authority is granted, must also be identified. Performance measures must be identified which will specifically involve mutual acknowledgement of desired goals and outcomes as well as a reciprocal understanding of the consequences of noncompliance with the original contract. This requires clarity about categories of satisfactory and unsatisfactory performance and how monitoring and assessment information will be reported.

If accountability procedures are to be significant, and not slide into commonplace reporting, administrative mechanisms must be established that hold voluntary agencies and private sector contractors responsible for performing according to agreed standards. One of the crucial problems in establishing contract monitoring procedures is how to combine the government's requirements – that the agency account for how contracted services are delivered – with the agency's desire to maintain independence and flexibility (Willis, 1984; Judge, 1982). Governments will need to consider the importance of three different forms of contracting and the respective monitoring and evaluation systems. First, one which is applicable to the already established and powerful voluntary agencies which are bureaucratically and managerially sophisticated. Secondly, another which is appropriate for those innovative and radical agencies which operate on consensual administrative models which have developed quite different forms of accountability. Thirdly, those monitoring and assessment systems which are culturally appropriate with respect to the provision of social service contracts to indigenous people, other ethnic groups and those groups which have a regional or specific community focus such as gender-orientated agencies.

The policies that support the introduction of contracted social services presume that a balance of accountability is held by the fiscal provider. These obligations, required of governments, also demonstrate that there are two sets of accountabilities required of agencies, one is to the clients and the other to the executive arm of government responsible for contracting out specific social services. In addition, there are substantial differences, both in priorities and service approaches, between public and non-public agencies, which suggests that the proprietary non-profit agencies should use public resources in a manner that is consistent with public intent (Jansson, 1979; Judge, 1982). However, despite writing specific clauses into contracts about monitoring and evaluation procedures, and how they will be applied, the procedures may never become operational. Where government monitoring reviews are dependent upon information provided by the contractors themselves the objective monitoring of contracts is constrained (De Hoog, 1985). Evaluations of contract performance can lose sight of this specific issue, either because the social problems are intransigent and there is a lack of information, or because they can be sidetracked onto the internal processes of the agency. This need not necessarily be a drawback, however, since it is part of the contract supervisor's role to assess the bias that might be built into the review procedures. Naturally enough, it is vital to social agencies that the conditions under which they may ensure maximum autonomy, consistent with equity in service provision and public accountability, are clarified. Consequently, effective evaluations must clearly demonstrate why the focus might shift to an analysis of process rather than outcome goals.

The usefulness of evaluation methods varies directly with the degree to which the findings reduce the uncertainty of action for specific policy-makers. The problem with determining precise social service goals is that they tend to be couched in ill-defined generalities which have eluded and even defied research measurement (Mushkat, 1982). However, if evaluation is understood as a co-operative process, in which the requirements of policy-makers play as important a role as the standards of research methodology, then more agreement about definable outcomes is possible (Berg and Theado, 1981; Crano and Brewer, 1986). The means of structuring the problem should not only specify the relevant criteria for evaluation but also offer an analysis of any uncertain events that may affect the outcomes, thus acknowledging the effect of random occurrence in social service evaluation (Dyer and Lorber, 1982). Therefore the nature of the problem should be a major determining factor in deciding which measure to use.

Several factors constrain the monitoring function of governments to issues of financial probity rather than the effectiveness of the agency programme. First, governments are dependent on certain powerful and political agencies to provide resources so that they can deliver scarce services (Hurl, 1986a). Secondly, the implementation of contracting is 'likely to be expensive, requires national legislative action, runs counter to virtually every vested interest in Social Welfare, and requires considerable explanation to gain support' (Reid, 1972: 54). Thirdly, there are inherent methodological difficulties involved in evaluating the outcomes of most social services. It is often not possible to specify needs in advance nor to assume that social agencies can schedule their programmes and guarantee an unbroken flow of information necessary for planned evaluations. Previous experience and participation in evaluations can increase future support for these investigations but only if they respect all sources of agency information and the results of these evaluations do not threaten significant personal or organizational interests. Problems also arise when evaluations are not really acceptable to the agency. Moreover, these evaluations may often only be undertaken in order to guarantee the continuation of grant monies. The fact that policy-makers and monitoring teams often reach such wide-ranging compromises suggests that the political demands are never far away!

*Fiscal Accountability in Monitoring and Evaluation*
How managers employ different funding mechanisms is central to the social policy debate about an appropriate structure necessary to identify needs and deliver social services. The fiscal accountability options available to managers are tax concessions, individual benefits and grants. Using tax concessions or tax deductions to support voluntary social services has been criticized on the ground that they tend to be regressive and inefficient. The vagaries of a system of tax concessions poses 'limitations on the abilities of government or voluntary planning bodies to plan a comprehensive and integrated service system' (Hurl and Tucker, 1986: 616). These fiscal mechanisms also tend to favour the large and established

welfare agencies over those that are smaller and more innovative. Tax concessions, therefore, do not allow for much accountability either to clients or to the government. Consequently, while allowing welfare agencies a certain degree of immunity from the kind of government regulations implicit in contract procedures, reliance on the taxation system to distribute resources evenly actually increases the existing inefficiencies within the social service system.

The classic neo-conservative argument, as we have seen, is that a private contract approach to welfare distribution is more efficient than a professional welfare bureaucracy. This maintains that problems of the 'monopoly structure' of state sector social services can be overcome by the use of a voucher system which gives purchasing power to the client and provides a way for clients and consumers to reject their continued dependency on the public agency. The arguments for a voucher system were proposed before the development of purchase of service contracting and may be seen to have contributed to the furthering of these proposals.

It is argued that the use of individual benefits, such as vouchers and a credit card or cash transfer system, provides clients with maximum participation and decision making in the determination of their own social service needs (Weddell, 1986). Vouchers may well offer governments the opportunity to develop innovative approaches. For example, they 'could be used to support indigenous service organizations' (Stoesz, 1988: 185). It is also argued that vouchers allow clients to choose from amongst a range of particular service delivery systems, thereby confirming an 'a priori' argument about market efficiency (cf., Reid, 1972; Brilliant, 1973; Wedel and Hardcastle, 1978; Rose-Ackerman, 1983; Savas, 1987; Stoesz, 1988). Judge and Matthews conclude their study on charging mechanisms by asserting that while some social administrators regard the market as 'a place of vulgar men and base motives' the fact that such views are commonly accepted has not diminished support for service charges in certain circumstances. Vouchers 'could be used in new ways to promote social policy objectives' (1980: 139).

There are two main criticisms of the use of voucher and credit card or cash transfer approaches. First, it is by no means clear that the market will respond either quickly or desirably to consumer demand. Private agencies which provide direct cash transfers to clients offer virtually no organizational accountability to government, despite the fact that it is the major provider of funds. Any monopoly will need to be constrained in order to preserve the public interest (Wedel and Hardcastle, 1978: 186). Secondly, because vouchers and credit cards are obviously redeemed after the service is purchased they can offer only partial accountability to the government, who actually provides the money in the first place. Brilliant argues that vouchers have the potential to favour select groups unless they are 'backed by intensive controls and expanded resources to counteract increased demands. Otherwise, vouchers may become a way for government to abrogate its responsibility for making and implementing social policy' (1973: 393). Hurl's (1986a) comment that clients are unable to make informed decisions because they 'seek out services when they are in crisis' is significant. Similarly to Hurl, Rose-Ackerman argues that the

> . . . reluctance of policy makers to endorse a pure, unregulated voucher plan reflects a pervasive difficulty. The premise underlying a pure voucher plan is that informed market decision by recipients of services will assure optimal quality. Yet in many contexts such informed choice is unlikely or impossible . . . . The efficacy of vouchers designed to aid such needy people would depend entirely on the choices of those who care for them. If many beneficiaries have no guardians, vouchers can be of no use at all. (1983: 1411)

There are various financial mechanisms which are subsumed under the general categories of grants, ranging from general grants to highly specific service contracts. In summary, the presumed benefits of allocating these grants to private agencies is that they cost less than direct governmental services. The use of a discretionary grant-allocation procedure increases the government's freedom to plan for and provide more flexible, accessible and higher quality services. The disadvantages are that the social agencies' perennial need for financial security suggests that they will tend to favour longer rather than shorter term contracts. This bias towards the longer contracts may run counter to a government's wish to terminate ineffectual services, which reinforce its preference for short-term contracts. The smaller agencies, particularly if they have had no experience of how to argue for substantial block grants, confront tactical and staff resource issues when attempting to negotiate such funding contracts. Tensions can also arise within agencies when resources that might have been spent on service delivery are used to satisfy government requirements for fiscal accountability (Berg and Wright, 1980; Kramer and Grossman, 1987). This is especially pertinent to the smaller, less wealthy or innovative agencies which operate on a more consensual administrative basis.

## Fiscal Accountability and Agency Autonomy?

In considering all the relevant patterns of fiscal accountability managers will need to take into account the various ways that agencies have of estimating costs (Willis, 1984). Financial account-ability is the most common form of accountability even though it may only involve, at least for small contractors, sending in annual accounts to government (Leat, 1986). However, recipients of larger grants are usually compelled to submit financial estimates, as well as on-going reviews, and be investigated by government representa-tives. Similarly, the length of time for which a contract is to operate will influence decisions about how the reporting of fiscal account-ability is to be determined. While issues of accountability, monitor-ing and evaluation are complex and diverse, in general fiscal accountability procedures are more clearly able to be established than those which involve monitoring and evaluating the professional practice aspects of service delivery.

## Graduated Fiscal Remuneration for Successful Contractors

Performance contracting focuses on the value to governments of creating a 'results and rewards' strategy in service delivery rather than the 'effort orientation' typical of conventional cost-orientated contracts (Weddell, 1986: 20). Ideally, with effective performance criteria and bonuses built into the funding mechanisms agencies may use this incentive to develop innovative and more efficient services. Carefully designed procedures of fiscal incentives can be developed in order to attract a supply of potential contractors. As we have seen, though, there may be conflict between a govern-ment's desire to offer only limited contracts and an agency's 'need' for a more secure funding-base. However, before performance contracting can be adequately applied, conventional cost-orientated contracts need to establish a base line cost of the particular services that governments want the private sector to deliver. This may involve the voluntary agency negotiating with government to provide services to specific clients for a fixed price based upon total or capitation costs, which are agreed to in advance. While govern-ments may guarantee total costs they might rather negotiate some system of partial reimbursement, which would allow for perform-ance bonuses within the contract terms. Performance contracting could also be extended to cover those situations in which the government wishes private contractors to offer services for more difficult and hard-to-reach clients. Performance bonus criteria would therefore relate not only to the efficient and effective delivery of services but also to the willingness of the agency to provide services for more difficult and exacting clients. Some form of graduated fiscal compensation may nullify criticisms of contracted social services that the voluntary and private sectors tend to serve only those cases where they are capable of being effective (Jansson, 1979: 371).

*Seeding Funding: Alternatives to Existing Agencies.*
Where some social services are contracted out, and there is no alternative supplier, some consideration might be given to providing development finance for enterprising or entrepreneurial groups who wish to establish a competing social service. There will always be a tendency for private agencies to act in collusion with each other against the government as the provider of the contract finance. Agencies make informal arrangements with one another to concentrate on certain areas and aspects of service delivery and inevitably create a form of monopoly (Hurl and Tucker, 1986). Given that contracting for services involves agencies in complex budgetary, monitoring and evaluation requirements it is inevitable that large agencies, with already established systems of managerial account-ability, are more able to fulfil contracting procedures. This is not the case for the smaller agency, which tends to be less bureaucratically sophisticated. This poses specific problems for governments if they wish to encourage those agencies which may be defined as innova-tive or radical. These agencies operate on financial 'shoestrings' and are almost totally committed to using all of their staff in direct service delivery. Servicing the fiscal accountability procedures of contracting may provoke undue strain within the particular agency. Nowhere in the current social policy literature is it suggested that government should play such a developmental role with respect to the financing of alternative agencies in order to provide competition when none has previously existed. However, despite the cautions, there seems to be no good reason why governments should not develop such policies.

## Managerial Procedures: The Practice of Change – Practical Strategies, Options and Choices

The actual implementation of purchase of service agreements reveals a plethora of questions about the prior administrative procedures that will be used to determine needs assessments. Management tasks can be grouped into four classic categories: how objectives are determined; what techniques will be selected for processing information; the training of contract supervision; and how the tasks will be performed. In practice, social services contracting compels governments to identify

> . . . the target group, what amount of service is to be purchased, what
> the service goals are, what the expected cost will be and how the service

will be monitored. The contract documents are much more explicit than the typical letters of exchange formalising most grants or core funding . . . . purchase of service contracting lends itself to the achievement of accountability objectives, because it establishes the terms and conditions of service and financial remuneration in an explicit, formalised manner which can then be evaluated. (Kettner and Martin, 1987: 23–24)

## Determining Appropriate Needs Assessment Strategies

Before the introduction of a contract system was promoted as a possible administrative option both private agencies and the government sector validated the priority of socially defined needs through local or specific agency intake policy. It was the clients who presented for service who, in some representative ways, defined the needs for services (cf., Hasenfeld, 1985a; 1985b). The state could deftly side-step the question of needs assessment by directly employing social workers and other social service workers to undertake individual assessments through statutory procedures of intake and assessment. The introduction of contracting procedures dictates a completely different system of needs assessment. Successive welfare state governments have demonstrated an increasing sensitivity to social and political pressures about the definition of appropriate social needs. As we have seen, identification and definition of social needs, and decisions about how those particular needs will be satisfied, represent political rather than solely managerial decisions (cf., Hurl, 1984; Johnson, 1986). Public opinion has demanded that the state provide certain social services, and the 'welfare lobby' has exercised considerable influence. Common assumptions about how expert needs assessments abrogate client rights and reinforce dependency have led individuals to join together to form consumer pressure groups, to define needs and advocate with the state to meet these specific social service needs (cf., Mishra, 1986b). It was the 'entrenched power' of this welfare lobby that a resurgent right wing has sought to attack.

## Procedures and Options in Contract Management

While the rhetoric associated with the establishment of social service contracting argues for the benefits of market competition this is very rarely what occurs. Distribution of social services through contract procedures has tended to interpret definitions of management within the narrower frame of implementation and to avoid the wider political aspects of policy formulation. The managerial questions implicit in decisions to contract out services to private for-profit or private voluntary agencies are not usually about competition between agencies, there often being too few for a truly

competitive market to exist, but about the procedures for implementation (Gilbert, 1983). The actual management of these new
policies does not determine which social agency has an inherently
superior service delivery system, but rather considers what specific
conditions are needed in order to decide whether profit- or non-
profit-orientated agencies are the most suitable provider of social
services. Managerial decisions, understood in this way, are about
the proper mix of these two forms of private social service delivery
systems, rather than the inherent superiority of one over the other
(Murray, 1975).

Four practical conditions impinge on administrative decisions
when choosing between for-profit and non-profit providers of
similar services. The first concerns the nature of the social service
and whether it is a standard service, with widespread or universal
entitlement, or whether it is specific and restricted. Standardized
services can be categorized and therefore merge well with the
economic planning and management skills of private business,
which tends to have established patterns of cost analysis, and are,
therefore, easier to control. The second pertains to how managers
view the personal competence of clients, some of whom are
defenceless, independently to select and use social services. However, because the ideas of 'public accountability and the charitable
ethos influence the behaviour of non-profit organizations more than
that of profit making organizations, the non-profit form is preferable for delivering services to these client groups' (Gilbert, 1983:
71). Thirdly, managers must assess the statutory authority of public
sector agencies and whether some of their services, which have the
potential to curtail personal freedoms, should be allocated to the
private sector. Curiously, the independence of the private sector
raises more issues than does the public sector, which has more open
systems of legislated accountability. Fourthly, where normative
responsibilities, as well as fiscal controls, are clear there is little to
choose between public or private agencies. Those circumstances
where the choice is more difficult usually reflect the dilemmas that
have arisen from equivocal or fragmented social planning (Gilbert,
1983: 71–72). In summary, where traditional areas of social services
are concerned, public and private non-profit agencies are better
able to provide more fitting services than are for-profit agencies. It
is the specific or more idiosyncratic social services which justify the
expenditure of public money on private social services.

*The Training of Contract Supervisors*
Contract monitoring and accountability depends upon the quality of
contract supervisors. As welfare bureaucracies have been restruc-

tured and contract management training implemented, relatively few middle-level managers have demonstrated the precise skills needed for contract management. Consequently, governments, wishing to pursue more extensive use of these alternatives to direct state provision of services, have had to initiate specific training programmes so that these management skills may be acquired (cf., Cooper, 1980; Kettner and Martin, 1986; Veit, 1987). Typically, in most social service departments a proportion of significant management positions have been held by former social workers; partly because management represented the only viable career path and there had not been the same promotional advantages for direct practice staff. Few who filled managerial positions had been professionally trained in management skills, let alone the more specific skills needed to manage contracts. They were trained to manage the provision of direct services not the delivery of these services via third-party contractors. Negotiating the terms and conditions of contracts, selecting suitable agencies, monitoring, evaluating and then either renewing or terminating contracts requires specialized administrative skills and competence in contract law (Veit, 1987: 25). Social work skills, shaped and given direction by the old welfare bureaucracies, are not readily transferable to the differing managerial roles. Those agencies and individual professionals who remain in a reactive mode rather than finding ways to be proactive in the new policy environment will be politically vulnerable (Pawlak et al., 1983: 9). Equally, because the statutory sector is bureaucratically structured, the professionals are rarely powerful enough to determine major resource allocation. Consequently, they rarely 'resist politically alluring calls for privatization of services, or calls for increased volunteer activity, calls which constitute contemporary mainstream rhetoric' (Pawlak et al., 1983: 387). Other staff with managerial skills are better suited to the administration of these new policies and roles. The social work category declines as the level of purchase of service contracting activity increases (Ghere, 1981). Rose argues that

> . . . if new, socially constructed paradigms and practice models are not forthcoming, the field is at risk from increasing exclusion in favour of less expensive, more acquiescent professions more amenable to medical models of care, medical hierarchies and medical institutions, all more immediately compatible with existing financing mechanisms and mandates. (1987: 257)

While the impetus of these policies is directed towards the efficient and effective market provision of social services, these expectations are often frustrated because contracting involves complex third-party negotiations (Gilbert, 1983). Ironically, this is precisely the benefit that neo-conservative social theorists wish to derive from a contract approach to welfare policy.

*Issues Involved in Third-Party Negotiations*
When third parties are introduced into the contract negotiations major problems arise which affect the distribution of social services. Clients of contracted services, particularly those provided by for-profit agencies, are vulnerable because third-party payments separate them from the government fiscal supplier. Contracts are not made between clients and governments but between governments and social service agencies. Third-party negotiations require contract managers and supervisors to make complex assessments which inevitably involve wider ethical and political issues. Consequently, because the administrative structures necessary to contract social services depend upon third-party negotiations and payments,

> . . . the entire transaction is perceived by neither the consumer who does not pay for the service, nor the purchaser who does not receive the service. Under these arrangements, the service provider is more accountable to the public body purchasing services than to the consumer. This indirect line of accountability often travels through two or three levels of government; the information costs are quite high; and the degree of accountability thus achieved is often limited. (Gilbert, 1984a: 68)

Several new layers of managerial responsibility are introduced by third-party negotiations, which blunts the effectiveness of any demands for accountability and transparent management. Services may be limited, or furnished unevenly, according to the budgetary constraints of the for-profit agency and may not follow the overall policy direction of government. Ethically, governments may not be able to move clients from agencies whose operating costs are greater to those whose administrative costs are lower (Hurl, 1986a). The priority interests of clients may have to be given pre-eminence over cost savings to governments 'even if this may seem a less than complete reliance on purely market considerations' (Veit 1987: 28). Emotionally complicated or specific social services are often subjectively assessed by clients and no standard formula for effective delivery can be established. As noted previously, where statutory powers are involved client choice is limited to public sector agencies. Similar arguments against the use of contracting apply when alternative service choices are not available (Gilbert, 1984a). These issues create difficulties for contract supervisors who deal with the inconsistent 'real world' of limited and incomplete services and have to reconcile them.

**Managerial Procedures: The Range of Practical
Techniques for Needs Assessment Research**

While there is some debate about the relevance of specific techniques to differing areas of needs assessment there is general
agreement about the nature of the broad range of applicable
techniques. The differences perhaps lie more in who initiates them,
either government or the social services sector. For example, the
research can either compile a summary of current social problems
and associated needs, or establish the political criteria for resource
allocation in order to bargain for increased agency or governmental
co-operation in meeting social needs (Gates, 1980: 121). Consequently, there are two possible approaches to the achievement of
effective assessments. The first is to concentrate on normative
comparisons. In this instance the contract supervisor compares the
agency's description of specific treatment activity to normative
standards of similar treatment established by other successful
programmes. The second is to rely on the judgements of independent experts about the theoretical approach to treatment and
intervention that the contracting agency espouses.

In order to estimate the success of treatment procedures, contract
supervisors must determine the congruence between the actual
treatment intervention, and how it is perceived by clients, with the
initial intention of the intervention (Moos and Finney, 1983). The
most commonly used methods of needs assessment research are
either overarching statistical analysis and survey techniques, which
provide an effective evaluation of current patterns of social service
delivery, or more specific advocacy techniques that seek to persuade
government or interest groups to accept the legitimacy of their
claims. Typical research techniques and guidelines include statistical
analysis, survey techniques and community-focused techniques.
Some aspects of each of these will be discussed in order further to
clarify the options managers must consider in deriving 'workable'
and accurate needs assessments.

**Statistical Analysis and Surveys**

There are eight generally accepted formal research techniques
which may be used to conduct surveys and compile statistical
information. These are general population surveys, target population surveys and agency-sponsored surveys which can be either
generalized or specific. Also discussed are rates under-treatment
surveys, key informant surveys, secondary information reviews,
social needs or social indicators series and administrative reviews,

which are typically an agency's annual report together with other managerial records (Olson, 1980; Meenaghan, 1982: 173).

**General Population Surveys: Macro-Perspectives**   This is the most common technique which is also most frequently used to support state social policy initiatives. For these surveys to be effective explicit and rigorous definitions of need must be determined, together with attitudinal surveys of how respondents actually view social needs. Information gathered by these surveys describes a range of individually identified social problems and provides governments with an overall assessment, aggregated from these individual needs descriptions. The reliability of community-based surveys depends upon non-subjective responses, therefore accurate judgements about the nature of social needs and how social services are to be provided necessitate numerical and statistical tests of reliability. The technique seeks to isolate the subjectivity of individual perceptions so that governments can make selective or targeted responses to these generally identified social needs. Significantly, it also provides a broad description of the patterns of how services are being used and whether those qualified to use them do so freely.

It may involve administering interviews or questionnaires to pre-selected group samples, which may be either selected population groups or respondents from defined geographical areas. The survey instrument includes questions about service eligibility in order to estimate the number of services required to meet the identified needs. These surveys also supply a synopsis about general public attitudes towards specific social agencies. They can indicate the rates of service use and offer some reasons why specific services may be under-utilized. Some allowance must be made for the prejudices of professional social service staff, who can provide an unwanted bias (Haskins and Gallagher, 1981). These problems can be initially overcome by using an open-ended survey

> . . . to identify the range of problems perceived in the community. A closed-ended survey instrument is then constructed based on the problem categories developed from the previous survey. The second instrument asks respondents if they have difficulties with each problem area, the severity of the difficulty, causes of the problem, solutions attempted, degree of resolution of the problem, and any suggestions respondents may have for services to address these problems. This technique provides an important check on the pre-conceptions of the professionals executing the community survey. (Reid and Smith, 1981: 304–305)

These survey questionnaires are flexible and the methodology can complement other techniques which might be used to target needs assessments on selected issues. They can, with minor adjustments, use the basic research designs of existing research methods and are therefore somewhat cheaper to administer, although wide-ranging surveys are inherently expensive. They need staff with specialist research skills and command significant amounts of time and staff resources (Reid and Smith, 1981: 304; Meenaghan et al., 1982: 174).

**Target Population Surveys: Searching for the Specific** This technique gathers information about social needs from those assumed to be a 'population at risk'. These 'at risk' groups usually demonstrate specific or selective characteristics, either because of the unique vulnerabilities of individuals, or because they constitute a distinct sub-group which can be identified and isolated from the general population. Other distinct groups can be specified by examining the patterns of how existing social services are used and comparing these with other communities and geographical areas. Target population surveys and general population surveys are similarly assessed. There is some complementarity in that the data which provide explicit detail about the problems recognized by the target population may be compared with information gathered by the general population survey. A target population sample may be stratified or, conversely, the sample may be isolated as a discrete example of specific problems. Target population surveys can therefore generate more significant and specific information than can general population surveys. This is a particular advantage when the target population is the same as the service population. In these circumstances more reliable information can be obtained about the difficulties clients may have in acquiring services and better strategies developed to pinpoint the type of service which may be desired.

Target population surveys also rely on existing survey research methods, thus complementing other techniques used. The disadvantages are that, similarly to the general population survey, they are relatively expensive and time consuming, requiring specialized skills not generally found in the planning or administrative staffs of most social services (Meenaghan et al., 1982: 175). When target populations are equated with the service population they reveal a higher concentration of problems in comparison to the general population survey. These 'at risk' groups already use existing services and are the likely clientele of any new programme that results from the needs assessment. However, precisely because of prior access to social service systems the information about needs and appropriate agency services is biased. Survey respondents will need reassurance that their information will not affect their present or future service eligibility, otherwise the reliability of target or client group information can be skewed by the fear of reprisal. Consequently, the data cannot be generalized beyond the target population. The identified problems may apply only to a small segment of the total population and may not be typical of the non-target population.

**Service-Provider Surveys and Rates Under-Treatment Surveys: The Search for Pragmatic Information** Information obtained from social agencies and service providers can be used to indicate specific patterns of current direct service provision and the extent of community resources. Direct service providers represent an important source of information about unmet service needs and can complement information provided by other respondent groups. Data can also be obtained on how agency services are actually used which can then be compared with that provided by general population or target group surveys (Meenaghan et al., 1982: 176). Given the political 'delicacy' associated with needs assessment it is important to obtain sensitive political information from those directly involved in the provision and delivery of social services. Agencies are presumed to be somewhat familiar with the type of social needs that might emerge from these surveys and can identify problems and needs for services which may not be widely recognized, or which may not yet have social or community acceptance. This involves the analysis of 'rates under-treatment data' which collate and describe the characteristics of those who have used a particular service (Olson, 1980: 129). The needs of the community can then be estimated from a sample of persons who have received care or treatment (Warheit et al., 1984: 48–49). This information will involve an analysis of referral sources, client characteristics, waiting lists, as well as some aspects about unmet needs in relation to the particular agency service. A rates under-treatment approach to needs assessment aims to determine the frequency or duration of the service and the possible outcomes of intervention (Gates, 1980: 134).

The main advantage of the rates under-treatment approach is that, since the data are already available, analysing them is relatively inexpensive. Secondly, where such analyses involve more than one agency the ripple-effect of shared information can be used by governments to stimulate and facilitate policy development in desired areas of service delivery. Specific work to accumulate this information in one agency can raise the general level of awareness about these particular needs in the wider social service community. Consequently, it has the potential to facilitate service integration and foster consultation. Given the limitations of the idiosyncratic concerns of specific agencies a rates under-treatment study provides a reliable overview of local social service delivery. If this approach is combined with community and expert forums, social indicators, surveys and rates under-treatment data, the overall validity and reliability of the needs assessment process is enhanced (cf., Gates, 1980). Problems arise because agency records are often confidential and therefore rates under-treatment surveys may only be useful as an appraisal of that particular agency's responses to needs assessment. The differing ways in which agencies store client information may curb comparative research (Olson, 1980: 129). For example, information may be collected for the purposes of accountability and managerial control and not primarily to assess social needs (Reid and Smith, 1981: 299). Generally, there is no standardized reporting system governing all social agencies and the data cannot therefore be uniformly categorized. Many of the records necessary to determine needs assessments may not be accessible to agency staff let alone outside researchers. Obtaining guarantees of complete anonymity and confidentiality is always difficult in exchanges between agencies, and this restricts any ability to undertake detailed comparisons of how they deliver services to their separate clients.

These research efforts must also contend with the fact that substantial differences occur between the characteristics of service clients and those which might be relevant to an assessment of wider community needs. Information gathered from agency surveys may reflect the needs of the service rather than of the non-service population. Equally, clients who are seen simultaneously by a large number of the public and private agencies may give a false picture of general community needs (Hurl, 1984). In addition, community members may seek services from agencies or people outside of the particular community where they happen to live. It is, therefore, difficult 'to extrapolate from populations receiving treatment or services to the population at large' (Warheit et al., 1984). The types of needs, and problems identified, may be more relevant to the interventive procedures and theoretical approaches intrinsic to specific agencies rather than to any normative expectations about how services are to be delivered or to how clients perceive need (Meenaghan et al., 1982).

**Key Informants Surveys: The 'Wise' Interpreters!**   The selection of key informants depends upon their knowledge of community needs and patterns of social service provision. Key informants can pinpoint which social problems are likely to become public issues and which will receive widespread exposure and discussion. Equally important is their leadership potential should the needs assessment project want to use these informants to secure political influence (Olson, 1980: 128; Rossi and Freeman, 1987). They are expected to have topical and relevant observations about which community and political leaders are likely to support as well as resist the introduction of new social programmes, or changes to existing ones. They are seen as interpreters of those important social issues which concern the politically active or vocal segment of the community (Hibbard, 1984). The research method involves the development of an interview schedule or questionnaire based on a checklist of needs and social service priorities prepared by the research steering committee. The informants are asked independently to rate local needs and service priorities. Only when that is completed are they permitted to discuss them with other informants. The inevitable variations in attitude and assumptions about community needs are discussed and an attempt is made to determine the elements of a consensus about community needs (Warheit et al., 1984: 43).

The major strengths of this particular technique are that it applies existing research methods, involves agency staff and is flexible and inexpensive. It may, however, require many interviewers because key informant surveys are more effective and produce more reliable information when undertaken personally, rather than when they are administered by a mailed questionnaire (Meenaghan et al., 1982: 177). While canvassing key informants has the advantage of stimulating community interest in social needs the disadvantage is that reliance on 'politically important' community figures can engender bias. Key informants' perceptions are not immune to the constraints of personal beliefs or their political sensitivities and they may therefore have only a selective or narrow view (Warheit et al., 1978). Key informants' evaluations may, similarly, reflect only sectorial opinion because they may be arbitrarily selected, with the result that some segments of the population may be excluded from fulfilling the role (Olson, 1980: 128). Key informants are therefore never statistically representative of the community and cannot satisfy empirical statistical tests of probability.

**Secondary Data Analysis: Inferring Social Need**   Secondary data analysis can be divided into the determination and assessment of social indicators, statistical reviews of administrative and agency records and collation of the information publicized by agencies about their theoretical approach to practice or their goals and clientele. It is collated from census surveys, demographic trends, annual reports and incidental reports on how clients use services. It also uses any statistical analysis of these services which can be validly associated with specific needs assessments. These data are used to list accurate needs assessments or, alternatively, to examine complicated areas of social concern. The location and severity of various types of social problems can be discerned and information given to policy-makers about where to locate new services designed to meet these needs. Valid social data include information that can be compared across communities and regions. The reliability of these comparisons depends upon the use of similar data collection methods gathered within a specific time frame. This allows the stream of information to be related to longitudinal studies of service delivery patterns, programme effectiveness and community trends. Longitudinal studies can discern whether the changes in particular social statistics relate to an increased efficiency in the established services to satisfy client need or to other, extraneous factors.

Needs assessments based only on the results of secondary data are questionable because the results are descriptive rather than analytical. Social data are often used to argue trends relevant to many areas of social planning and are not conceptually specific to the assessment of social needs. Similarly, because they are used to predict trends which existed prior to the design and implementation of specific needs research they are essentially retrospective. The discursive and general or, conversely, narrowly statistical nature of the available data may not sufficiently address the requirements of a valid community needs assessment. For example, they may be inadequate to assess gaps in particular social services and because the data cannot be broken into such discrete analytical categories they cannot be used to determine the distinct or idiosyncratic nature of individual need or to identify individuals with more than one problem. Similarly, they may not provide sufficient information to describe specific patterns of existing services or the willingness of clients to use those services.

**Social Indicators: Statistics and Correlations, Signposts of Community Need?**   Social indicators are typically aggregate measures relying upon statistical analysis of the rates of incidence of specific social needs and their geographical location. These statistical averages are used to determine the social service characteristics of particular communities and subsequently to establish service patterns for the general population (Burdge, 1983; Verwayen, 1984). Social indicators help to define specific 'at risk' community groups with a concentration of particular social problems (Gates, 1980; Goodman and Craig, 1982). These indicators are more accurate measures of social need if they characterize general populations 'rather than the deprived, the deviant or the handicapped, and the degree to which . . . [the research] embodies implicit rather than explicit judgments about resource allocation or vice versa' (Bebbington and Davies, 1980: 147).

This is a flexible research instrument because it is based primarily upon information drawn from statistics. One advantage of this approach is that it uses a wide range of readily accessible information such as census reports or government statistics (Warheit et al., 1984: 54). It may involve a simple design using only one or two indicators or it may involve a very complex strategy from which estimates of needs can be projected by analysing statistics on factors found to be highly correlated with persons in need (Orthner and Smith, 1986). The primary disadvantage in the use of social indicators is that the information used can only be an indirect measure of the needs they represent. Many phenomena about which trend data are desired are not readily quantified. Information which can be gathered from social indicators may be used to define levels of social well-being perceived as minimally acceptable by various groups when assessing community and individual goals (Fear, 1978). However, minimally acceptable standards of community well-being are often politically determined rather than established by needs assessment research (Taylor, 1980). Social indicators are broad-based methods that should be used with some degree of care. Consequently, the assembling of valid social indicators requires a sensitivity to the biases implicit in personal, class, ethnic or gender differences. Conclusions about the disposition of social need based on local community characteristics, on statistical correlations or on indicators of social class values ought to be interpreted with caution (Warheit et al., 1978). The existence of a need based upon social indicators should be verified with other evidence to see how convergence or triangulation of data might obtain a more balanced result (cf., Hawkins, 1980; Rossi and Freeman, 1987).

**Administrative Records: Agency Information Reviews** Such reviews yield valuable information about client characteristics, providing a means to assess the range of clients and the nature of the problems addressed by particular services. One of the most frequently used needs assessment techniques is to collate the annual information reviews from other government departments, from the private and voluntary sector as well as direct service agencies. These records and agency reviews often indicate needed services which the agency or service organization intends to address but which are not yet available. They provide a partial survey of inter-agency programme co-ordination and can identify duplication and gaps in the services they separately provide. This information can also be used to document agency referral patterns. The technique complements other needs assessments and is relatively inexpensive since the information has already been collected. It can also be used to corroborate or identify discrepancies with other information, the usefulness of which may be restricted to those 'individuals who have participated in the formal service delivery system' (Meenaghan et al., 1982: 182). These reviews are developed to present the strategic 'public face' of the agency and they may not be available in a form that may be useful for needs assessment. This information may not be comparable or capable of being generalized from agency to agency. Lack of comparability makes it difficult to track clients or service patterns across agencies and there is 'little or no awareness of the subtleties of those statistics in terms of cross-referencing for trends' (Peters and Sibbison, 1980: 418–419).

*Community-Focused Research Techniques*
These community-based evaluations stress client 'satisfaction' with current services. They involve evaluations of either direct social service provision or needs assessment research. They reflect a predominant trend towards welfare rights and are undertaken in order to protect the rights and interests of clients (cf., Kilburg, 1978). Therefore, it is only possible to discuss consumer-based needs assessment models if the questions that are asked with respect to that particular needs analysis have in fact been formulated by the community members themselves and not by the service providers or by the researchers (Hawkins, 1980: 139; Ife, 1980). These ad hoc evaluations often result from a community action approach which gathers complaints and dissatisfactions about social services. They are used by community pressure groups to urge agencies to remedy deficiencies. Given their limited financial resources, expertise and methodology, it is rare for such mutual aid groups to undertake comprehensive evaluation research. Several commonly accepted protocols are required if researchers are to respect a community's needs and activities.

Commitments must first be gained from the community about the subsequent use of the information. The research must clearly identify funding sources and demonstrate why particular research methods are deemed to be the most appropriate assessment technique. Finally, community-based research must 'apply convergent analysis to multiple sources of data to arrive at final interpretations' (Hawkins, 1980: 140). Convergent analysis of community needs depends upon two main assumptions. First, neither administrators, agency managers, client advocacy groups nor clients can offer a complete view of the health and social needs of a particular community. Second, community research illustrates that the needs of a particular community or target group are essentially unique (Gates, 1980: 122). Convergent analysis sifts a range of information in order that the community needs be 'identified, defined, evaluated, and given priority in a progressive manner' (Siegel et al., 1978). It seeks to integrate this range of community perceptions about successive needs assessments with an analysis of the constant attitudinal and perceptual issues that accompany community-based research. The 'winnowing' of this material helps communities to identify the most urgent and pressing social problems and provides a mechanism by which policy options can be rank ordered in terms of community priority. The process of convergent analysis demonstrates that no one technique is superior, rather that they represent a 'series of useful tools integrated into an assessment plan' (Hawkins, 1980: 141). For example, in order to develop more comprehensive community-based needs assessments, the two strategies of key informant and community forum may be operated sequentially. Alternating key informant surveys and community forums utilizes and incorporates the benefits of an impressionistic and subjective approach. Measurements of community group-based needs assessments can complement the formal gathering of needs assessment information. They can identify unacceptable proposals and determine which approach has the highest community priority.

However, while these techniques can be used as part of a larger convergent process that incorporates the hard data of statistical analysis to complement and strengthen the overall results, some issues still remain. While they may not need researchers to rely solely on the idiosyncrasy and subjectivity of self-contained needs assessments, these client evaluations are usually informal. They can be argued passionately, are non-systematic and are not easily validated by empirical research. More formal needs assessments often gather data which are of little or no importance to the studied community. Despite the professed value of having clients participate in assessing patterns of needs assessment, conceptual and methodological problems occur when consumers are directly involved in systematic research. Most services are individualized and the valid assessment of social needs is left to professional judgement, and it is this intrinsic subjectivity which hampers research. Such services cannot be standardized nor can they easily be monitored for deficiencies. Development of true consumer-based research is hampered because social agencies accord clients relatively little power to change current service patterns. Professional staff may equally resist client involvement because it involves some loss of status or power. Their 'professed' concern for the efficient discharge of organizational responsibilities can hamper the involvement of clients in needs assessments. For example, there are the vexed and complex issues of client dependency on professional expertise while there is, simultaneously, an increasing community rejection of paternalistic welfare traditions (Taylor-Gooby, 1985c).

Global judgements of satisfaction with social agencies are likely to be strongly influenced by the 'halo-effect' of positive feelings about particular practitioners, rather than by a dispassionate assessment of the general effectiveness of the service. Favourable responses by clients to inexact questions about their satisfaction with services must be interpreted warily because the degree of satisfaction expressed may reflect the range of congruence between their expectations of the service and their experience of it. These expectations are influenced by previous experiences of both formal and informal assistance and their prior knowledge and recollection of specific services. They are also influenced by their beliefs about what assistance is possible and their personal feelings of self-worth and their willingness to endure social deprivation, or the view that the practitioner was a kind person (cf., Stipak, 1979; Hasenfeld, 1985a; 1985b). Other difficulties surface because some clients are depressed or socially alienated which limits their effective participation. Analysis of the more objective obstacles to client involvement indicates that barriers are created by the specific theoretical approach adopted by distinctive agencies. Bureaucratic structures have subtle ways of withstanding external influences. Martin has argued that in a 'communally mandated and resourced service, accountability is not only to those served but also to the sources of legitimacy and resources' (1986: 188–189). The obscure professional or theoretical procedures used to evaluate agency services limit the influence of clients to improve services. The specific techniques of community-based research are community forums, nominal group techniques, the delphi technique, community impressions and jury panels (Siegel et al., 1978; Burdge, 1983).

**Community Forums – A Vexatious Public Voice?** Community forums represent a quick and effective method for initial impressions and perspectives to be gained about the accessibility, availability, acceptability and organization of services within particular communities (Siegel et al., 1978). These forums usually follow the pattern of an open community meeting where opinions can be expressed publicly about particular issues in order to elicit quickly a range of views about them. Community forums very rarely involve concrete decision-making. Rather, they are used to establish current problems, to determine the ways that needs are identified and to elicit comments about existing patterns of service delivery. The process of problem identification is only the initial phase of a problem-solving process. An important and perhaps self-evident caveat is that 'care may need to be taken to avoid raising unrealistic expectations among consumers' (Martin, 1986: 193). These forums usually mobilize the radical elements of the community and heighten the awareness of existing social service needs. As a result, the expectations of community members may be raised in ways which cannot or will not be met.

The validity and usefulness of community forums depends upon wide representation of diverse opinion and it may be necessary to develop incentives for all invited individuals and groups to attend. Community forums help to identify potential community leaders (Warheit, 1984: 44). The usefulness of these forums also depends upon respecting the procedures and protocols of that particular community, establishing a neutral venue and having the meeting chaired by a generally respected member of the community. More specifically, the success of these forums depends upon agreement about the rules for participation and how any issues raised at the meeting will be subsequently considered (Siegel et al., 1978: 240–241). Community forums are comparatively economical and they provide policy planners and agency administrators with an opportunity to gauge the views of those who have fallen into the 'underserved' or 'non-served' category in the community (Olson, 1980: 124). They stimulate the identification of social service needs and provide those responsible for needs assessment with an opportunity, not only to hear from many different elements of the community about unmet needs, but also to identify those participants and agencies most interested in resolving them (Siegel et al., 1978: 241). Given the inevitable group dynamics of large meetings it is unlikely that everyone who wishes to speak will have a chance to do so. The vocally strong and 'group-wise' will tend to dominate. Community forums therefore represent an impressionistic and probably incomplete picture of the needs of the community. There are inherent problems in adequately recording and reflecting all the responses made at a community forum which undermine the determination of priorities.

**The Nominal Group Technique: Structured Community Opinion**
The nominal group process provides a way in which to evaluate, within a group setting, individual reactions about the appropriate assessment of social needs. Nominal groups are used to identify a wide range of problem areas and to draft various practical sugges-

tions. The technique provides an opportunity to develop a greater range of innovative and different solutions to community problems. Group members might be asked to specify their own social service needs, to consider those that are relevant to other groups in the community or, more broadly, to identify the significant issues that new welfare policies ought to address. Nominal groups can be used to involve clients and direct social agency staff in joint exploration of these problems and policies. They can also draw upon the expertise of resource people who are not intrinsic to the community as well as using the experience of internal specialists who are already involved in solving problems and establishing new policies. Nominal groups can be used to diffuse difficult and conflictual community issues. They provide an added political benefit because these methods of needs assessment and policy recommendation involve governments, agency staff and clients in the formation and implementation of new social policy.

Nominal groups usually include small working groups of participants who do not initially interact. An issue or a series of questions is placed before the group, to which the participants are invited, without discussion, to provide succinct responses. After the initial period of private reflection all individual ideas are shared with the total group. The process is strictly controlled as each participant is asked to comment on only one issue at a time. These comments are recorded exactly and subsequently opened to group review. The nominal group then adopts a 'round robin' process until each participant's ideas are canvassed. A strictly controlled discussion period follows in which participants are invited to clarify or elaborate the ideas which have been presented. Nominal groups attempt to isolate and remove controversy in order to elicit as wide a range of opinion as possible. Ideas are clarified and not defended; this is sustained by the group process which strictly limits group discussion and considers only one idea at a time. Only when all possible issues relating to that specific question are addressed are further questions entertained. Consequently, there is freedom to add new ideas, to eliminate others and to highlight duplication. Once the process of separate clarification is completed each participant is required to compile a short list of the most important ideas and rank order them. These are collated and a group rank ordering is determined on the basis of the individual weighting. Following this initial process, when problems and solutions are identified and rank ordered, the nominal group can be used as a key reference group to monitor subsequent stages of policy planning and development.

One of the major advantages of nominal groups is that the

procedure avoids 'group-think' (Lauffer, 1984: 68). Some of the perennial problems of group dynamics are avoided: namely, the dominating 'guru'; those who come with a prearranged or hidden agenda; and those with high social or organizational status who might use that position to control the discussion (Burdge, 1983: 198–199). The initial silent period is a creative opportunity for 'lateral thinking' and is essential for the presentation of minority ideas, and the controlled group dynamics cut through the usual power of hidden agendas. An equal burden is placed on all members to participate in the work of the group and to share responsibility for the group's success (Hairston, 1979: 14). However, the technique lacks precision, as individual rank ordering can be idiosyncratic, or compiled without thoroughly and carefully sorting all the ideas of other participants into categories which are appropriate to the original issue of the needs assessment. Some members may feel 'manipulated' by their experience of such a highly structured and unfamiliar process, and the nominal group is only as good as the people selected.

**The Delphi Technique: Information and the 'Wise Judges'**   This research procedure involves the systematic gathering and ordering of informed judgements on a particular topic (Delbecq et al., 1975; Linstone and Turoff, 1975; Burdge, 1983; Raskin, 1983). It usually involves the careful design and distribution of a set of sequential questionnaires where each subsequent questionnaire provides a summary of the information and opinion derived from earlier questionnaires. This method is dynamic and constantly elaborates and focuses material on specific areas (Reid and Smith, 1981). The sequential questionnaires provide for a structured dialogue between persons who do not meet, but whose opinions are valuable to the issue being assessed. The delphi method demands anonymity and systematic feedback. Questionnaires relative to an important issue or set of issues are distributed to a panel of experts or key individuals. Since it is not necessary and, in certain circumstances, not desirable to have these experts meet, questionnaires can be mailed. When the questionnaires are returned, the results are compared and areas of agreement and disagreement noted. If there is still substantial disagreement other questionnaires are distributed which describe the various conflicting opinions. This procedure is repeated until an agreement can hopefully be reached (Burdge, 1983: 199). The technique is used by those who expect that participation in the exercise will assist their own responsibilities for policy formulation and management. It can also be initiated by a group of expert respondents who constitute a community 'watchdog' or monitoring group which produces the initial questionnaire and summarizes the returns and designs follow-up questionnaires. It is typically used to determine broad-based or long-range policy and to evaluate corporate planning. In the current economic and social climate, when welfare and social services are formulating strategic plans, the delphi technique is a useful method to determine targeted social policy. The summarized information is carefully organized to provide a common reference point against which the delphi technique judges base their responses.

Although the original experiments relating to the delphi technique centred on questions that required specific or factual answers, the originators believe that the technique is also appropriate to social areas where 'value judgements' occur and where there are no preset 'answers'. The usual presentation of this controlled feedback is through statistical analysis, although less empirical responses can be generated thus providing more personal information to the participants (Lauffer, 1984: 68). It can be used to determine or develop a typology of social service needs as well as to explore or expose the underlying assumptions which have led to different judgements about social service needs. The delphi technique also aims to correlate informed judgements about specific topics from a broad section of the community in order to demonstrate to the respondent group that social service needs are diverse yet interconnected. However, because participation can be anonymous, and the feedback controlled systematically, the inhibiting influences of personally or politically dominant and more verbal participants are minimized, and vested interests reduced to a minimum (Hawkins, 1980: 142). The delphi is an efficient user of the respondent's time involving individuals who might otherwise have rejected more time-consuming procedures.

This procedure yields concise results that can be tested on a much larger community sample, applying exactly the same methods of scoring and statistical analysis to make the two sets of data analogous. The main disadvantage of the technique is the lack of certainty in establishing guidelines for its use and design. For example, there are a number of important questions for which general agreement does not exist. Whether the delphi should be used only in conjunction with the same respondent group or be administered to a series of separate respondent groups is an important question that may well be settled only by the relative size of the sample community. The respondents may not be completely anonymous either to each other or to the policy team which designed the research. However, since the aim of the delphi technique is to elicit opinion in isolation so that there is no undue influence or pressure it may not be appropriate in small well-knit communities (Reid and Smith, 1981: 301). A further disadvantage is that extreme positions may be dropped in order to obtain agreement. Consequently, many outrageous and divergent yet creative ideas may be lost. This problem is also shared by the nominal group approach and other similar approaches.

**The Community Impressions Approach**   This involves three steps: using key informants, integrating existing information and conducting a community forum. There are a number of advantages and disadvantages. It requires minimal expenditure of time and resources and dovetails well with apparently different research information. It has the potential to unite empirical 'hard data' with the range of 'impressionistic hunches', usually generated by those 'outsiders' who are traditionally alienated from policy-making about community needs identification and service provision. Those who may be identified as being 'at risk', or having 'unmet needs', are able to apply their own perspective to these judgements. They may, similarly, comment on the introduction of better procedures for meeting their needs or on ways that these needs may be reduced. This approach is tangible and specific and it has the capacity to develop a more efficient network among different social agencies resulting in a more effective, broad-based, community approach to needs assessment. It can also contribute to the establishment of priorities and to procedures for the allocation of resources.

Despite the usefulness of a combined community impressions approach to needs assessment the results must be subjected, as far as possible, to the same tests of reliability and validity that are applied to empirical surveys. However, reasonable standards of statistical reliability and validity can rarely be confirmed because the results are generally impressionistic. There is no way to ensure that every group with social service needs will be identified, or that they might have been identified and recorded previously. The community impressions approach is most useful when the focus is on an inexpensive and expeditious assessment of those who have 'unmet' needs in different groups within the community. The approach can be related to the results of other surveys as well as to the thoughts and feelings of various community members. The approach is particularly useful if there is a commitment to involving those with greatest needs in processes which will help reduce their needs.

**Jury Panels – The Dispassionate Assessors?**   Jury panels are a random community selection of people who are interested in and involved with the processes of how groups make decisions (Burdge,

1983). Using a sequential random sampling technique, each potential juror receives a call to jury duty. People continue to be contacted until the required number of jurors have agreed to participate. They receive a modest fee and expenses in return for several days of listening to the descriptions of proposed new social service policies. The researchers discover the jurors' perspective on community problems. At the end of a defined period they are asked to give their verdict on what they see as major community impacts or needs. Since selection is random, it may be assumed that all gender, racial and class positions in the community are asked to participate. Jury panels are an excellent way to obtain representative public input, at acceptable costs and in a timely manner. They have the disadvantage of requiring considerable advance planning and a leader who is trained in group dynamics. Finally, those who refuse to participate may have done so for ideological reasons, which may skew the significance of the jury sample.

### Managerial Procedures: Contract Formulation, Offer and Acceptance?

Perhaps the most detailed description of purchase of service contracting procedures is contained in the joint work of Kettner and Martin (1987). Their book is a veritable compendium of useful and practical 'how-to-do-it' suggestions. Paradoxically, its strength is is its weakness in that, written as a type of manual, it is relatively uncritical of its own presumptions. However, given political decisions to implement a contracted welfare system, there is much welcome practical advice for management. Careful negotiation of all these stages of the contracting process is administratively costly. Once decisions are made to contract with the private sector, governments will need to weigh several factors before deciding which agencies to use. They will need to ensure that the contract does not omit or disadvantage any clients for whom the public sector had a prior public responsibility. This will hold true as well for contracts which may displace voluntary agencies in favour of the proprietary sector. Clear programme and delivery guidelines, together with specific outcome assessment measures, must be defined, as well as the expected duration of the programme. Governments will need to be reassured about the agency's intake policy, the practical expertise of its staff and how it proposes to deliver the services. Finally, both parties must explicitly agree to consult with each other about the progress of cases and respect routine procedures such as fiscal review and audit in order to ensure public fiscal accountability (Kramer, 1983: 426).

More practically, when considering whether to award contracts to particular agencies, managers must resolve four questions that relate specifically to the principles of accountability. The first is how appropriate are the practice-interventive theories employed by the agency applying for government contracts to those services that governments wish to have contracted. While this is always important it assumes an added significance when governments attempt to respond innovatively to the demands for non-sexist and culturally appropriate social services. The second question, almost a coda on the first, involves the types of research instruments which may be used to measure the usefulness of the practice theory adopted by the particular agency. The third involves the creation of agency assessment procedures by which separate practice performance will be compared to that of other agencies who might be possible contenders for the contract. The principles of administrative transparency require that contracts must go to the demonstrably more efficient agency in order to avoid charges of favouritism. The final question involves the assortment of contract rules that link agency performance to service and client improvements (Poertner and Rapp, 1985).

**Managerial Procedures: Contract Monitoring and Evaluation**

The success of a social service contracting relationship depends on the ability of the government contractor to design, administer and enforce contracts that have clearly specified objectives (cf., Judge, 1982; Wortman, 1984; Veit, 1987). Evaluations will be useful if the terms of the evaluation are agreed on by all parties. Specific goals are needed since the research is focused on a particular dimension of the programme. Evaluations will have to be completed within a period of time that is relevant to the decisions that have to be made about the programme (Berg and Theado, 1981). Effective evaluation requires clear definition of the initial problem and the objectives used to solve it, which includes non-measurable goals and outcomes (cf., Wortman, 1984). Alternatives must be identified and effective procedures instituted to undertake cost-benefit analysis and consider the ethical issues that might be involved. Kettner and Martin's (1987) practical schema suggests specific checklists for contract management and describes the explicit categories within which investigation would indicate successful contract compliance. Monthly progress reports would reveal possible problems in vital areas like the service provision programme, financial accountability and specific contract claims. Rigorous, on-site monitoring would involve a member of the contract evaluation team visiting the agency within a predetermined period after the agency had completed its first monthly report. Monitoring requires periodic reports and review statements which are prepared using objective evidence based on the direct monitoring procedures established at the time of contract negotiation. The contract itself provides the criteria by which the contractor's performance is monitored and areas are identified where alterations in service delivery are wanted. These monitoring reports include an estimation of the contractor's progress in fulfilling the initial terms and conditions of the contract. If the contract is altered on the basis of these compliance reports then new follow-up procedures will need to be introduced to ensure compliance with the restated contract (Kettner and Martin, 1985b). It is clear that the motivation behind the introduction of such tight procedures was to institute the rigour of a management by objectives approach, and to instil in the social services arena the logic of the market-place.

**Managerial Procedures: Treatment Monitoring and Evaluation**

One of the criticisms that can be levelled at purchase of service contracting is that it is more involved in procedural review than in any substantive analysis and review of actual programme or treatment effectiveness. Evaluation and monitoring of treatment effectiveness depends on the existence of a valid model of how the particular deficiency, problem or disadvantage is produced or maintained. The inherent conceptual problem which this presents relates to the difficulties in separating out the treatment objective from the method of delivery. However, social science research methods can be used to evaluate and assess whether given social policies can achieve or are achieving their intended aims (Rossi, 1979). Successful evaluations and effective treatment monitoring depend on definite, non-contradictory and measurable goals. Managers will need to consider whether the treatment is effective in achieving its goals given the most favourable delivery method. It is always possible to take 'worst-case' scenarios and use these to invalidate overall programmes. Managers must also determine if the services are actually being delivered to the appropriate groups and within a reasonable budget. Of equal importance is a judgement about whether specific agencies can deliver the proposed services effectively and earn the trust and acceptance of the proposed client population.

The clients' role in the choice of outcome measures will depend on the extent to which their definitions of the problem are taken into account. In general clients like social service programmes, evaluate them favourably and think that they are beneficial irrespective of whether measurable behavioural changes towards stated programme goals occur (Scheirer, 1979). This reflects the halo-effect previously discussed in Chapter 4. If the social service programme is intended to influence actual behaviours then Scheirer believes that it is inappropriate to use attitude and other subjective measures as primary indicators of programme effectiveness. In systems theory terms, the solution becomes part of the problem. Once state resources are specifically committed it is highly likely that the programme will be continued regardless of its facility actually to address the problem. The orientation of programme administrators towards successful management of their programme, irrespective of outcome, as well as political pressure from recipients participating in that programme, engender an in-built conservatism. Managers will need to consider that the legitimate roles of contract monitoring supervisors and agency managers differ and that evidence of effective completion of a contracted programme ought to depend not on subjective impression but rather on specific evidence (Scheirer, 1979: 420).

### Managerial Procedures: Contract Termination

Very little is written about the conclusion of contract arrangements. It is generally assumed that the results of an unsatisfactory evaluation will be used to implement changes in agency procedures, to raise standards of service delivery and to alter, where necessary, the direction of the agency's efforts at client out-reach. Irrespective of how ineffective a specific programme might be, political considerations or the lack of viable alternatives may ensure its continuation. Consequently, decisions to renew or terminate contracts are often influenced by the relative political pressures of the enduring demand for services (Kramer and Grossman, 1987). We have seen how intrinsic to the contracting process is the assumption that criteria for monitoring and effectiveness be established as part of the negotiation of the contract. Ideally, contracts should not only outline what mechanisms would be used to resolve disputes, but also prescribe the methods and processes of contract termination, thus guidelines for the 'separation phase' should be considered at the contract drafting stage (Cooper, 1980).

**Conclusion: The 'Never-Ending' Objective!**

Social service managers will always have to deal with the paradox that certain problems cannot be eliminated without creating others. No incongruity can be resolved simply because the process of resolving one set of disparities produces further contradictions (cf., Gilliatt, 1984: 357). The constant danger is that social services have an intrinsic conservative effect in that they tend to take on a life of their own. The consequence is a reduction in the flexibility of social service managers to initiate change through either experimentation or the development of new and innovative social policy. In this situation, importance is placed on organizational survival and social services 'become solutions whose benefits are rarely questioned' (Moroney, 1977: 131). Faced with the problems of organizational survival social service managers either adopt policies that resist further decline or they may be forced to make decisions that smooth the transition to lower levels of welfare funding. One consequence of budgetary restraints is that managers will be under less pressure to extend the benefits of programmes to clients because they experience a correspondingly greater pressure to withhold benefits or to tighten access criteria (Lipsky, 1984). There is much debate about what are the most appropriate strategies to pursue in the face of resource cutbacks and possible programme decline. In general, management theory has not been able to develop appropriate responses to the problems of organizational decline or zero economic growth (Hasenfeld, 1985b: 78)

Senior managers in the social services will be required to continue major reviews of the reasons why the established patterns of welfare policy have engendered an inertia in the policy debate. In this new policy climate managers will have to develop legislative policy to provide short-lived and 'self-liquidating' programmes for both the private sector, where such policies are expected and wanted, and the public sector, where they are decried. In addition, they will have to provide a rationale for how these experimental programmes will contribute to and enhance the long-term social policy objectives of governments. There will need to be more emphasis, in the short term, on the design of administrative measures which aim to overcome the particular organizational blocks which impede adaptation. New systems of financial accounting are required, particularly in the current political climate which constantly emphasizes the limited resources available for welfare spending. These fiscal pressures and potential cutbacks have highlighted the value of contracted social services as both a procedural and a regulatory strategy. Similarly, these policies serve a political purpose in that they are also an administrative alternative to the proliferation of centrist social institutions (Klein and O'Higgins, 1985). The transition for traditional managers of social services has been traumatic indeed.

# 6

# Conclusion

# Epistemology, knowledge and meaning

The nature of political discourse reflects epistemological questions about how social 'knowledge' is created by paradigmatic beliefs. Within this theory of knowledge it is argued that we all seek to explain the world from within the constraints of how we seek to know it. What can be 'known' is the result of a patterning or ordering of experience and the punctuation of that pattern by 'difference'. To argue for the truth of only one set of social beliefs constructs the preconditions for dichotomous and dualistic assumptions. Recent developments in epistemology, from cybernetics and systems theory, attempt to reveal the presumptions that have structured social and political perceptions of social policy. Furthermore, the argument that what counts as knowledge is based on metaphor (Bateson, 1972; Keeney, 1983) undermines the claim that it is a reflection of absolute reality or the 'truth'. The implication of this is a challenge to the rhetorical assumptions of the classic protagonists in the welfare state debate. The hollow rhetoric of the neo-conservatives, based on a presumption about the normative reality of economics, that 'there is no alternative' and that the 'social' is a troublesome fiction, attempts to constrain the social policy debate to a narrow definition of private obligation (Ignatieff, 1989). In the light of these developments it is important therefore to understand how the 'silences of social and economic policy' – epistemological strategies to shut down debate – (Katznelson, 1986) influence the current restructuring of the welfare state. At least for the moment – as a consequence of the epistemological sleight of hand that does away with values in social policy – the high hopes that Titmuss and others (cf., Abel-Smith and Titmuss, 1987) have held about the transformation of the welfare state into a welfare society seem illusory (Robertson, 1988).

It is the 'language' of this debate that I wish to stress. One of the commonplace 'facts' about the current restructuring of welfare policy is that it has been undertaken almost entirely on the basis of economic pragmatism. Such pragmatic views reject both the former rhetoric of grand political visions and its implicit value structure which supported the theory of citizenship. Perhaps one of the dominant aspects of the welfare state 'crisis' debate, and of the success of the neo-conservative rejection of the role of values, is that it has not really been a debate. The 'language' of necessary economic reform has isolated the normative aspects of welfare state politics. As I have argued previously, the dovetailing of neo-conservatism and welfare rights about a lesser public role for government formed an intellectual coalition against the rhetoric of welfare. Both the neo-conservatives and those supporting a leftist anti-bureaucratic organization jointly attacked what they called a 'malign bureaucracy'. This provided a political opportunity for governments to introduce major social policies without any clear basis in political philosophy as a guiding principle. Consequently, once in office political parties have been prepared to abnegate their traditional political platforms. They have championed what are presented as the 'hard and necessary decisions' of paradigmatic neo-conservative economic theory. In this they have dramatically restructured those patterns of social and citizenship relationships that typified welfare states.

While not gainsaying the importance of these economic 'facts', the rhetorical 'language' of neo-conservatism, which has dominated public discussion, denies citizenship rights to those unwilling or unable to participate in their 'brave new world'. In that world acceptable political speech is a language of 'players' and 'winners'. It involves an arena of strategic play and counterplay which scorns the sentimentality of liberal democracy and seeks only to serve the welfare interests of citizen 'friends', denying any significance to the citizen 'stranger'. As Balibar has argued, neo-conservatism idealizes

> . . . the pragmatic and technocratic values of decisiveness, efficiency [and] entrepreneurial spirit . . . [This idealization] presupposes an aesthetic sublimation . . . it is not by chance that the modern executive, whose enterprises must dominate the planet, is both an athlete and a seducer. (1990: 292)

The motivations that underpin political activity and social analysis cannot be explained away by neo-conservative analysis that has no respect for the personal and phenomenological subjectivity that supports political activity. It is important in this to remind the separate protagonists that they speak a 'political language' – the 'domains of political speech and political silence'. The 'meanings' that we ascribe to economics, social policy and politics are subjective and ontological. They reflect not a neutral social science but how various parties perceive and act within the world. Significantly, the neo-conservative language of 'winners' and 'players' also embraces the 'silences' of 'losers'.

Similarly, the language of rights alone, which reflects the reifications of the new welfare rights paradigm, provides no political guide to the future because it too can only point to the defensive selfishness of a different pattern of strategic winning and playing. Thus the epistemology of welfare rights has to be seen as the 'socially committed standpoints' of social administration. This is, as Mishra (1984) has argued, where knowledge and theorizing about the welfare state has no intrinsic value but is presented as a way to understand the world and as a lever to change it (cf., Robertson, 1988). This also has constrained the debate about welfare provision so that privatization is inevitably defined as 'bad' (cf., Block, 1987a; Esping-Andersen, 1987). From an epistemological perspective the left and the right present us with opposing sides of the coin which forces an illusory choice.

## Normative Beliefs, Ideology and 'Right Action'

The origin and nature of strongly held opinions, especially in relationship to contracting and privatization policies, become a central issue in the analysis of the debate about welfare policy. Social policy analysis reflects the centrality of moral values and political philosophy (Pearson, 1975a: 66). The conflictual nature of the separate 'worlds' that these positions reflect is obvious. The understanding of this approach as ideological raised fundamental questions about the validity of professional theoretical approaches to policy analysis based on 'abstracted empiricism' (Rein, 1981). Equally, other critiques of professional ideology suggested that it arose only out of the philosophy of the free market and the 'logic' of corporate capitalism (Mishra, 1984). The origin of this anti-professional bias could be located partly in the intellectual criticisms of a positivistic approach to knowledge building in the social sciences. Social administration had been dominated by the idea, at the heart of a positivistic philosophy, that theoretical understanding precedes the acquisition of practice skills and wisdom. However, the acquisition of practical knowledge does not only depend upon the positivistic notion of theoretical preparation. The very sense of what is practical is sustained by virtue of an acquired epistemology. Both the theoretical ground and the process of how knowledge is used and applied reflect epistemological assumptions and silences. The use of power both in the personal and public spheres suggests that it involves the ability to remove from public focus issues that are not to be discussed. We can never be entirely sure that the currently topical issues are necessarily the most important, but only that they represent the ones that we are free to discuss. Conceptual thinking can never be presumed to be innocent because statements of explicit value can mask implicit and more fundamental operating values (Mishra, 1984).

Ideological approaches to social policy which depend upon the certainty of their prescriptive analysis can be seen as suspect in a world in which the intellectual justification for objectivity and a positivistic philosophy are no longer so easily sustainable. For example, there are conceptual difficulties in defining the altruism of the welfare exchange. To discuss them reifies altruistic acts and robs them of their essential specific ('here and now') character (Arendt, 1959). Part of the reason for the ideological debate about welfare is that it is conceptually difficult to provide definitions of social obligation that can be couched in the managerial language of efficient resource usage. For example, in social work and the social services both the clinical (function) and community advocacy (cause) arguments for change stumble over the administrative demand for explicit 'measurable outcomes'.

The challenge of systems thinking is to see that all 'knowledge' is interrelated and not essentially separate. Current assumptions about the possibility of 'abstracted empiricism' protect dualistic thinking and allow for the continuation of rigid categories of right and wrong. If it can be argued that knowledge is a metaphor for the organized pattern of experience, then it becomes highly idiosyncratic and personal. Commonsense experience suggests that people seek confirmation from others that what they see, think or feel is what others see, think or feel. It is the apparent similarity of this experience that allows us to assert that we know the truth. The awareness that beliefs are in fact beliefs – and not 'knowledges' – must replace the assumption of moral rightness and earnestness which so far has characterized the debates on welfare. It is only this understanding, that belief is a socially produced reality, which can prevent the foreclosing of policy debates by those who assert that they know the 'truth'. If we see knowledge as a negotiated reality other people then become the means to validate subjective views of the world. The process is that 'my' beliefs are therefore true because 'you' also believe them. It is only then that people will have the courage to accept the statement that 'I believe that my beliefs are beliefs'. This can be described as a 'meta'-position, that is, one in which it is possible to stand 'extra to' the process of the debate and comment on it. It can be asserted that this is not possible; that by definition it is only possible to observe ourselves from within ourselves. The apparent circularity of this position is important. Social policy theory is full of the same recursive arguments which lead either into passivity or into angry and impotent grandiosity.

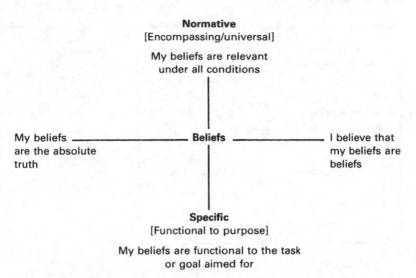

Figure 6.1   *Intersecting Patterns of Beliefs*

Both of these options are created by the same set of assumptions that what we believe is in fact the truth. The way out of this circular pattern and process is a renewed sense of the ontology that supports differing sets of assumptions about the role of values, the subjectivity of values, and the political nature of policy-making.

We can see from Figure 6.1 that there are two intersecting continuums in this debate. Each continuum expresses the range of opinion that is possible with respect to belief. There is a horizontal axis ranging from the rigidity of 'My beliefs are the absolute truth' to the flexibility of 'I believe that my beliefs are beliefs'. There is also a vertical axis ranging from the normative position that 'My beliefs are relevant under all conditions' to the specific position that 'My beliefs are functional to the task or goal aimed for'.

There is a logical connection between disparate systems of belief and the arguments used to validate these apparently uniquely different belief systems. That which is asserted to be 'true' can only be understood in the context of that which is denied. Extending these concepts further we can apply both Weber's (1947) notion of a *typology of rationality*, and Robertson's (1970) *typology of religious belief*. Weber divides rationality into two categories, formal (or technique-orientated) and substantive (or value-orientated). Robertson divides belief systems into those which are uniquely legitimate and those which are pluralistically legitimate. The conflict about the use of privatized and contracted social services has

| Freudian psychoanalysis | Professional specialities | Formal [Technique orientated] |
|---|---|---|
| Single technique | Plurality of technique | |
| Radicalism | Genericism | Substantive [Value orientated] |
| One set of values | Plurality of values | |
| Uniquely legitimate | Pluralistically legitimate | |

Figure 6.2   *Professional Belief Systems in Social Work*

emphasized how social work services are in fact professional reifications of political belief systems about a just society and citizenship. Applying Weber's distinction between formal and substantive rationality to a horizontal axis and Robertson's distinction between uniquely and pluralistically legitimate belief systems to a vertical axis a four by four analysis about professional belief systems in social work practice can be developed (Figure 6.2).

   Many of the major political debates about the nature of a just society are played out in the internal clash about the appropriateness of these ideological positions. The debate is, as we have seen, not so much about practice competence as it is about appropriate belief. It is only an examination of the function and nature of practice based upon belief that will admit an analysis that is not developed from within positions that are explicitly ideological. However, it is possible to 'push' the reflexiveness of this argument to the point of absurdity. For example, it can be argued that if all professional assumptions are based solely on belief then even this position is only a belief and therefore not worthy of respect! To acknowledge that our beliefs are beliefs engenders the respect for difference that is essential in seeking to point beyond the 'classic' ideological divide. We will need, as Katznelson has suggested, to 'develop a taste for thinking about possible worlds that are not very far away, but seen to be just beyond our grasp' (1986: 325).

## Privatization: The 'Eclipse' of Social Work?

The epistemological dilemmas have specific implications for social work practice. In order for social work to respond effectively to purchase of service contracting and the privatization of social services it must reclaim some of the central ground that is implied by a professional stance. To stand totally against these developments will condemn social work to obscurity and hasten the transformation of social work practice positions to those that can be performed by a new managerial elite (cf., Ghere, 1981). The welfare rights paradigm which reinforced an anti-professional bias has argued that the only effective and true 'healing' occurs in situations where 'like cures like'. The attack upon the relevance of professional detachment inherent in this position is apparent. The welfare paradigm shift has reinforced an assumption that only community-based practice has any moral 'high ground' in the continued search for socially just and effective intervention. On the face of it the debate looks finished. Practice assumptions rest upon encoding extraordinarily complicated perceptions into personal belief systems. Part of the movement against professionalism has attacked the 'hidden' value stance of those who espoused a professional approach and has called into question the possibility of professional neutrality. The enormous pressure exerted by practice realities is apparent. The tendency therefore is to establish a set of assumptions that will allow the social welfare professions to function both under pressure and with scarce resources.

While there is an inherent inadequacy in the existing system of social service provision constant criticism of it may not just reflect its inherent deficiency but may also indicate a failure to accept the limited nature of the changes that are possible. The cycle of poverty, issues of gender and racism, while reflected in social work practice, cannot essentially be challenged by social service practice and delivery. These are part of the whole structure of society. Social work activism has blithely assumed that prevention is the only morally justifiable practice stance. That it is desirable and morally and ethically an important goal is obvious. There is, however, very little examination of how social work per se can bring about the massive restructuring that would allow it to assume a mandate and responsibility for such a preventative role. It is possible to see preventative functions with respect to specific areas of practice, but not with respect to the overall mission and function of social work. Social work has no mandate for such global responsibility, and if there are no limits to be placed upon areas of responsibility then the profession assumes a megalomaniac vision that is ultimately destructive. A more reasonable assumption is that the origin of disadvantage, injustice and oppression lies with the total political and economic structure and not just with a part of it that is termed social work. Radical rhetoric within the social services constantly attacks residual concepts as antiquated and ineffective but rarely demonstrates how the social services are capable of effectively acting in a preventative role. Thus an enormous burden of guilt and obligation is wrongly laid on those who work within the statutory social services. The political and moral pressure generated both internally and externally by this radical critique has not been able to develop an analysis that can yet transcend statements of imperative obligation. For such arguments to be intellectually and morally sustainable they must reveal not only the imperatives for action but also the possibility of transformation. It is at this point that arguments for purchase of service contracting and privatization of social services must be taken seriously.

The question remains, how can institutional systems of helping which were established to respond to alienation, oppression, injustice and disadvantage be held solely accountable for the fact of these situations? If social work is to maintain a publicly mandated purpose in a 'restructured' world then it will need to develop a practice analysis that more clearly starts with the premise of what it *can* do rather than what it *ought* to do. The emergence of these moral imperatives in social work is clearly not a current dilemma. The fact that the profession grew out of a social movement that was essentially religious in origin, together with the emergence of various left-wing orientations that have been structurally critical of the social control function of social work, contributes to this sense of moral obligation.

The normative conjunction of the modern national state and the church created a paradigm of social welfare that was essentially paternalistic. This old paradigm created the institutions of education, health and social welfare as the means by which the redistributive functions of the welfare state and other forms of social services were established. This old paradigm has been superseded by one in which welfare is to be mediated not on the basis of the obligation to care for the stranger but on the basis of the social legitimacy of the claim rights that various groups can espouse. With the disappearance of the old paradigm, then, there is even more reason to look at the professional role in a new way. Future analysis of the professional role must respond to the difficult issue that knowledge is relative. It will not be possible to adhere to the old pattern whereby theory preceded practice, but it will be incumbent on social work to 'do our knowledge' (Rein 1981). To continue to argue for the essential 'rightness' of one position or view of the world as against another is to miss the point.

The rhetoric of radical change, irrespective of precise content, depends upon the exclusive power of its own internal logic in order to preserve the integrity of the desired change. In some profound ways the meta-position of the professional vision, the stance of detachment, has occasioned much rage and it is some aspects of this anger that I now want to explore. The rhetoric of anger attempts to destroy the possibility of detachment. There are numerous appeals to commitment and group obligation. Within the impetus for social change (of whatever kind) there are group dynamics which emphasize the supremacy of the dominant belief system. Colloquially, whatever is good and perfect, holistic and beautiful is contained within; while whatever is bad, divisive, stupid or destructive lies without. Pursuit of an angry righteous vision does indeed break the old paradigm, the systems of thought that were constraining. Yet, in social work radicalism, the praxis of the new vision, the mechanisms by which the new knowledge is actually used in practice draw upon metaphors of reflection, evaluation and tangible workability that seem 'dangerously' like the old professional stance of detachment!

Part of the justification for professionalism lies with the realization that social change and the pursuit of social justice are not specifically realizable goals. It is clearly not the case that we could all agree or accept that we had arrived at such a place of contentment. As Bitensky comments, the commitment to never resolving these issues within the professional paradigm maintains 'the ridiculous exercise in expanding vacuity' (1978: 72). To translate new metaphors into practice realities take us to the paradox at the heart of professional knowledge. The need to translate new visions into practice immediately freezes them or reduces them to something other (Arendt, 1959). We are here at the core of Rein's assertion that social policy must 'do its knowledge'. What can be known arises out of the act of knowing. As soon as such knowledge is assumed to be the 'truth' the process of the social debate is forestalled because any attempt to step outside of the constant relativism of ideas and establish unquestioning truths will freeze the debate. Here is the origin for some of the ideological rage and anger that has constantly divided social work and left it floundering in the wake of the introduction of purchase of service contracting and arguments for the complete privatization of social services.

If the professional stance of detachment is criticized as an effect of 'false consciousness', and this to hide a position of power, so too must be the rigidity of other ideologies which have different fixed stances of right belief and right action. The constant projection of the role of the oppressor onto any external figure, and especially to vilify the stance of professional detachment, is not intellectually sustainable. For better or worse the internal logic of the professional position is that the three roles of 'oppressor', 'rescuer' and 'victim' are equally to be found within the boundaries of the self. The ideals of liberation and justice require social workers to work both with the ceaseless internal individual restlessness as well as with specific social contexts. There is some justification for a renewed professional vision because it is accepting of difference. Clearly, it uses different metaphors to define membership. Professional bodies of theory and knowledge and ethical codes of practice are not too dissimilar from the rhetoric of commitment to right action and right belief. There are rules and patterns that apply to membership of professional organizations and radical caucuses, of whatever sort, that have the same group dynamic functions: both are ever only partial explanations.

Ideas must become action in order to sustain the integrity of the new vision yet praxis seems always to corrupt the clarity and purity of the righteous vision. Out of the heart of this paradox arises the logic for a professional stance that respects the essential relativism of social and individual process. Bitensky concludes his polemic about the social work profession by arguing that while it

> . . . has delusions of grandeur about effecting social change, it will be unable to make the modest contribution to human welfare possible within its scope. For since the just society is not yet around the corner, there is a temporary role for the profession in contributing to alleviating human misery. However, it must be recognised, also, that the basic development of the individual and even the alleviation of present suffering means the mounting of a massive political struggle for broad social and economic opportunities, which essentially is a civic rather than a professional responsibility. (1978: 72)

## Conclusion

One of the most important consequences of the advent of privatization proposals and purchase of service contracting strategies in social policy is that the perennial antagonisms between left and right have been refashioned into a different 'frame'. Privatization is not simply, as some would have us believe, the triumph of classic liberalism recast in the neo-conservative mould. These proposals have shown that the state, having accepted the notion of citizenship rights and obligation intrinsic to a welfare rights paradigm, cannot easily retreat from welfare (Klein, 1980). As we have seen, the arguments for dismantling welfare are largely rhetorical. This is not to deny that there have been instances of cutbacks, but the overall pattern is that sets of structured obligations remain (O'Higgins, 1985: 303; Morris, 1988). Mishra (1984) suggested that the corporate welfare state provided a resolution for the historic antagonisms between left and right. The development of corporatism hastened the arguments in favour of privatization and purchase of service contracting, but these proposals have pointed the way beyond the corporate state. As Turner (1986) argues, the 'anarchy of the market place', which establishes and protects the practical bases for profit-making, also protects the development of social rights. As a result the capitalist system is transformed by precisely those institutions that capitalism established for its defence. Turner suggests that the capitalist welfare state will be constantly transformed because of the 'social struggles of a variety of social movements which are not class-based'. As he asserts:

> The state in capitalist society is popular rather than bourgeois in the sense that the state arises from popular conflict and struggle to enlarge and democratize state institutions against the interests of capital. (1986: 142)

Goodin's (1985b; 1988) arguments for the morality of responding to social vulnerability are part of the recasting of mutual obligation that will be necessary for the state to survive. The political ascription of rights and citizenship criteria have changed the ways that power can be politically defined. Feminist theory, systems theory and epistemological theory have redrawn the nature of the social debate. We can no longer justifiably avoid dealing with the essential relativity of those beliefs that we hold to be normative. To deny the contingent and relative nature of our social and personal beliefs condemns us to stagnation. Systems theory shows that those people who or institutions which are the most flexible and responsive to change are likely to have the most power. For those who would defend the validity of the welfare state it is necessary to couch their responses in a proactive rather than reactive way. The neo-conservative challenge to the welfare debate must be engaged non-defensively. To argue for the truths of the past is to institutionalize an inflexibility. Moral defensiveness and the rhetoric of exhortation are ineffective. What form of social obligation will be established will not be like the old.

I have discussed how it might be possible to rethink philosophical justifications for aspects of collective responsibility and obligation. There are vital reasons for these issues to be discussed on a broad philosophical scale. Obligation to each other must be based upon a recognition of mutual vulnerability. What is clear in the breaking of the traditional welfare paradigm is that new explanations will need to be found for those visions and ideals that were at the heart of the initial expectations of a mutual welfare state. What is also clear is that this will never again be achieved by coercive rhetoric that will not tolerate difference. Social policies will need to be flexible and less effort will need to be put into attempting to establish legislation that is 'once-for-all' and never again to be questioned. The ideals of citizenship and mutual obligation are not yet totally discredited. How they are to be rekindled and reinvented remains to be seen. What seems inevitable, despite the enormous power of the neo-conservative argument, is that social and economic survival depends in part on further resolving the classic political problem of the proper relationship between individual autonomy and public obligation. Political cynicism and even dispassionate analysis might justifiably lead to the conclusion that such broad-based social visions are no longer tenable. Yet, it is possible to rethink moral and ethical justifications for social obligation based upon respect for vulnerability; in particular, how vulnerabilities are defined, recognized and responded to, and how social structures selectively enhance certain lives at the expense of others.

# Bibliography

Abel-Smith, B. and Titmuss, K. (1987) *The Philosophy of Welfare: Selected Writings of Richard M. Titmuss*. London: Allen & Unwin.

Abramovitz, M. (1986) 'The Privatization of the Welfare State: A Review', *Social Work*, 31(4): 257–264.

Abramovitz, M. and Epstein, I. (1983) 'The Politics of Privatization: Industrial Social Work and Private Enterprise', *Urban and Social Change Review*, 16(1): 13–19.

Anderson, D., Lait, J. and Marsland, D. (1981) *Breaking the Spell of the Welfare State: Strategies for Reducing Public Expenditure*. Cambridge: The Social Affairs Unit.

Arendt, H. (1959) *The Human Condition*. Chicago: University of Chicago Press.

Armstrong, P. (1982) 'The Myth of Meeting Needs in Adult Education and Community Development', *Critical Social Policy*, 2(2): 24–37.

Ascher, K. (1988) *The Politics of Privatisation : Contracting Out Public Services*. London: Macmillan.

Ashford, D.E. (1986) *The Emergence of the Welfare States*. Oxford: Basil Blackwell.

Austin, M.J. (1984) 'Managing Cutbacks in the 1980's', *Social Work*, 29(5): 428–434.

Baldock, C.V. and Cass, B. (1988) *Women, Social Welfare and the State*. Sydney: Allen & Unwin.

Baldock, J. (1989) 'United Kingdom – A Perpetual Crisis of Marginality', in Munday, B. (ed.), *The Crisis of Welfare*. Hemel Hempstead: Harvester Wheatsheaf. pp. 23–50.

Balibar, E. (1990) 'Paradoxes of Universality', in Goldberg, D.T. (ed.), *Anatomy of Racism*. Minneapolis: University of Minneapolis Press. pp. 283–294.

Barker, R.L. (1987) 'Private and Proprietary Services', *Encyclopedia of Social Work*. Silver Spring, MD: NASW (18th edition), 2: 324–329.

Barry, N. (1987) 'Understanding the Market', in Loney, M. and Bocock, R. (eds), *The State or the Market: Politics and Welfare in Contemporary Britain*. London: Sage. pp. 161–171.

Bateson, G. (1972) *Steps to an Ecology of Mind*. New York: Ballantine.

Bebbington, A.C. and Davies, B. (1980) 'Territorial Need Indicators: A New Approach Part I', *Journal of Social Policy*, 9(2): 145–168.

Beedle, P. and Taylor-Gooby, P. (1983) 'Ambivalence and Altruism: Public Opinion about Taxation and Welfare', *Policy and Politics*, 11(1): 15–39.

Beesley. M. and Littlechild, S. (1983) 'Privatization: Principles, Problems and Priorities', *Lloyds Bank Review*, 149: 1–29.

Bennett, J.T. and Johnson, M.H. (1980) 'Tax Reduction without Sacrifice: Private-Sector Production of Public Services', *Public Finance Quarterly*, 8(4): 363–396.

Benton, S. (1987) 'Death of the Citizen', *New Statesman*, 114(2956): 21–22.

Beresford, P. and Croft, S. (1986) *Whose Welfare: Private Care or Public Services?*, Brighton: Russell Press.

Berg, W.E. and Theado, R. (1981) 'The Utilisation of Evaluative Research in Social Welfare Programmes', *Social Service Review*, 55(2): 183–192.

Berg, W.E. and Wright, R. (1980) 'Program Funding as an Organisational Dilemma – Goal Displacement in Social Work Programs', *Administration in Social Work*, 4(4): 29–39.

Berger, P.L. and Luckmann, T. (1967) *The Social Construction of Reality*. London: Penguin.

Biggs, S. (1987) 'Local Authority Registration Staff and the Boundary between Public and Private Sector Care', *Policy and Politics*, 15(4): 235–244.

Bitensky, R. (1978) 'Social Work: A Non-Existent Profession in Search of Itself', *New Universities Quarterly*, Winter: 65–73.

Blackham, H.J. (1976) 'The Concept of Need in Social Policy', *Social Service Quarterly*, XLIX(4): 122–126.

Blanchard, W. (1986) 'Evaluating Social Equity: What Does Fairness Mean and Can We Measure It?', *Policy Studies Journal*, 15(1): 29–54.

Blau, J. (1989) 'Theories of the Welfare State', *Social Service Review*, 63(1): 26–38.

Block, F. (1987a) 'Rethinking the Political Economy of the Welfare State', in Block, F., Cloward, R.A., Ehrenreich, B. and Piven, F.F. (eds), *The Mean Season: The Attack on the Welfare State*. New York: Pantheon Books. pp. 109–160.

Block, F. (1987b) 'Social Policy and Accumulation: A Critique of the New Consensus', in Rein, M., Esping-Andersen, G. and Rainwater, L. (eds), *Stagnation and Renewal in Social Policy: The Rise and Fall of Policy Regimes*. Armonk, NY: M.E. Sharpe. pp. 13–31.

Borenzweig, H. (1981) 'Agency vs. Private Practice: Similarities and Differences', *Social Work*, 26(3): 239–244.

Born, C. (1983) 'Proprietary Firms and Child Welfare Services: Patterns and Implications', *Child Welfare*, LXII(2): 109–117.

Bosanquet, N. (1983) *After the New Right*. London: Heinemann.

Bosanquet, N. (1984a) 'Social Policy and the Welfare State', in Jowell, R. and Airey, C. (eds), *British Attitudes: The 1984 Report*. Aldershot: Gower. pp. 75–96.

Bosanquet, N. (1984b) 'Is Privatisation Inevitable?', in Le Grand, J. and Robinson, R. (eds), *Privatisation and the Welfare State*. London: Allen & Unwin. pp. 58–69.

Boston, J. (1988) 'From Corporatisation to Privatization: Public Sector Reform in New Zealand', *Canberra Bulletin of Public Administration*, 57: 71–86.

Bradshaw, J. (1972) 'The Taxonomy of Social Need', *New Society*, 19(496): 640–642.

Bradshaw, J. (1977) 'The Concept of Social Need', in Gilbert, N. and Specht, H. (eds), *Planning for Social Welfare: Issues, Models and Tasks*. Englewood Cliffs, NJ: Prentice Hall. pp. 290–296.

Bradshaw, J. and Deacon, A. (1986) 'Social Security', in Wilding, P. (ed.), *In Defence of the Welfare State*. Manchester: Manchester University Press. pp. 81–97.

Brewer, C. and Lait, J. (1981) *Can Social Work Survive?* London: Temple Smith.

Brilliant, E. (1973) 'Private or Public: A Model of Ambiguities', *Social Service Review*, 47: 384–396.

Brown, R.E., Cousineau, M.R. and Price, W.T. (1985) 'Competing for Medi-Cal Business: Why Hospitals Did, and Did Not, Get Contracts', *Inquiry – Chicago*, 22(3): 237–250.

Bulmer, M. (1987) 'Privacy and Confidentiality as Obstacles to Interweaving Formal and Informal Social Care: The Boundaries of the Private Realm', *Journal of Voluntary Action Research*, 16(1 & 2): 112–125.

Burdge, R.J. (1983) 'Community Needs Assessment and Techniques', in Finsterbusch, K., Llewellyn, L.G. and Wolf, C.P. (eds), *Social Impact Assessment Methods*. London: Sage. pp. 191–213.

Burkitt, B. and Davey A.G. (1980) 'Choice and Markets: The "New Right's" Approach to Welfare', *Social Policy and Administration*, 14(3): 257–265.

Burkitt, B. and Davey A.G. (1984) *Radical Political Economy: An Introduction to the Alternative Economics*. Brighton: Wheatsheaf Books.

Bush, M. and Gordon, A. (1978) 'The Advantages of Client Involvement', in Cook, T. et al. (eds), *Evaluation Studies Review Annual*, 3. Beverly Hills: Sage. pp. 767–783.

Challis, L., Fuller, S., Henwood, M., Klein, R., Plowden, W., Webb, A., Whittingham, P. and Wistow, G. (1988) *Joint Approaches to Social Policy*. Cambridge: Cambridge University Press.

Chamberlain, J.R. and Jackson, J.E. (1987) 'Privatization as Institutional Choice', *Journal of Policy Analysis and Management*, 6(4): 586–604.

Clayton, S. (1983) 'Social Need Revisited', *Journal of Social Policy*, 12(2): 215–234.

Collin, R.W. (1987) 'Toward a New Theory of Nonprofit Liability', *Administration in Social Work*, 11(1): 15–24.

Cooper, J. (1980) 'Government Contracts in Public Administration: The Role and Environment of the Contracting Officer', *Public Administration Review*, 40: 459–468.

Crano, W.D. and Brewer, M.B. (1986) *Principles and Methods of Social Research*. Boston: Allyn and Bacon.

Creed, H. and Tomlinson, J. (1984) 'The Role of Ideology in Community Work: Contributions from Feminism and the Left', *Australian Journal of Social Issues*, 19(4): 273–283.

Croft, S. and Beresford, P. (1989) 'User-Involvement, Citizenship and Social Policy', *Critical Social Policy*, 9(2): 5–18.

Cullis, J.G. and Jones, P.R. (1983) 'The Welfare State and Private Alternatives: Towards an Existence Proof', *Scottish Journal of Political Economy*, 30(2): 97–113.

Culyer, A.J. (1981) 'Economics, Social Policy and Social Administration: The Interplay between Topics and Disciplines', *Journal of Social Policy*, 10(3): 311–329.

Culyer, A.J. (1983) 'Economics without Economic Man?', *Social Policy and Administration*, 17(3): 188–203.

Culyer, A.J. (1985) 'Privatization and the Welfare State. Le Grand, J. and Robinson, R. (Book Review)', *Economica*, 52(208): 533–534.

Davies, B. (1977) 'Needs and Outputs', in Heisler, H. (ed.), *Foundations of Social Administration*. London: Macmillan. pp. 129–162.

Davies, S. (1987) 'Towards the Remoralization of Society', in Loney, M. and Bocock, R. (eds), *The State or the Market: Politics and Welfare in Contemporary Britain*. London: Sage. pp. 172–188.

Day, P. (1985) 'Regulating the Private Sector of Welfare', *Political Quarterly*, 56: 282–285.

Deakin, N. (1985) 'Editorial: A Future for Welfare?', *The Quarterly Journal of Social Affairs*, 1(2): 89–92.

De Hoog, R.H. (1984) *Contracting Out for Human Services*. Albany, NY: State University of New York Press.

De Hoog, R.H. (1985) 'Human Services Contracting – Environmental, Behavioral and Organizational Conditions', *Administration and Society*, 16(4): 427–454.

de Kok, A. (1984) 'Crisis in the Welfare States', *Social Policy and Administration*, 18(2): 157–164.

Delbecq, A.L. and Van de Ven, A.H. (1971) 'A Group Process Model for Problem Identification and Program Planning', *Journal of Applied Behavioral Science*, 7: 466–492.

Delbecq, A.L., Van de Ven, A.H. and Gustafson, D.H. (1975) *Group Techniques for Program Planning: A Guide to Nominal Group and Delphi Processes*, Glenview, IL: Scot and Foresman.

Demone, Jr, H.W. and Gibelman, M. (1984) *Purchasing Human Services, Policies, Programs and Procedures*. New York: Human Sciences Press.

Dobell, A.R. (1981) 'Social Policy Making in the 1980s: Elements and Issues', in *The Welfare State in Crisis: An Account of the Conference on Social Policies in the 1980s*. Paris: OECD. pp. 227–239.

Domberger, S. and Piggott, J. (1986) 'Privatization Policies and Public Enterprise – A Survey', *Economic Record*, 62(177): 145–162.

Dominelli, L. and McLeod, E. (1989) *Feminist Social Work*. London: Macmillan.

Donnison, D. (1984) 'The Progressive Potential of Privatisation', in Le Grand, J. and Robinson, R. (eds), *Privatisation and the Welfare State*. London: Allen & Unwin. pp. 45–57.

Dorwart, R.A., Schlesinger, M. and Pulice, R.T. (1986) 'The Promise and Pitfalls of Purchase-of-Service Contracts', *Hospital and Community Psychiatry*, 37(9): 875–878.

Downie, R.S. (1980) 'The Market and Welfare Services: Remedial Values', in Timms, N. (ed.), *Social Welfare: Why and How?* London: Routledge & Kegan Paul. pp. 42–54.

Doyal, L. and Gough, I. (1984) 'A Theory of Human Needs', *Critical Social Policy*, Issue 10, 4(1): 6–38.

Drucker, P. (1969) 'The Sickness of Government', *The Public Interest*, 14: 3–23.

Dryzek, J. and Goodin, R.E. (1986) 'Risk-Sharing and Social Justice: The Motivational Foundations of the Post-War Welfare State', *British Journal of Political Science*, 16(1): 1–34.

Duke, V. and Edgell, S. (1987) 'Attitudes to Privatization: The Influence of Class, Sector and Partisanship', *The Quarterly Journal of Social Affairs*, 3(4): 253–284.

Dunleavy, P. (1982) 'Is There a Radical Approach to Public Administration?', *Public Administration*, 60(2): 215–225.

Dunleavy, P. (1986) 'Explaining the Privatization Boom: Public Choice versus Radical Approaches', *Public Administration*, 64: 13–34.

Dyer, J.S. and Lorber, H.W. (1982) 'The Multiattribute Evaluation of Program-Planning Contractors', *Omega – International Journal of Management*, 10(6): 673–678.

Ehrenreich, B. (1987) 'The New Right Attack on Social Welfare', in Block, F., Cloward, R.A., Ehrenreich, B. and Piven, F.F. (eds), *The Mean Season: The Attack on the Welfare State*. New York: Pantheon Books. pp. 161–195.

Eisenstadt, S.N. and Ahimeir, O. (1985) *The Welfare State and Its Aftermath*. London and Sydney: Croom Helm.

Elim, P. and Taylor-Gooby, P. (1987) *The Private Provision of Public Welfare: State, Market and Community*. Brighton: Wheatsheaf Books.

Epstein, W.M. (1988) ' "Our Town": A Case Study of Ideology and the Private Welfare Sector', *Journal of Sociology and Social Welfare*, XV(3): 101–123.

Esping-Andersen, G. (1982) 'After the Welfare State', *Working Papers*, May/June: 36–41.

Esping-Andersen, G. (1985) *Politics against Markets: The Social Democratic Road to Power*. Princeton, NJ: Princeton University Press.

Esping-Andersen, G. (1987) 'Citizenship and Socialism: De-Commodification and Solidarity in the Welfare State', in Rein, M., Esping-Andersen, G. and Rainwater, L. (eds), *Stagnation and Renewal in Social Policy: The Rise and Fall of Policy Regimes*. Armonk, NY: M.E. Sharpe. pp. 78–101.

Evans, C. (1985) 'Privatization of Local Services', *Local Government Studies*, 11(6): 97–110.

Fear, F. (1978) 'A Systems Approach to Needs Assessment', *Social Development Issues*, 2(1): 52–69.

Ferber, R. and Hirsch, W.Z. (1982) *Social Experimentation and Economic Policy*. Cambridge: Cambridge University Press.

Ferris, J.M. (1986) 'The Decision to Contract Out: An Empirical Analysis', *Urban Affairs Quarterly*, 22(2): 289–311.

Fisk, D.D., Kiesling, H. and Muller, T. (1978) *Private Provision of Public Services: An Overview*. Washington: The Urban Institute.

Florestano, P.S. and Gordon, S.B. (1980) 'Public vs Private: Small Government Contracting with the Private Sector', *Public Administration Review*, 40: 29–34.

Flynn, N. (1989) 'The "New Right" and Social Policy', *Policy and Politics*, 17(2): 97–109.

Frankfather, D.L. (1981) 'Welfare Entrepreneurialism and the Politics of Innovation', *Social Service Review*, 55(1): 129–146.

Fraser, D. (1984) *The Evolution of the British Welfare State*. London: Macmillan.

Fraser, N. (1987) 'Women, Welfare and the Politics of Need Interpretation', *Hypatia: A Journal of Feminist Philosophy*, 2(1): 103–121.

Fraser, N. (1989) 'Talking about Needs: Interpretive Contests as Political Conflicts in Welfare-State Societies', *Ethics*, 99(2): 291–313.

Frieden, K. (1986) 'Public Needs and Private Wants', *Journal of Social Policy*, 17(2): 19–29.

Friedman, K.A. (1981) *Legitimation of Social Rights and the Western Welfare State: A Weberian Perspective*. Chapel Hill: University of North Carolina Press.

Gardner, J.R. (1987) 'The Ethics and Responsibilities of the Not-for-Profit Manager', *Journal of Voluntary Action Research*, 16(4): 6–14.

Gates, B.L. (1980) *Social Programme Administration: The Implementation of Social Policy*. Englewood Cliffs, NJ: Prentice Hall.

George, P. (1985) 'Towards a Two-Dimensional Analysis of Welfare Ideologies', *Social Policy and Administration*, 19(1): 33–45.

George, V. and Wilding, P. (1985) *Ideology and Social Welfare*. London: Routledge & Kegan Paul.

Ghere, R.K. (1981) 'Effects of Service Delivery Variations on Administration of Municipal Human Services Agencies: The Contract Approach versus Agency Implementation', *Administration in Social Work*, 5(1): 65–78.

Gibelman, M. (1981) 'Are Clients Served Better When Services Are Purchased?', *Public Welfare*, 39(4): 26–33.

Gibelman, M. (1983) 'Using Public Funds to Buy Private Services', in Dinerman, M. (ed.), *Social Work in a Turbulent World*. Seventh NASW Symposium. pp. 101–113.

Gibelman, M. and Demone Jr, H.W. (1983) 'Purchase of Service: Forging Public–

Private Partnerships in the Human Services', *The Urban and Social Change Review*, 16(1): 21–26.

Giddens, A. (1979) *Central Problems in Social Theory*. London: Macmillan.

Gilbert, N. (1977) 'The Transformation of Social Services', *Social Service Review*, 51: 624–641.

Gilbert, N. (1983) *Capitalism and the Welfare State*. New Haven: Yale University Press.

Gilbert, N. (1984a) 'Welfare for Profit: Moral, Empirical and Theoretical Perspectives', *Journal of Social Policy*, 13(1): 63–74.

Gilbert, N. (1984b) 'Moral Objections to Welfare for Profit: A Reply', *Journal of Social Policy*, 13(3): 339–340.

Gilbert, N. (1985) 'The Commercialisation of Social Welfare', *Journal of Applied Behavioral Science*, 21(4) 365–376.

Gilbert, N. (1986) 'The Welfare State Adrift', *Social Work*, 31(4): 251–256.

Gilbert, N. and Moon, A. (1988) 'Analyzing Welfare Effort: An Appraisal of Comparative Methods', *Journal of Policy Analysis and Management*, 7(2): 326–340.

Gilbert, N., Specht, H. and Lindeman, D.A. (1981) 'Social Service Planning Cycles: Ritualism or Rationalism?', *Social Service Review*, 55(3): 419–433.

Gilliatt, S. (1984) 'Public Policy Analysis and Conceptual Conservatism', *Policy and Politics*, 12(4): 345–367.

Glazer, N. (1981) 'Roles and Responsibilities in Social Policy', in *The Welfare State in Crisis: An Account of the Conference on Social Policies in the 1980s*. Paris: OECD. pp. 240–255.

Glazer, N. (1983) 'Towards a Self–Service Society', *The Public Interest*, 70: 66–90.

Glazer, N. (1988) *The Limits of Social Policy*. Cambridge, MA: Harvard University Press.

Glennerster, H. (1983) (ed.), *The Future of the Welfare State: Remaking Social Policy*. London: Heinemann.

Glennerster, H. (1985) *Paying for Welfare*. Oxford: Basil Blackwell.

Goodin, R.E. (1982a) 'Freedom and the Welfare State: Theoretical Foundations', *Journal of Social Policy*, 11(2): 149–176.

Goodin, R.E. (1982b) *Political Theory and Public Policy*. Chicago: University of Chicago Press.

Goodin, R.E. (1985a) 'Self–Reliance versus the Welfare State', *Journal of Social Policy*, 14: 25–47.

Goodin, R.E. (1985b) 'Vulnerabilities and Responsibilities: An Ethical Defense of the Welfare State', *The American Political Science Review*, 79(3): 775–787.

Goodin, R.E. (1988) *Reasons for Welfare: The Political Theory of the Welfare State*. Princeton, NJ: Princeton University Press.

Goodin, R.E. and Le Grand, J. (1987) *Not Only the Poor: The Middle Classes and The Welfare State*. London: Allen & Unwin.

Goodman, A.B. and Craig, T.J. (1982) 'A Needs Assessment Strategy for an Era of Limited Resources', *American Journal of Epidemiology*, 115(4): 624–632.

Goodsell, C.T. (1980) 'Conflicting Perceptions of Welfare Bureaucracy', *Social Casework*, 61(6): 354–360.

Gough, I. (1979) *The Political Economy of the Welfare State*. London: Macmillan.

Graycar, A. (1981) 'Social and Political Constraints', in Henderson, R.F. (ed.), *The Welfare Stakes: Strategies for Australian Social Policy*. Melbourne: University of Melbourne. pp. 106–146.

Graycar, A. (1982) 'Agencies, Services and Government Funding', *Australian Rehabilitation Review*, 69(3): 48–53.

Graycar, A. (1983a) 'The Interrelationship of Voluntary, Statutory and Informal Services', *British Journal of Social Work*, 13(4): 379–393.

Graycar, A. (1983b) *Retreat from the Welfare State*. Sydney: Allen & Unwin.

Gronbjerg, K.A. (1982) 'Private Welfare in the Welfare State: Recent U.S. Patterns', *Social Service Review*, 56(1): 1–26.

Gronbjerg, K.A. (1983) 'Private Welfare: Its Future in the Welfare State', *American Behavioral Scientist*, 26(6): 773–793.

Grosser, R.C. and Block, S.R. (1983) 'Clinical Social Work Practice in the Private Sector: A Survey', *Clinical Social Work Journal*, 11(3): 245–262.

Guberman, N. (1987) 'State–Family Relations: Privatising Social Services', *Perception*, 10(3): 16–18.

Gurin, A. (1978) 'Conceptual and Technical Issues in the Management of Human Services', in Sarri, R.C. and Hasenfeld, Y. (eds), *The Management of Human Services*. New York: Columbia University Press. pp. 289–308.

Hairston, C.F. (1979) 'The Nominal Group Technique in Organizational Research', *Social Work Research and Abstracts*, 15(3): 12–17.

Hairston, C.F. (1985) 'Costing Nonprofit Services: Developments, Problems and Issues', *Administration in Social Work*, 9(1): 47–56.

Hamilton-Smith, E. (1975) 'Issues in the Measurement of "Community Need" ', *Australian Journal of Social Issues*, 10(1): 35–44.

Hansmann, H.B. (1980) 'The Role of Nonprofit Enterprise', *Yale Law Journal*, 89(5): 880–881.

Harris, D. (1987) *Justifying State Welfare: The New Right versus the Old Left*. Oxford: Basil Blackwell.

Harris, R. and Seldon, A. (1979) *Over-Ruled on Welfare*. London: Hobart Paperback No. 13: The Institute of Economic Affairs.

Hartley, K. (1984) 'Policy towards Contracting-Out: The Lessons of Experience', *Fiscal Studies*, 5(1): 98–105.

Hasenfeld, Y. (1984) 'The Changing Context of Human Services Administration', *Social Work*, 29(6): 522–529.

Hasenfeld, Y. (1985a) 'Citizens' Encounters with Welfare State Bureaucracies', *Social Service Review*, 59(4): 622–635.

Hasenfeld, Y. (1985b) 'The Administration of Human Services', *The Annals of the American Academy of Political and Social Science*, 479: 67–81.

Haskins, R. and Gallagher, J.J. (1981) *Models for Analysis of Social Policy: An Introduction*. Norwood, NJ: Ablex.

Hawkins, M.R. (1980) 'Dynamic Needs Assessment: An Example', in Davenport III, J. and Davenport, J.A. (eds), *The Boom Town: Problems and Promises in the Energy Vortex*. Laramie, WY: University of Wyoming Press. pp. 139–144.

Heald, D. (1980) 'The Rehabilitation of the Market in Social Policy', in Timms, N. (ed.), *Social Welfare: Why and How?* London: Routledge & Kegan Paul. pp. 55–92.

Heald, D. (1985) 'Will the Privatization of Public Enterprises Solve the Problem of Control?', *Public Administration*, 63: 7–22.

Heald, D. and Steel, D. (1981) 'The Privatization of UK Public Enterprises', *Annals of Public and Co-operative Economy*, 52(3): 351–367.

Heald, D. and Thomas, D. (1986) 'Privatization as Theology', *Public Policy and Administration*, 1(2): 49–66.

Heclo, H. (1981) 'Toward a New Welfare State?', in Flora, P. and Heidenheimer, A.J. (eds), *The Development of Welfare States in Europe and America*. New Brunswick, NJ: Transaction Books. pp. 383–406.

Heclo, H. (1986) 'General Welfare and Two American Political Traditions', *Political Science Quarterly*, 101(2): 179–198.

Hibbard, M. (1984) 'Empowerment through the Needs Assessment Process', *Journal of Sociology and Social Welfare*, 11(1): 112–133.

Higgins, J. (1981) *States of Welfare*. Oxford: Basil Blackwell.

Higgins, J. (1982) 'Public Welfare: The Road to Freedom', *Journal of Social Policy*, 11(2): 177–199.

Higgins, J. (1986) 'Comparative Social Policy', *The Quarterly Journal of Social Affairs*, 2(3): 221–242.

Hill, M. and Bramley, G. (1986a) *Analyzing Social Policy*. Oxford: Basil Blackwell.

Hill, M. and Bramley, G. (1986b) 'The Future of Welfare: A Review Article', *Policy and Politics*, 14(3): 405–412.

Hill, M. and Bramley, G. (1988) *Understanding Social Policy* (3rd edition). Oxford: Basil Blackwell.

Hindess, B. (1987) *Freedom, Equality, and the Market: Arguments on Social Policy*. London: Tavistock.

Hoshino, G. (1973) 'Social Services: The Problem of Accountability', *Social Service Review*, 47(3): 373–383.

Hurl, L.F. (1984) 'Privatized Social Service Systems: Lessons from Ontario Children's Services', *Canadian Public Policy*, 10(4): 396–405.

Hurl, L.F. (1986a) 'Privatization of Social Services: Time to Move the Debate Along', *Canadian Public Policy*, 12(3): 505–512.

Hurl, L.F. (1986b) 'Keeping on Top of Government Contracting: The Challenge to Social Work Educators', *Journal of Social Work Education*, 22(2): 6–18.

Hurl, L.F. and Tucker, D.J. (1986) 'Limitations of an Act of Faith: An Analysis of the MacDonald Commission's Stance on Social Services', *Canadian Public Policy*, 12(4): 606–621.

Ife, J. (1980) 'The Determination of Social Need – A Model of Need Statements in Social Administration', *Australian Journal of Social Issues*, 15(2): 92–107.

Ignatieff, M. (1984) *The Needs Of Strangers*. London: Chatto & Windus.

Ignatieff, M. (1989) 'Citizenship and Moral Narcissism', *The Political Quarterly*, 60(1): 63–74.

Jansson, B.S. (1979) 'Public Monitoring of Contracts with Nonprofit Organizations: Organizational Mission in Two Sectors', *Journal of Sociology and Social Welfare*, 6: 362–374.

Jayasuriya, D.L. (1985) 'Multiculturalism: Fact, Policy and Rhetoric', in Poole, M.E., de Lacey, P.R. and Randhawa, B.S. (eds), *Australia in Transition: Culture and Life Possibilities*. Sydney: Harcourt Brace Jovanovich. pp. 23–34.

Jayasuriya, D.L. (1987) 'Ethnic Minorities and Social Justice in Australian Society', *Australian Journal of Social Issues*, 22(3): 481–497.

Johnson, D.E., Meiller, L.R., Miller, L.C. and Summers, G.F. (1987) *Needs Assessment: Theory and Methods*. Ames, IA: Iowa State University Press.

Johnson, G.W. and Heilman, J.G. (1987) 'Meta Policy Transition Policy Implementation: New Federalism and Privatization', *Public Administration Review*, 47(6): 468–478.

Johnson, N. (1987) *The Welfare State in Transition: The Theory and Practice of Welfare Pluralism*. Brighton: Wheatsheaf Books.

Johnson, N. (1989) 'The Privatization of Welfare', *Social Policy and Administration*, 23(1): 17–30.

Johnson, P. (1986) 'Some Historical Dimensions of the Welfare State "Crisis" ', *Journal of Social Policy*, 15(4): 443–465.

Jones, K., Brown, J. and Bradshaw, J. (1978) *Issues in Social Policy*. London: Routledge & Kegan Paul.

Judge, K.A. (1982) 'The Public Purchase of Social Care: British Confirmation of the American Experience', *Policy and Politics*, 10(4): 397–416.

Judge, K.A. and Knapp, M. (1985) 'Efficiency in the Production of Welfare: The Public and Private Sectors Compared', in Klein, R. and O'Higgins, M. (eds), *The Future of Welfare*. Oxford: Basil Blackwell. pp. 131–149.

Judge, K.A. and Matthews, J. (1980) *Charging for Social Care: A Study of Consumer Charges and the Personal Social Services*. London: Allen & Unwin.

Judge, K.A. and Smith, J. (1983) 'Purchase of Service in England', *Social Service Review*, 57(1): 209–233.

Judge, K.A. Smith, J. and Taylor-Gooby, P. (1983) 'Public Opinion and the Privatization of Welfare: Some Theoretical Implications', *Journal of Social Policy*, 12(4): 469–490.

Kammerman, S.B. (1983) 'The New Mixed Economy of Welfare: Public and Private', *Social Work*, 28(1): 5–10.

Katznelson, I. (1986) 'Rethinking the Silences of Social and Economic Policy', *Political Science Quarterly*, 101(2): 307–325.

Kay, J., Mayer, C. and Thompson, D. (eds) (1986) *Privatization and Regulation: The UK Experience*. London: Clarendon Press.

Kaye, L.W., Monk, A. and Litwin, H. (1984) 'Community Monitoring of Nursing Home Care: Proprietary and Non-Profit Association Perspectives', *Journal of Social Service Research*, 7(3): 5–19.

Keeney, B.P. (1983) *Aesthetics of Change*. New York: The Guildford Press.

Kettner, P.M. and Martin, L.L. (1985a) 'Purchase of Service Contracting and the Declining Influence of Social Work', *Urban and Social Change Review*, 9(2): 8–11.

Kettner, P.M. and Martin, L.L. (1985b) 'Issues in the Development of Monitoring Systems for Purchase of Service Contracting', *Administration in Social Work*, 9(3): 69–82.

Kettner, P.M. and Martin, L.L. (1986) 'Making Decisions about Purchase of Service Contracting', *Public Welfare*, 44(4): 30–37.

Kettner, P.M. and Martin, L.L. (1987) *Purchase of Service Contracting*. Sage Human Services Guide, 44. Newbury Park, CA: Sage.

Kettner, P.M. and Martin, L.L. (1989) 'Factors Affecting Competition in State Contracting for Human Services', *Journal of Sociology and Social Welfare*, XVI(2): 181–194.

Kilburg, R. (1978) 'Consumer Survey as Needs Assessment Method: A Case Study', *Evaluation and Program Planning*, 1(4): 285–292.

King, D.S. and Waldron, J. (1988) 'Citizenship, Social Citizenship and the Defence of Welfare Provision', *British Journal of Political Science*, 18(4): 415–443.

Klein, R. (1977) 'The Conflict between Professionals, Consumers and Bureaucrats', *Journal of the Irish College of Physicians and Surgeons*, 6(3): 88–91.

Klein, R. (1980) 'The Welfare State: A Self-Inflicted Crisis?', *The Political Quarterly*, 51: 24–34.

Klein, R. (1981) 'Values, Power and Policies', in *The Welfare State in Crisis: An*

*Account of the Conference on Social Policies in the 1980s*. Paris: OECD. pp. 166–178.

Klein, R. (1984a) 'Privatization and the Welfare State', *Lloyds Bank Review*, 151: 12–29.

Klein, R. (1984b) 'Review of Offe, C. Contradictions of the Welfare State', *Journal of Social Policy*, 3(4): 485–487.

Klein, R. and O'Higgins, M. (eds) (1985) *The Future of Welfare*. Oxford: Basil Blackwell.

Knapp, M. and Missiakoulis, S. (1982) 'Inter–sectorial Cost Comparisons: Day Care for the Elderly', *Journal of Social Policy*, 11(3): 335–354.

Kolderie, T. (1986) 'The Two Different Concepts of Privatization', *Public Administration Review*, 46(4): 285–291.

Kramer, R.M. (1966) 'Voluntary Agencies and the Use of Public Funds: Some Policy Issues', *Social Service Review*, 40(1): 15–26.

Kramer, R.M. (1979) 'Voluntary Agencies in the Welfare State: An Analysis of the Vanguard Role', *Journal of Social Policy*, 8(4): 473–488.

Kramer, R.M. (1981) *Voluntary Agencies in the Welfare State*. Berkeley, CA: University of California Press.

Kramer, R.M. (1983) 'Contracting for Human Services: An Organisational Perspective', in Kramer, R.M. and Specht, H. (eds), *Readings in Community Organisation Practice* (3rd edition). Englewood Cliffs, NJ: Prentice Hall. pp. 421–432.

Kramer, R.M. (1985a) 'Toward a Contingency Model of Board–Executive Relations', *Administration in Social Work*, 9(3): 15–33.

Kramer, R.M. (1985b) 'The Future of the Voluntary Agency in a Mixed Economy', *Journal of Applied Behavioral Science*, 21(4): 377–391.

Kramer, R.M. (1985c) 'The Welfare State and the Voluntary Sector: The Case of the Personal Social Services', in Eisenstadt, S.N. and Ahimeir, O. (eds), *The Welfare State and Its Aftermath*. London: Croom Helm. pp. 132–140.

Kramer, R.M. and Grossman, B. (1987) 'Contracting for Social Services: Process Management and Resource Dependencies', *Social Service Review*, 61: 32–55.

Kuhn, T. (1962) *The Structure of Scientific Revolutions*. Chicago: University of Chicago Press.

Kutchins, H. and Kutchins, S. (1987) 'Advocacy and the Adversary System', *Journal of Sociology and Social Welfare*, XIV(3): 119–133.

Lane, R.E. (1987) 'Market Justice, Political Justice', in Shadish Jr, W.R. and Reichardt, C.S. (eds), *Evaluation Studies Review Annual*, 12: 343–362.

Lauffer, A. (1984) 'Assessment and Program Development', in Cox, F.M., Urlich, J.L., Rothman, J. and Tropman, J.E. (eds), *Tactics and Techniques of Community Practice* (2nd edition). Itasca, IL: F.E. Peacock. pp. 60–75.

Leat, D. (1986) 'Privatization and Voluntarization', *The Quarterly Journal of Social Affairs*, 2(3): 285–320.

Lewis, H. (1989) 'Ethics and the Private Non-Profit Human Service Organizations', *Administration in Social Work*, 13(2): 1–14.

Lightman, E.S. (1987) 'Welfare Ideology, the Market and the Family', *International Social Work*, 30(4): 309–316.

Linowes, D.F. (ed.) (1988) *Privatization: Towards More Effective Government*. Chicago: University of Illinois Press.

Linstone, H.A. and Turoff, M. (eds) (1975) *The Delphi Method: Techniques and Applications*. Boston, MA: Addison-Wesley Co.

Lipsky, M. (1981) 'The Assault on Human Services: Street-Level Bureaucrats,

Accountability, and the Fiscal Crisis', in Gruber, M.L. (ed.), *Management Systems in the Human Services*. Philadelphia: Temple University Press. pp. 342–356.

Lipsky, M. (1984) 'Bureaucratic Disentitlement in Social Welfare Programs', *Social Service Review*, 58(1): 3–27.

Loney, M. (1986) *The Politics of Greed: The New Right and the Welfare State*. London: Pluto Press.

Loney, M. and Bocock, R. (eds) (1987) *The State or the Market: Politics and Welfare in Contemporary Britain*. London: Sage.

Lourie, N.V. (1978) 'Purchase of Service Contracting: Issues Confronting the Governmental Sponsored Agency', in Wedel, K.R., Katz, A.J. and Weick, A. (eds), *Proceedings of the National Institute on Purchase of Service Contracting*. University of Kansas. pp. 17–27.

Lowery, D. (1982) 'The Political Incentives of Government Contracting', *Social Science Quarterly*, 63(3): 517–527.

Lowi, T.J. (1986) 'The Welfare State: Ethical Foundations and Constitutional Remedies', *Political Science Quarterly*, 101(2): 197–220.

Lundqvist, L.J. (1988) 'Privatization: Towards a Concept for Comparative Policy Analysis', *Journal of Public Policy*, 8(1): 1–19.

McCready, D.J. (1986) 'Privatized Social Service Systems: Are There Any Justifications?', *Canadian Public Policy*, XII(1): 253–257.

McDonald, C. (1989) 'Privatisation in the Human Services Sector: It's Time We Had a Decent Debate on the Subject', *Impact*, 19(3): 13–14.

McDonald, T.P. and Piliavin, I. (1981) 'Impact of Separation on Community Social Service Utilisation', *Social Service Review*, 55(4): 625–635.

McKnight, J.L. (1985) 'A Reconsideration of the Crisis of the Welfare State', *Social Policy*, 16(1): 27–30.

Manning, N. (1987) 'What Is a Social Problem?', in Loney, M. and Bocock, R. (eds), *The State or the Market: Politics and Welfare in Contemporary Britain*. London: Sage. pp. 8–23.

Manser, G. (1974) 'Further Thoughts on Purchase of Service', *Social Casework*, 55: 421–427.

Marshall, T.H. (1972) 'Value Problems of Welfare-Capitalism', *Journal of Social Policy*, 1(1): 15–32.

Martin, E. (1982a) 'A Framework for Exploring Different Judgements of Social Need', *Australian Journal of Social Issues*, 17(3): 190–201.

Martin, E. (1982b) 'Flowchart for Evaluation in Service Organisations', *Australian Social Work*, 35(2): 23–31.

Martin, E. (1985) 'Human Service Organisations: Useful Category or Useless Jargon?', *Australian Journal of Social Issues*, 20(2): 124–135.

Martin, E. (1986) 'Consumer Evaluation of Human Services', *Social Policy and Administration*, 20(3): 185–200.

Mayntz, R. (1983) 'The Conditions of Effective Public Policy – A New Challenge for Policy Analysis', *Policy and Politics*, 11(2): 123–143.

Means, R. (1982) 'Some Ethical and Practical Problems in the Construction of Policy Recommendations from Implementation Research', *Policy and Politics*, 10(2): 205–215.

Meenaghan, T.M., Washington, R.O. and Ryan, R.M. (1982) *Macro Practice in the Human Services*. New York: The Free Press.

Meissen, G.J. and Cipriani, J.A. (1983) 'A Needs Assessment of Human Service Agencies in an Urban Community', *Prevention in Human Services*, 2(4): 123–133.

Mercer, J.L. (1983) 'Growing Opportunities in Public Service Contracting', *Harvard Business Review*, 61(2): 178–186.

Millar, A. and Glendinning, C. (1989) 'Gender and Poverty', *Journal of Social Policy*, 18(3): 363–381.

Minford, P. (1987) 'The Role of the Social Services: A View from the New Right', in Loney, M. and Bocock, R. (eds), *The State or the Market: Politics and Welfare in Contemporary Britain*. London: Sage. pp. 70–82.

Minogue, M. (1983) 'Theory and Practice in Public Policy and Administration', *Policy and Politics*, 11(1): 63–85.

Minogue, M. and O'Grady, J. (1985) 'Contracting Out Local Authority Services in Britain', *Planning and Administration*, 12(1): 82–90.

Mishra, R. (1984) *The Welfare State in Crisis*. Brighton: Harvester Press; and New York: St Martin's Press.

Mishra, R. (1986a) 'The Left and the Welfare State: A Critical Analysis', *Critical Social Policy*, 15(3): 4–19.

Mishra, R. (1986b) 'Social Policy and the Discipline of Social Administration', *Social Policy and Administration*, 20(1): 28–38.

Mishra, R. (1986c) 'Social Analysis and the Welfare State: Retrospect and Prospect', in Oyen, E. (ed.), *Comparing Welfare States and Their Futures*. Aldershot: Gower. pp. 20–32.

Mishra, R. (1987) 'Social Welfare: National and International Dimensions', *International Social Work*, 30(2): 151–158.

Mishra, R. (1989) 'Riding the New Wave: Social Work and the Neo-Conservative Challenge', *International Social Work*, 32(3): 171–182.

Moe, R.C. (1987) 'Exploring the Limits of Privatization', *Public Administration Review*, 47(6): 453–460.

Moe, R.C. (1988) ' "Law" versus "Performance" as Objective Standard', *Public Administration Review*, 48(2): 674–675.

Moore, C. and Pierre, J. (1988) 'Partnership or Privatisation? The Political Economy of Local Economic Restructuring', *Policy and Politics*, 16(3): 169–178.

Moos, M.R.H. and Finney, J.H. (1983) 'The Expanding Scope of Alcoholism Treatment Evaluation', *American Psychologist*, 38(10): 1036–1044.

Morgan, D.R. and England, R.E. (1988) 'The Two Faces of Privatization', *Public Administration Review*, 48(6): 979–987.

Moroney, R.M. (1977) 'Needs Assessment for Human Services', in Anderson, W. and Frieden, B.J. (eds), *Managing Human Services*. Boston International City Management Association. pp. 128–154.

Moroney, R.M. (1983) 'Editorial – Special Issue on the Privatization of Social Work – The New Federalism', *Urban and Social Change Review*, 16(2): 2.

Morris, R. (1982a) 'Government and Voluntary Agency Relationships', *Social Service Review*, 56(3): 333–345.

Morris, R. (1982b) 'Persistent Issues and Elusive Answers in Social Welfare Policy, Planning and Administration', *Administration in Social Work*, 6(2/3): 33–47.

Morris, R. (1986) *Rethinking Social Welfare: Why Care for the Stranger?* New York: Longman Paul.

Morris, R. (ed.) (1988) *Testing the Limits of Social Welfare: International Perspectives on Policy Changes in Nine Countries*. Brandeis: University Press of New England.

Munday, B. (ed.) (1989) *The Crisis in Welfare*. Hemel Hempstead: Harvester Wheatsheaf.

Murray, M.H. (1975) 'Comparing Public and Private Management: An Exploratory Essay', *Public Administration Review*, 35(4): 364–371.

Mushkat, M. (1982) 'In Quest of Control – MBO Options for Monitoring System Performance in the Social Services', *Journal of General Management*, 7(4): 53–69.

Neuber, K.A. (1980) *Needs Assessment: A Model for Community Planning*. Sage Human Services Guide 14. Beverly Hills, CA: Sage.

Nevitt, D.A. (1977) 'Demand and Need', in Heisler, H. (ed.), *Foundations of Social Administration*. London: Macmillan. pp. 113–128.

Obler, J. (1986) 'Moral Duty and the Welfare State', *The Western Political Quarterly*, 39(2): 213–235.

O'Connor, J. (1973) *The Fiscal Crisis of the Welfare State*. London: St Martin's Press.

Offe, C. (1982) 'Some Contradictions of the Modern Welfare State', *Critical Social Policy*, 2(2): 7–16.

Offe, C. (1984) *Contradictions of the Welfare State*. London: Hutchinson.

O'Higgins, M. (1984) 'Privatisation and Social Security', *Political Quarterly*, 55(2): 129–139.

O'Higgins, M. (1985) 'Inequality, Redistribution and Recession: The British Experience, 1976–1982', *Journal of Social Policy*, 14(3): 279–307.

O'Higgins, M. (1987) 'Egalitarians, Equalities and Welfare Evaluation', *Journal of Social Policy*, 16(1): 1–18.

Olson, J.K. (1980) 'Needs Assessment and Program Evaluation in Impacted Communities', in Davenport III, J. and Davenport, J.A. (eds), *The Boom Town: Problems and Promises in the Energy Vortex*. Laramie, WY: University of Wyoming Press. pp. 123–138.

Orthner, D.K. and Smith, S. (1986) 'Measuring Program Needs: A Strategic Design', *Evaluation and Programme Planning*, 9: 199–207.

Pack, J.R. (1987) 'Privatization of Public Sector Services in Theory and Practice', *Journal of Policy Analysis and Management*, 6(4): 586–604.

Papadakis, E. and Taylor-Gooby, P. (1986) 'Positional Satisfaction and State Welfare', *The Sociological Review*, 34(4): 812–827.

Parham, T.M.J. (1982) 'Social Service Issues and Challenges in the 1980's', *Administration in Social Work*, 6(2–3): 91–105.

Parker, D. (1987) 'The New Right, State Ownership and Privatization: A Critique', *Economic and Industrial Democracy*, 8(3): 349–378.

Parry, G. (1985) 'Welfare State and Welfare Society', *Government and Opposition*, 20(3): 287–296.

Parry, N., Rustin, M. and Satyamurti, C. (1979) *Social Work, Welfare and the State*. London: Edward Arnold.

Pascal, A.H. (1981) 'User Charges, Contracting Out, and Privatization in an Era of Fiscal Retrenchment', *Urban Interest*, 3(1): 6–12.

Pascall, G. (1986) *Social Policy: A Feminist Analysis*. London: Tavistock.

Paul, S. (1985) 'Privatisation and the Public Sector – Relevance and Limits', *Economic and Political Weekly*, XX(8): M4–M8.

Pawlak, E.J., Jeter, C.S. and Fink, R.l. (1983) 'The Politics of Cutback Management', *Administration in Social Work*, 7(2): 1–10.

Pearson, G. (1973) 'Social Work as the Privatised Solution of Public Ills', *British Journal of Social Work*, 3(2): 209–227.

Pearson, G. (1975a) 'The Politics of Uncertainty: A Study in the Socialization of the Social Worker', in Jones, H. (ed.), *Towards a New Social Work*. London: Routledge & Kegan Paul. pp. 45–68.

Pearson, G. (1975b) *The Deviant Imagination: Psychiatry, Social Work and Social Change*. London: Macmillan.

Peters, D.L. and Sibbison, V. (1980) 'Considerations in the Assessment of Community Child Care Needs', *Residential and Community Care Administration*, 1(4): 407–420.

Plant, R., Lesser, H. and Taylor-Gooby, P. (1980) *Political Philosophy and Social Welfare*. London: Routledge & Kegan Paul.

Plattner, M.F. (1979) 'The Welfare State versus the Redistributive State', *The Public Interest*, 55: 28–48.

Poertner, J. and Rapp, C.A. (1985) 'Purchase of Service and Accountability: Will They Ever Meet?', *Administration in Social Work*, 9(1): 57–66.

Poole, D.L. (1985) 'The Future of Public–Private Sector Partnerships for the Provision of Human-Services-Problems and Possibilities', *Journal of Applied Behaviour*, 21(4): 393–406.

Poole, R.W. (1983) 'Objections to Privatization', *Policy Review*, 24(Spring): 105–119.

Popple, P.R. (1984) 'Negotiation: A Critical Skill for Social Work Administrators', *Administration in Social Work*, 8(2): 1–12.

Popple, P.R. (1985) 'The Social Work Profession: A Reconceptualisation', *Social Service Review*, 59(4): 560–577.

Pringle, R. (1981) 'Training for the Eighties: Some Pointers', *Community Development Journal*, 16(3): 176–187.

Pruger, R. and Miller, L. (1973) 'Competition and the Public Social Services', *Public Welfare*, 31: 16–25.

Quadagno, J.S. (1984) 'Welfare Capitalism and the Social Security Act of 1935' *American Sociological Review*, 49: 32–64.

Randall, R. and Wilson, C. (1989) 'The Impact of Federally Imposed Stress Upon Local-Government and Nonprofit Organizations', *Administration and Society*, 21(1): 3–19.

Rapp, C. (1982) 'Needs Assessment: Who Needs It?', *Journal of Social Welfare*, Spring/Summer: 49–60.

Raskin, M. (1983) 'A Delphi Study in Field Instruction: Identification of Issues and Research Priorities by Experts', *Arete*, 8(2): 38–47.

Reamer, F.G. (1983) 'Social Services in a Conservative Era', *Social Casework*, 64(8): 451–458.

Rees, A.M. (1988) *T.H. Marshall's Social Policy* (5th Edition). London: Hutchinson.

Reichert, K. (1977) 'The Drift Toward Entrepreneurialism in Health and Social Welfare', *Administration in Social Work*, 1(2): 123–133.

Reichert, K. (1982) 'Human Services and the Market System', *Health and Social Work*, 7: 173–182.

Reid, P.N. (1972) 'Reforming the Social Services Monopoly', *Social Work*, 17(4): 44–45.

Reid, P.N. and Gundlach, J.H. (1983) 'A Scale for the Measurement of Consumer Satisfaction with Social Services', *Journal of Social Science Research*, 7(1): 37–54.

Reid, W.J. and Smith, A. (1981) *Research in Social Work*. New York: Columbia University Press.

Rein, M. (1977) 'Social Planning: The Search for Legitimacy', in Gilbert, N. and Specht, H. (eds), *Planning for Social Welfare: Issues, Models and Tasks*. Englewood Cliffs, NJ: Prentice Hall. pp. 50–69.

Rein, M. (1981) 'Private Provision of Welfare: From Welfare State to Welfare Society', in Henderson, R.F. (ed.), *The Welfare Stakes: Strategies for Australian Social Policy*. Melbourne: University of Melbourne. pp. 9–44.

Rein, M. (1983) 'Value-Critical Policy Analysis', in Callahan, D. and Jennings, B., *Ethics, The Social Sciences, and Policy Analysis*. New York: Plenum Press. pp. 83–111.

Rein, M. and Peattie, L. (1981) 'Knowledge for Policy' *Social Service Review*, 55(4): 525–543.

Rein, M. and Rainwater, L. (1986) *Public/Private Interplay in Social Protection: A Comparative Study*. Armonk, NY: M.E. Sharpe.

Rein, M. and White, S.H. (1977) 'Can Policy Research Help Policy', *The Public Interest*, 49: 119–136.

Rein, M. and White, S.H. (1981) 'Knowledge for Practice', *Social Service Review*, 55(1): 1–41.

Rein, M., Esping-Andersen, G. and Rainwater, L. (eds) (1987) *Stagnation and Renewal in Social Policy: The Rise and Fall of Policy Regimes*. Armonk, NY: M.E. Sharpe.

Rice, R.M. (1975) 'Impact of Government Contracts on Voluntary Social Agencies', *Social Casework*, 56: 386–395.

Richan, W.C. and Mendelsohn, A.R. (1973) *Social Work: The Unloved Profession*. New York: New Viewpoints.

Richter, B. and Ozawa, M. (1983) 'Purchase of Service Contracts and the Functioning of Private Agencies', *Administration in Social Work*, 7(1): 25–38.

Robertson, A. (1980) 'The Welfare State and "Post-Industrial" Values', in Timms, N. (ed.), *Social Welfare: Why and How?* London: Routledge & Kegan Paul. pp. 27–41.

Robertson, A. (1988) 'Welfare State and Welfare Society', *Social Policy and Administration*, 22(3): 222–234.

Robertson, R. (1970) *The Sociological Interpretation of Religion*. Oxford: Basil Blackwell.

Robinson, R. (1986) 'Restructuring the Welfare State: An Analysis of Public Expenditure', *Journal of Social Policy*, 15(1): 1–21.

Rose, N.E. (1989) 'The Political Economy of Welfare', *Journal of Sociology and Social Welfare*, XVI(2): 87–108.

Rose, S.M. (1987) 'Deinstitutionalisation – A Structurally Generated Opportunity for Social Work', *International Social Work*, 30(3): 251–257.

Rose-Ackerman, S. (1983) 'Social Services and the Market', *Columbia Law Review*, 83(5): 1405–1428.

Rossi, P.H. (1979) 'Issues in the Evaluation of Human Services Delivery', in Sechrest, L. et al. (eds), *Evaluation Studies Review Annual*, 4. Beverly Hills: Sage. pp. 68–95.

Rossi, P.H. and Freeman, H.E. (1987) *Evaluation: A Systematic Approach* (3rd edn). Beverly Hills: Sage.

Salamon, L.M. (1987) 'Of Market Failure, Voluntary Failure, and Third-Party Government: Toward a Theory of Government-Nonprofit Relations in the Modern Welfare State', *Journal of Voluntary Action Research*, 16(1 & 2): 29–49.

Saleeby, D. (1989) 'The Estrangement of Knowing and Doing: Professions in Crisis', *Social Casework*, 70(9): 556–563.

Sapiro, V. (1986) 'The Gender Basis of American Social Policy', *Political Science Quarterly*, 101(2): 221–238.

Sappington, D.E.M. and Stiglitz, J.E. (1987) 'Privatization, Information and Incentives', *Journal of Policy Analysis and Management*, 6(4): 567–582.

Sarri, R.C. (1982) 'Management Trends in the Human Services in the 1980's', *Administration in Social Work*, 6(2–3): 19–30.

Sarri, R.C. and Hasenfeld, Y. (eds) (1978) *The Management of Human Services*. New York: Columbia University Press.

Sarri, R.C. and Lawrence, R.J. (eds) (1980) *Issues in the Evaluation of Social Welfare Programs: Australian Case Illustrations*. Kensington: N.S.W. University Press.

Savas, E.S. (ed.), (1977) *Alternatives for Delivering Public Services: Towards Improved Performance*. Boulder, CO: Westview Press.

Savas, E.S. (1982) *Privatizing the Public Sector: How to Shrink Government*. Chatham, NJ: Chatham House.

Savas, E.S. (1987) *Privatization: The Key to Better Government*. Chatham, NJ: Chatham House.

Scheirer, M.A. (1979) 'Program Participants' Positive Perceptions: Psychological Conflict of Interest in Social Program Evaluation', in Sechrest, L. et al. (eds), *Evaluation Studies Review Annual*, 4. Beverly Hills: Sage. pp. 407–424.

Schorr, A.L. (1985) 'Professional Practice as Policy', *Social Service Review*, 59(2): 178–196.

Seldon, A. (1985) 'The Idea of the Welfare State and Its Consequences', in Eisenstadt, S.N. and Ahimeir, O. (eds), *The Welfare State and Its Aftermath*. London: Croom Helm. pp. 132–140.

Shackleton, J.R. (1984) 'Privatization: The Case Examined', *National Westminster Bank Review*: 59–73.

Shalev, M. (1983a) 'The Social Democratic Model and Beyond: Two "Generations" of Comparative Research on the Welfare State', *Comparative Social Research*, 6: 315–351.

Shalev, M. (1983b) 'Class Politics and the Western Welfare State', in Spiro, S.E. and Yuchtman-Yaar, E. (eds), *Evaluating the Welfare State*. New York: Academic Press. pp. 27–50.

Sharkansky, I. (1980) 'Policy Making and Service Delivery on the Margins of Government: The Case of Contractors', *Public Administration Review*, 40: 116–123.

Shaw, I.F. (1984) 'Literature Review: Consumer Evaluations of the Personal Social Services', *British Journal of Social Work*, 14(5): 277–284.

Sherraden, M.W. (1988) 'Rethinking Social Welfare: Toward Assets', *Social Policy*, 18(3): 37–43.

Siegel, L.M., Attkisson, C.C. and Carson, L.G. (1978) 'Need Identification and Program Planning in the Community Context', in Attkisson, C.C., Hargreaves, W.A., Horowitz, M.J. and Sorenson, J.E. (eds), *Evaluation of Human Service Programs*. New York: Academic Press. pp. 215–252.

Smith, B.L. (1971) 'Accountability and Independence in the Contract State', in Smith, B.L. and Hague, D. (eds) *The Dilemma of Accountability in Modern Government*. New York: Macmillan. pp. 3–69.

Smith, G. (1980) *Social Need: Policy, Practice and Research*. London: Routledge & Kegan Paul.

Smith, G. (1986) 'Service Delivery Issues', *The Quarterly Journal of Social Affairs*, 2(3): 265–283.

Smith, G. and Harris, R. (1972) 'Ideologies of Need and the Organization of Social Work Departments', *The British Journal of Social Work*, 2(1): 27–45.

Soper, K. (1981) *On Human Needs*. Brighton: Harvester.

Sosin, M.R. (1984) 'Do Private Agencies Fill Gaps in Public Welfare Programs? "A Research Note" ', *Administration in Social Work*, 8(2): 13–24.

Sosin, M.R. (1985) 'Social Problems Covered by Private Agencies: An Application of Niche Theory', *Social Services Review*, 58(1): 75–94.

Sosin, M.R. (1987) 'Private Social Agencies: Auspices, Sources of Funds, and Problems Covered', *Social Work Research and Abstracts*, 23(2): 21–29.

Sosin, M.R. and Caulum, S. (1983) 'Advocacy: A Conceptualization for Social Work Practice', *Social Work*, 28(1): 12–17.

Specht, H. (1981) 'British Social Services under Siege: An Essay Review', *Social Service Review*, 55(4): 593–602.

Spicker, P. (1987) 'Concepts of Need in Housing Allocation', *Policy and Politics*, 15(1): 17–27.

Spicker, P. (1988) *Principles of Social Welfare*. London: Routledge & Kegan Paul.

Spiro, S.E. and Yuchtman-Yaar, E. (eds) (1983) *Evaluating the Welfare State: Social and Political Perspectives*. New York: Academic Press.

Springborg, P. (1981) *The Problem of Human Need and the Critique of Civilisation*. London: Allen & Unwin.

Steel, D.R. and Herald, D.A. (1982) 'Privatising Public Enterprise – An Analysis of the Government's Case', *Political Quarterly*, 53(3): 333–349.

Stipak, B. (1979) 'Citizen Satisfaction with Urban Services: Potential Misuse as a Performance Indicator', in Sechrest, L. et al. (eds), *Evaluation Studies Review Annual*, 4. Beverly Hills: Sage. pp. 441–447.

Stoesz, D. (1981) 'A Wake for the Welfare State: Social Welfare and the Neoconservative Challenge', *Social Service Review*, 55(3): 398–410.

Stoesz, D. (1987) 'Privatization: Reforming The Welfare State', *Journal of Sociology and Social Welfare*, XIV(3): 3–19.

Stoesz, D. (1988) 'Why Not Social Service Vouchers?', *Social Casework*, 69(3): 184–185.

Stoesz, D. (1989) 'A New Paradigm For Social Welfare', *Journal of Sociology and Social Welfare*, XVI(2): 127–150.

Stone, C.N. (1983) 'Whither the Welfare State? Professionalization, Bureaucracy, and the Market Alternative', *Ethics*, 93: 588–595.

Stoner, M. (1986) 'Marketing of Social Services Gains Prominence in Practice', *Administration in Social Work*, 10(4): 41–52.

Straussman, J.D. and Farie, J. (1981) 'Contracting for Social Services at the Local Level', *Urban Interest*, 3(1): 43–50.

Sugden, R. (1986) *The Economics of Rights, Co-operation and Welfare*. Oxford: Basil Blackwell.

Sullivan, H.J. (1987) 'Privatization of Public Services: A Growing Threat to Constitutional Rights', *Public Administration Review*, 47(6): 461–467.

Taylor, D. (1989) 'Citizenship and Social Power', *Critical Social Policy*, 9(2): 19–31.

Taylor, R.W. (1980) 'The Problems with Social Indicators', *Australian Journal of Social Issues*, 15(3): 230–245.

Taylor-Gooby, P. (1981a) 'The Empiricist Tradition in Social Administration', *Critical Social Policy*, 1(2): 6–21.

Taylor-Gooby, P. (1981b) 'The State, Class Ideology and Social Policy', *Journal of Social Policy*, 10(4): 433–451.

Taylor-Gooby, P. (1983) 'Moralism, Self Interest and Attitudes to Welfare', *Policy and Politics*, 11(2): 145–160.

Taylor-Gooby, P. (1985a) *Public Opinion, Ideology and State Welfare*. London: Routledge & Kegan Paul.

Taylor-Gooby, P. (1985b) 'The Politics of Welfare: Public Attitudes and Behaviour', in Klein, R. and O'Higgins, M. (eds), *The Future of Welfare*. Oxford: Basil Blackwell. pp. 72–91.

Taylor-Gooby, P. (1985c) 'Pleasing Any of the People, Some of the Time: Perceptions of Redistribution and Attitudes to Welfare', *Government and Opposition*, 20(3): 396–406.

Taylor-Gooby, P. (1986a) 'Privatisation, Power and the Welfare State', *Sociology*, 20(2): 228–246.

Taylor-Gooby, P. (1986b) 'Consumption Cleavages and Welfare Politics', *Political Studies*, XXXIV(4): 592–606.

Taylor-Gooby, P. (1987) 'Welfare Attitudes: Cleavage, Consensus and Citizenship', *The Quarterly Journal of Social Affairs*, 3(3): 199–211.

Taylor-Gooby, P. and Dale, J. (1981) *Social Theory and Social Welfare*. London: Edward Arnold.

Terrell, P. (1979) 'Private Alternatives to Public Human Services Administration', *Social Service Review*, 53(1): 56–74.

Terrell, P. (1987) 'Purchasing Social Services', *Encyclopedia of Social Work* Silver Springs, MD: NASW. (18th edition), 2: 434–442.

Terrell, P. and Kramer, R.M. (1984) 'Contracting with Non-Profits', *Public Welfare*, 42(1): 31–37.

Thane, P. (1986) 'History and the Future of Welfare', *The Quarterly Journal of Social Affairs*, 2(3): 171–195.

Thayer, R. (1977) 'Measuring Need in the Social Services', in Gilbert, N. and Specht, H. (eds), *Planning for Social Welfare: Issues, Models and Tasks*. Englewood Cliffs, NJ: Prentice Hall. pp. 297–310.

Thurow, L.C. (1981) 'Equity, Efficiency, Social Justice, and Redistribution', in *The Welfare State in Crisis: An Account of the Conference on Social Policies in the 1980's*. Paris: OECD. pp. 137–150.

Timms, N. and Mayer, J. (1971) *The Client Speaks*. London: Routledge & Kegan Paul.

Tucker, D. (1980) 'A Quantitative Assessment of the "Parallel Bars" Theory of Public–Voluntary Collaboration', *Administration in Social Work*, 4(2): 29–48.

Tucker, D. (1981) 'Voluntary Auspices and the Behavior of Social Service Organisations', *Social Service Review*, 55(4): 603–627.

Tulloch, P. (1978) 'Normative Theory and Social Policy', *Australia and New Zealand Journal of Sociology*, 14(1): 65–75.

Tulloch, P. (1983) 'Theory, Reformism and Retrenchment', *Australian Social Work*, 36(2): 15–22.

Turner, B.S. (1986) *Citizenship and Capitalism: The Debate over Reformism*. London: Allen & Unwin.

Turner, B.S. (1988) 'Individualism, Capitalism and the Dominant Culture: A Note on the Debate', *Australia and New Zealand Journal of Sociology*, 24(1): 47–64.

Veit, S. (1987) *Purchase of Service Contracting in the Social Services in Canada*. Ministry of Social Services and Housing, Government of British Columbia.

Verwayen, H. (1984) 'Social Indicators: Actual and Political Uses', *Social Indicator Research*, 14: 1–27.

Vettenranta, J. (1986) 'Restructuring Welfare Policy by Means of Privatization', *Acta Sociologica*, 29(3): 255–264.

Vigilante, F.W. and Mailick, M.D. (1988) 'Needs-Resource Evaluation in the Assessment Process', *Social Work*, 33(2): 101–104.

Volland, P.J. (1980) 'Costing for Social Work Services', *Social Work in Health Care*, 6(1): 73–87.

Walker, A. (1984) 'The Political Economy of Privatisation', in Le Grand, J. and Robinson, R. (eds), *Privatisation and the Welfare State*. London: Allen & Unwin. pp. 19–44.

Wallace, M.E. (1982) Private Practice: A Nationwide Study, *Social Work*, 27(3): 262–267.

Warheit, G.J., Bell, R.A. and Schwab, J.J. (1984) 'Selecting the Needs Assessment Approach', in Cox, F.M., Urlich, J.L., Rothman, J. and Tropman, J.E. (eds), *Tactics and Techniques of Community Practice* (2nd edition), Itasca, IL: F.E. Peacock. pp. 41–59.

Warheit, G.J., Buhl, J.M. and Bell, R.A. (1978) 'A Critique of Social Indicators Analysis and Key Informants Surveys as Needs Assessment Methods', *Evaluation and Program Planning*, 1: 239–247.

Warren, R. (1987) 'Coproduction, Volunteerism, Privatization, and the Public Interest', *Journal of Voluntary Action Research*, 16(3): 5–10.

Watson, D. (1980) *Caring for Strangers: An Introduction to Practical Philosophy for Students of Social Administration*. London: Routledge & Kegan Paul.

Watson, D. (1983) 'Making Reality Intelligible: The Relation between Philosophical Analysis and the Study of Social Policies', *Journal of Social Policy*, 12(4): 491–514.

Watson, D. (1984) 'Moral Objections to Welfare for Profit', *Journal of Social Policy*, 13(3): 333–337.

Weale, A. (1978) *Equality and Social Policy*. London: Routledge & Kegan Paul.

Weale, A. (1983) *Political Theory and Social Policy*. London: Macmillan.

Weale, A. (1985a) 'Why Are We Waiting? – The Problem of Unresponsiveness in the Public Social Services', in Klein, R. and O'Higgins, M. (eds), *The Future of Welfare*. Oxford: Basil Blackwell. pp. 150–165.

Weale, A. (1985b) 'The Welfare State and Two Conflicting Ideals of Equality', *Government and Opposition*, 20(3): 315–327.

Weale, A. (1986) 'Ideology and Welfare', *The Quarterly Journal of Social Affairs*, 2(3): 197–219.

Weber, M. (1947) *The Theory of Social and Economic Organizations*. New York: The Free Press.

Weddell, K. (1986) 'Privatising Social Services in the USA', *Social Policy and Administration*, 20(1): 14–27.

Wedel, K.R. (1974) 'Contracting for Public Assistance Social Services', *Public Welfare*, 32(Winter): 57–62.

Wedel, K.R. and Hardcastle, D.A. (1978) 'Alternatives to Monolithic Public Social Services', *Midwest Review of Public Administration*, 12(3): 177–188.

Wedel, K.R. and Katz, A.J. (1980) 'Purchase of Service Contracting in Human Services', *Journal of Health and Human Resources Administration*, 2(3): 327–341.

Wedel, K.R., Katz, A.J. and Weich, A. (eds) (1978) *Proceedings of the National Institute on Purchase of Service Contracting*. Lawrence: University of Kansas School of Social Work.

Wedel, K.R., Katz, A.J. and Weich, A. (eds) (1979) *Social Services by Government Contract: A Policy Analysis*. New York: Praeger.

Wilding, P. (ed.) (1986), *In Defence of the Welfare State*. Manchester: Manchester University Press. pp. 98–126.

Wilensky, H.L. and Lebeaux, C. (1958) *Industrial Society and Social Welfare*. New York: Russell Sage.

Williams, A. (1974) ' "Need" as a Demand Concept (with Special Reference to Health)', in Culyer, A.J. (ed.), *Economic Policies and Social Goals: Aspects of Public Choice*. London: Martin Robertson. pp. 60–76.

Williams, F. (1987) 'Racism and the Discipline of Social Policy: A Critique of Welfare Theory', *Critical Social Policy*, 7(2): 4–29.

Willis, D.C. (1984) 'Purchase of Social Services – Another Look', *Social Work*, 29(6): 516–520.

Withorn, A. (1984) *Serving the People: Social Services and Social Change*. New York: Columbia University Press.

Wortman, P.M. (1984) 'Cost-Effectiveness: A Review', in Connor, R.F. et al. (eds), *Evaluation Studies Review Annual*, 9. Beverly Hills: Sage. pp. 308–322.

# Index